OXSTALLS UNIVERSITY OF

AND ROMY TIONGCO

Doing Theology
and
Development

MEETING
THE CHALLENGE
OF POVERTY

WINDOWS ON THEOLOGY

SAINT ANDREW PRESS

First published in 1997 by
SAINT ANDREW PRESS
121 George Street, Edinburgh EH2 4YN

on behalf of
WINDOWS ON THEOLOGY

ISBN 0 86153 233 3

British Library Cataloguing in Publication Data
A catalogue record for this book
is available from the British Library.

ISBN 0861532333

The Authors would like to acknowledge the following sources:
- 'Depoliticising Development', reprinted from *Development in Practice*, Volume 6, No 1, with permission of Oxfam UK and Ireland – for material quoted in Chapter Five of this book.
- 'I wanna have a little bomb like you' by Sydney Carter, from *In the Present Tense* Book 2, reproduced by permission of Stainer & Bell, Ltd – as quoted in extract form on page 184 of this book.

Cover by Mark Blackadder.
Cover photograph courtesy of Sarah White.
Printed and bound by Athenaeum Press Ltd, Gateshead, Tyne & Wear.

Contents

Preface

The Authors

This book is the product of two unlikely colleagues, separated by age, gender, culture, nationality, religious background, work experience, marital status and academic training. It traces the path of our search towards an approach to development, which weaves a common meaning out of our differences. The book does not reflect a point of arrival. The journey is ongoing. We hope simply that our thoughts will encourage others to tell their own stories.

Romy Tiongco was born in a remote village in Bukidnon, Southern Philippines, in 1944. He was ordained a Jesuit in 1973 and served as a parish priest for six years. In 1979 he decided to become again a lay person, in solidarity with the married people and women, who could not be ordained in the Catholic Church. He did not lose his faith, nor his love for the priesthood or the Church. He got married in 1981. He co-founded an organisation called the Muslim Christian Agency for Rural Development (MuCARD) and continued working until 1989 as a community organiser in poor farming and fishing villages. In the following two years he worked for Christian Aid in development education in the UK. In August 1991 he joined the teaching team of the MTh in Theology and Development in Edinburgh University and served as the course coordinator of the programme until September 1994.

Sarah White was born in a small town in Southern England in 1963, the daughter of a Baptist minister. After studying theology and social science, she went and lived in a village in Bangladesh in 1985-6 to do field research for a PhD in sociology. Since then she has made a number of visits back, working on appraisal and evaluation of aid projects. In 1990 she joined the Department of Sociology in Edinburgh, and became a member of the teaching team on the new course in Theology and Development. In 1992 she moved to the University of East Anglia to join the School of Development Studies there.

The idea of writing a book came out of the experience of working together with others to design and teach the Theology and Development course. We had not chosen each other as colleagues, but now we made a decision to become co-authors. We recognised that each of us brought strengths and weaknesses to the partnership. Romy had theological training and long experience in community organising and practical development work, but had never written anything of any length before. Sarah had done more academic writing, but had much less practical experience to share. One of our friends teased us: one is a peasant and the other a heretic. We have often laughed over that, but also found potentials in ourselves and each other that we did not expect. At other times we had to admit our weaknesses and allow ourselves to be vulnerable, trusting that the other would give support. It took some patience and a lot of openness to listen to one another as we groped for the words to formulate our thoughts. Both being hard-headed, there have also been conflicts. We did not foresee all that would be involved when we started to write: maybe in any joint venture there is an element of surprise.

When we began to tell people that we were writing a book, the first question we were asked was: who was going to write which parts? This did not correspond to our thinking. What we wanted was not just a joint product, but a joint process. Some sections we have actually written together, the others we have talked through in detail before one of us prepared a draft, which served as the basis for further discussion. We opted for this process so the book would not just be a compilation of different perspectives, but a dialogue between us through which we could forge a common view. Looking back, neither of us alone could have written what is in these pages. In some strange way, the whole is more than the sum of us, its parts.

The students taking Theology and Development at Edinburgh are all people experienced in development work, who come to take time out to reflect more deeply on their own situations. We have benefited greatly from the insights and friendship they have shared with us. In working together with students from many different places, we have come to see our differences from one another not as stumbling blocks but as stepping stones. We have found ourselves affirmed and enriched by recognising and accepting what has made us who we are. Hand in hand with this personal experience, came the awareness that development also is about overcoming apparent barriers, celebrating the diversity, and coming to see that we belong to one another in a new way.

A Note about Structure

In this book we present our attempt to do theology and development. We believe that the core of this is reflection and action built on our own particular contexts. As a result, we draw heavily on our own experiences of doing development, and the action that this has involved. As far as possible, we begin with stories. This has the advantage of starting from the concrete, but also the disadvantage that we have a strong bias towards the contexts we know best: the Philippines, Bangladesh, and the UK. When the experience is particularly personal, we indicate this by citing one of our names directly in the text. Since we are both Christians, the scope of the book is restricted to Christianity rather than taking in also other faiths. In none of this do we mean to suggest that our own stories or religious tradition are of particular importance. Rather, it is an acknowledgement of our own limitations. We have to begin where we are. We hope, however, that people of other backgrounds and beliefs will respond by putting forward their own perspectives to broaden and enrich the dialogue.

In our analysis and reflection, we draw on perspectives from both social science and theology. In both we follow the essential insight that knowledge is always from a particular point of view. The challenge is to be with the oppressed, to see how things look from the bottom-up, as a means to critique the dominant perspectives from the top-down, and to promote different kinds of practice. This involves looking at how society is structured, in terms of what makes and keeps poor people poor. But it also means a closer examination of ourselves, to see what it is within us as well as outside us, that keeps these structures in place.

In the introductory chapter we set out our understanding of what doing theology and development means. Chapter Two then starts with the question: Who are the poor? This is the first of three chapters in which we consider the key issue in theology and development, the problem of poverty. We present the stories of poor people we have known, and try by 'being with' them to understand something of what poverty means. The second of these chapters asks the question: Why are the poor poor? In exploring this, we introduce the four basic world-views which we believe structure the answers to this question. We begin with an outline of the first three perspectives, their assumptions and the social and development policies to which they lead. We then consider how well their diagnoses of poverty match the experience of poor people. In the following chapter we critically present our own option; revising and deepening these understandings of poverty by pointing out the connections between inner, spiritual poverty and the global reproduction of want and scarcity.

In the next four chapters we explore in more detail four core commitments that are central to our understanding of theology and development. Chapter Five takes a look at the issue of power to find a way how the dualism it creates can be overcome. Chapters Six and Seven concern gender and the environment respectively. We consider how theology and development have operated against the interests of women and the natural world, and review the attempts that have been made to put this right. Through reflection on the 'problem' and 'solutions', we suggest also the direction of our own approach. A similar pattern is followed in the next chapter, in which we set out our commitment to nonviolent strategies to achieve change. We close the book with some final reflections on where we have got to and possible ways forward.

Theology and development is potentially a huge subject. We do not pretend to offer a general survey of the literature, but aim to present a method for doing theology and development as we present our own reflections. This is itself incomplete. We wished, for example, to include a chapter on race and ethnicity, which has been taken up in Black theology, but is largely absent from development discourse. Time did not permit us to do this. Altogether, rather than containing any 'answers' in itself, our hope is that the book will help to point other people outwards to other texts and inwards towards their own experience, and so encourage them to do something similar in their own context.

This book has been in many ways a joint project. We are deeply grateful to all the friends who have helped us on its way. In particular, however, we would like to thank three sets of people. First, those responsible for establishing the course in Theology and Development at Edinburgh, which first inspired us to write this book. These are Christian Aid, represented especially by Michael Taylor and Paul Spray; and the Departments of Christian Ethics and Practical Theology, Sociology, and Social Anthropology in the University of Edinburgh, represented by their professors, Duncan Forrester, Colin Bell, and Anthony Cohen. Special thanks are also due to John Parratt, of New College, Edinburgh, who first suggested that we write this book, and to Lesley Taylor of Saint Andrew Press who brought it finally to birth. Second, our students and those who have shared with us on the teaching team. Finally, we are most grateful to those kind friends who painstakingly went through all or part of an earlier draft of this book. These are: Marcella Althaus-Reid, Christina Arthurton, Charles Elliott, Charlotte Heath, Jude Howell, Linda McClintock-Tiongco, Livingstone Ngewu, Chris Rowland, Joan Sharples, Michael Taylor, Bridget Walker, Barrie and Margaret White, and Richard Woodham. Throughout, Bible references are given in the New Revised Standard Version.

CHAPTER ONE

Why Theology and Development?

Introduction

Putting theology and development together may seem an odd thing to do. Development is concerned with the immediate, practical challenge of tackling world poverty. Those working in development may be agriculturalists, engineers, doctors and nurses, economists, or social scientists – but theologians? Theology seems too abstract, too removed, more concerned with the hereafter than the here and now. Even to religious people, theology can seem obscure, distant, with little to say to the everyday. For those with no religious belief, it is simply irrelevant. Theology belongs to the 'childhood of humankind', where development represents humankind 'come of age'. If they have any place at all, such beliefs and values are a purely private matter. Highly personal and subjective, they have no place in the concrete world of development, where the urgent need is to get something done.

At the same time, it is clear that religion has always been a feature of the development scene. Historically, development is the successor to colonialism, in which Christian missions played an important part. One legacy of this is evident even today in Christian schools and hospitals all over Asia, Africa and Latin America. Many contemporary non-governmental aid agencies (NGOs) are also religiously inspired, and even some official aid. A significant proportion of Saudi aid, for example, goes into the building of mosques and Muslim religious schools. Religion has also been important in anti-colonial movements. A famous example is Mahatma Gandhi, who drew heavily on Hindu tradition to provide ideology and strategies for the Indian nationalist struggle against the British. Finally, the current rise of fundamentalism in all of the major religions overturns assumptions that religion and politics can be kept apart. The Iranian revolution of 1979 is the most obvious indicator of a general pattern, that when people search for an alternative model of development they often turn to their religion for answers.

To look at theology with development is not, therefore, as strange as it at first appears, but it still raises a number of questions. Looking at religion is one thing, but why go further to consider theology? What does 'doing theology' mean? And what is 'development'? What might the two have in common, and how are they distinct? Will doing theology make a difference to our development practice, or being involved in development affect our theology? Must they be done separately, or is there a single process that we can call 'doing theology and development'?

The questions are difficult ones, not because there are no answers, but because there are too many. There are many theologies, and many kinds of development. In Autumn 1993 a short article appeared in one of the British daily newspapers. It was headed: 'Portillo conjures up Christian lessons for welfare cutback.' The Conservative MP Michael Portillo was calling on Christian tradition to justify his government's cuts in welfare spending. Individual moral responsibility and neighbourly charity, he claimed, had been undermined by people becoming over dependent on the state. While he admitted that Christian teaching urges us to share our wealth, this did not mean taxation or public welfare spending. Instead, he went on: 'The call to do good that lies at the heart of Christianity demands an individual response.'

This is theology and development, of a kind. Political and religious values come together in a particular view of what human beings are, or should be. Having defined the 'problem' in this way, in turn leads on to the advocacy of certain policies to solve it. In making the case for these policies people may further develop their political and religious world-view. The fundamental point here is that theology and development *are* together. Our basic beliefs and attitudes are not split up into boxes with different labels. We cannot separate out the 'religious bits' from the others. Both our ideas of development and our religion say something about the way the world is, and should be. Sometimes they may be in tension, our religious understanding challenges our social and political commitments, or vice versa. But more often they reinforce one another. We hear those parts of our religious tradition and see those aspects of society that confirm our basic orientation. It is when we come to explain our position to others that we may abstract a 'theology' or a view of 'development' that can be stated in simply religious or secular language.

These points become clearer if we consider how they apply in this particular case. Here, Michael Portillo believes that human beings are, or should be, morally responsible individuals. It is people's failure to measure up to this that causes social problems such as rising crime or inadequate support for the elderly. This failure is again due to the state having taken over the provision of care that people should bear responsibility for as individuals. A political strategy follows clearly from this: cutting state welfare services is the way to achieve a better society. This is, of course, in line with his party's economic priorities and ideology. This is not coincidental; theology and development is never done entirely alone. On the one hand Michael Portillo's understanding of the world reflects his own background and experience, the people he has known, and the books he has read. On the other hand, it is also formed in response to people who take a different stand. His speech is a reaction against those who attack Conservative party policy on moral grounds – particularly some radical bishops in the Church of England. In opposing their understanding of Christian teaching he consolidates his own. In the process of making the argument, both his views of development and his theology thus become more clearly defined.

The same basic framework holds for those who do not believe in God. While they do not have a theology as such, they do have a cosmology, a basic world-view made up of beliefs and values about how the world is and how it should be. For everyone there are sacred moments of love, beauty, being moved beyond words. In their own way, everyone has also to face the questions that are at the core of all religions: the search for community; for guidelines by which to live; and for meaning, in the face of suffering and death. Looked at more closely, therefore, there may be less difference than at first appears between the world-views of those who believe in God and those who do not. This has a practical dimension also. When it comes to development, people may find that they have more in common in their basic approach across the believer/non-believer divide, than they do with those of very different politics, who happen to belong to the same religion.

Doing theology and development, then, begins with the recognition that all development policies are inevitably built on a particular world-view. This may or may not include reference to God, but it will always go beyond what is simply observable to make statements about how the world is and should be. Seeing development in this holistic way means that policies need to be examined not in isolation, but in the context of the broader perspective which they reflect. Similarly, analysing theology means looking not only at its internal consistency, but also at its implications for social and political action.

The context of this is quite practical: theology and development is already being done. The failure of development policies of East and West to deliver the prosperity they promised, has led many people in the South – Asia, Latin America and Africa – to question the existing package and seek alternatives. The answers they find are very different, ranging from the radical populism of Liberation Theology on the left to Islamic theocratic states on the right. In common, however, they have a profound rejection of the disregard for spiritual and moral dimensions in the dominant model of development.

This indicates a deep crisis in the modernist/development worldview, that cannot just be ignored. It is a crisis about where we are going, where we ought to be going, and how we can get there. Since the late 1980s it has been taken as proved that socialism 'doesn't work'. But does the capitalist development model that is being exported the world over 'work', and if so for how many, and at what cost? In the North – Europe and the United States – it is in the green movement that these questions are being asked most sharply. Here again, the boundaries between spiritual and material are being questioned, as people catalogue the disastrous environmental costs of the all-out pursuit of economic growth and seek a new relationship between the human and natural worlds. At the 1992 Earth Summit, for example, the language of many papers was mystical or prophetic rather than cold-blooded scientific. The search for a new understanding of development is already begun. This means not just tinkering with the system, but a fundamental re-evaluation of the values and assumptions on which that system is based.

There is a story that Jesus tells (Matthew 12:43-45) about an evil spirit that goes out of a man and looks for somewhere else to rest. Finding nowhere, it goes back and finds the house swept clean and empty. Then it goes out and brings back with it seven other spirits even worse than itself. This could stand as a picture of our current development crisis. The spirit of secular modernism cleansed its home of the old household gods of conservative religion. The 'age of reason' banished religious faith to a small, locked room, well away from the mainstream of life. But the new belief in progress and development is now itself under attack. The spiritual vacuum it left has brought the evil spirits of authoritarian religion and ethno-nationalism pounding at the door. The last thing that should be done is to leave the house swept and spiritually empty and so invite them to come in.

What is Theology?

In the previous section we made clear that when we talk about theology and development we begin with the understanding that the two cannot be entirely separated from each other. Our theology informs our understanding of development, and what we see as development influences our theology. Nonetheless, the two are plainly not the same. In this section and the next therefore, we spell out further what we mean by each of these terms.

In defining what we mean by theology we have been greatly helped by the way Dorothy Solle puts it in her book *Thinking about God*. She quotes the classical way of defining theology, *fides quaerens intellectum,* faith seeking understanding. As she goes on, she expresses again how deeply theology and development are entwined:

> *Quaerens* (in search of) also means that faith cannot exist without its shadow, doubt. Faith without doubt is not stronger, but merely more ideological. The search into which living faith throws us cannot be content with cheap grace, naive trust that all will go well, superficial charity which does not get to the root of things. A faith which seeks practical understanding of itself as participation in the reality of God cannot spare itself the trouble of rational grappling with the conditions for a worthwhile human life.
>
> ~ Solle (1990:4-5) ~

Faith, in this context, does not mean simply a disembodied belief; an intellectual assent to a set of prescribed doctrines. Faith is a pledge of oneself to God. We could as well say love, or hope. *Doing* theology, therefore, is not just an academic exercise, trying to deduce minor principles from major premises. It is an active commitment to live one's faith, critically and questioningly, lovingly and hopefully. Latin American theologians have described this process as the pastoral cycle, in constant revolution from experience to analysis to reflection to action and on again.

It is this cycle that we have had in mind as a pattern in writing this book. But as it stands, there is nothing particularly theological about it. It could as well be a description of scientific experiments, or counselling practice. What makes it theological is the context in which the experience, analysis, reflection and action take place.

A contemporary translation of 'theology' is 'God-talk'. If God is, then the one thing that we can be sure of is that God is utterly beyond our 'talk'. This is the insight of the Jewish tradition of God as Yahweh, 'I am'; or the Buddhist tradition of negation, 'not this, not this'; or the Islamic rejection of figurative pictures; or recent Christian descriptions of God as 'absolute reality' or 'the ground of our being'. Another way of expressing this is found in Hindu thought and practice. Here the 'beyondness' of God means that God may appear in many different forms, or in none. The many different deities in human or animal form are thus seen as manifestations of the ultimate One. There is also space within Hindu, like Buddhist, tradition for a non-theistic path, in which God does not appear in a particular form at all. This finds echoes in the current impulse of many people in the West to find a spirituality through which they can seek personal wholeness, outside the confines of institutional religion.

God-talk is a finite, human activity. It cannot comprehend the infinite reality of God. But what we can talk about is our relationship with God, however we understand God to be. If the context of our experience, analysis, reflection and action is this relationship, then we can rightly call it 'doing theology'.

It is this engagement in the process that makes doing theology different from simply studying religion or cosmologies. In doing theology, we put ourselves and our commitments on the line, seeking to find a way forward in our understanding of the world and our response to it. In this way, we hope to open up dialogue with people of very different experience and religious traditions. This is very different from the sociological study of religion, which brackets off 'truth questions' and keeps a stance of academic distance and objectivity. We make this option for a number of reasons. First, we want to ground our analysis in experience, and follow it through to action. Second, we believe that in practice much sociology of religion *has* assumed a particular view of how the world is. Like much of Western thought, its starting point is the separation of spiritual and material, which contradicts our own understanding of the way the world is. This means that it analyses religion in purely materialist terms, with the result that rather than simply explaining religion, it has often explained it *away*. Finally, we believe that knowledge is always from a particular point of view. Everybody is committed to a certain view of reality, and claims of objectivity are only a way of masking this. It is only in being aware of our own basic assumptions that we can subject them too to rigorous analysis.

It is all very well to talk about being in relation to God, but what does this mean in practice? *How,* that is, do we do theology? The fundamental process is one of critical reflection on our experience in the light of our religious tradition, and on our religious tradition in the light of our experience. As we are both Christians, our sense of God is embodied in the Christian tradition. In line with the pastoral cycle, our starting point is our own experience. This gives us the questions which we bring to our religious tradition for answers. Our experience itself, of course, is not ours alone, but reflects our families and the societies in which we were born, the people we have met and the answers they have sought and found. The religious tradition, similarly, is not something set and unchanging, but living and growing, made up of the experience and reflection of many people down the ages. The basic story-line of this great history is given in the key Christian text, the Bible. For Christians, therefore, the Bible is an important reference point, as it offers a kind of distillation of how people have explored their experience in relation to God and how they have found God to be revealed.

As the example of Michael Portillo suggests, however, there are many ways of reading the Bible. There are even many ways of answering the same question. We explore this in Chapter Three in relation to the key question of development: Why are the poor poor? This shows the importance of viewing theology as something *to be done*. Neither in the Bible, nor in Christian tradition, is there a blueprint theology which can simply be lifted out and applied to the present context. There are, for example, no exclusively *Christian* values. What is authentically human cannot be foreign to Christians; and what is truly Christian must be inclusive and universal. The essential values of Christianity are common to all the world religions, and to committed humanists. What Christianity gives, as do these other faiths, is a *particular witness* to certain core *human values*. It is in relation to our understanding of these – which of course bears the imprint of our own religious background – that we must reflect critically both on our own experience and on the religious tradition to which we belong.

For Christians, the life and teaching of Jesus provide the key witness to these universal human values. These are summed up by Jesus in the 'new commandments': to love God with all your heart and to love your neighbour as yourself (Mark 12:29-30). Love, then, is central to the Christian understanding of how the world is and should be. This indicates what is perhaps the distinctive insight of the Jewish and Christian tradition. For there to be love, there must be personal encounter. The Jewish and Christian witness, therefore, makes the dual affirmation: that the personal is at the heart of reality; and that persons exist not in isolation, but essentially in relation to one another.

Just as love affirms that we belong fundamentally to one another, so it also entails justice. We cannot love our neighbour as ourselves if we behave unjustly to him or her. The Christian Church itself stands judged by this in its tolerance of racism, sexism, and exploitation of the poor. But the teaching is clear. The love of God cannot be separated from the love of our neighbour. There is no separate sacred realm, but the sacred is there to be encountered in the ordinary, the everyday. This is shown most clearly in the person of Jesus, who Christians believe was both human and God. But all human beings are made in God's image. We realise God's presence in as much as we live in love.

The Christian picture of how the world is also includes the cross. This shows the cost of loving, and the reality of injustice. The struggle to live life lovingly is a threat to the power structures and they respond with violence and cruelty. Human beings have the capacity for evil, or 'sin', for choosing to suppress, rather than express, the image of God in themselves and in others. As Dorothy Solle says, there is no easy optimism here, no naive faith that all will go well. But there is a message of hope. For the crucifixion is also the key symbol of Grace, of the power of love to redeem and make new. It holds the promise that the cross is not the end, that after the cross is resurrection. That through death comes life, and through suffering, liberation.

What is Development?

Whereas in theology the main emphasis tends to be on reflection, in development the chief focus tends to be on action. How can the poor become less poor? What part should the non-poor play in making this happen? The urgency of the need for change can make us impatient to be doing something. No development agency report is complete without a section on 'recommendations for policy'. But just as doing theology demands action, so doing development requires reflection. In the first place this is about strategy: how do we bring about the changes that we want? What will be the consequences of making this move, rather than that? But in and through this, we also 'seek understanding' at a deeper level. We need to understand what poverty means before we can know how to tackle it. We need to analyse development experience to see what has worked, how and why. We need to reflect on whether this confirms the assumptions we began with, or whether our understanding of development needs to be revised. And of course, we need to act on this understanding to bring about change.

Doing development then, like theology, involves engagement in the action-reflection cycle. The principal focus, however, is not our relationship to God, but to one another, and how this is shaped by the context of poverty.

The conventional notion of development says little about the relationship of poor to non-poor. Instead, it sees development as the movement from 'traditional' to 'modern' society. A country's 'stage of development' is assessed by national figures on income, generation of savings, growth rates of industrial output, availability of public utilities, or rates of literacy, infant mortality and life expectancy. There is no suggestion that relations between rich and poor countries might be responsible for the huge differences of wealth and welfare that such national figures reveal. *Doing* development means drawing up national plans to expand agricultural and industrial production, plus, perhaps, health and welfare services. At a more local level, development programmes are also established to enable poor communities to generate better standards of living. Richer countries may then enter the scene with aid programmes to support such plans with finance, technology and know-how. Although they may admit some commercial and political interests in such involvement, the dominant motivation, it is claimed, is humanitarian.

The history of different development approaches is given in more detail in Chapter Three. The dominant view of development has not gone unchallenged. Particularly in the 'voluntary' sector of the Non-Governmental Organisations (NGOs) such as Christian Aid and Oxfam, there is a very different analysis of both the 'problem' and the 'solutions'. Here, we outline some of the basic elements in this critique, to set down some markers for our own approach.

National figures of course give important evidence of the widely unequal distribution of wealth between different countries. But ranking countries in this way implies that development is an end to be achieved, an end which some countries have already reached. This is backed up by the way we commonly talk of 'developed' and 'under-developed' or 'developing' countries. In this view, the challenge for poor countries is to 'catch up' with those 'in front'. Development is seen as a pre-determined model that holds for all times and all places.

There are two issues here. First, seeing development as a goal for countries to aim at is at odds with the root meaning of the word itself, as the *process* of developing. This may seem obvious, but it is often forgotten. Development is something that *happens* and goes on happening, unless there is decline. It is not an end-point that can be achieved. This means that there is no blueprint which all individuals and societies must follow. Instead, there must be openness for poorer people and countries to define development in their own terms. This has a further implication. Seeing it as a process makes clear that development is not an issue for the poor alone, but for all people and countries. It can be pictured not as a line in which those 'behind' struggle to move forward, but as a spiral in which the problems and solutions of rich and poor are vitally intertwined.

Second, the word 'development' is not neutral. It suggests growth, progress, improvement, something to be desired. Development, therefore, is about *values*. Put crudely, this means that in the conventional view the 'advanced' North is not only richer, but also *morally* superior to the 'backward' South. Economic growth, material accumulation and Western-style modernity are the ideals to be desired, by countries and individuals. Ironically, however, being so value-laden also gives development a certain openness. So long as the reality differs from the ideal, the ideal can be used as a judgement on the system, to question the existing model. If their quality of life does not improve, then people can protest that what is on offer is 'not genuine development' and call for an alternative. The argument is not only about strategy, but also values, assumptions, and ways of seeing the world.

Like other histories, the story of development tends to be told by the winners. If we want to understand what it means, we need to read the small print, not just scan the headlines. In particular, we need to question the accepted definitions, and to learn what development looks like 'from below', from the viewpoint of the poor.

The industrial revolution of the late eighteenth and nineteenth century Britain is often taken as a model of national development. It seems, therefore, a fitting place to start to piece together a view on development 'from below'. For most people in the West, the image the industrial revolution conjures up first is the steam engine, followed perhaps by the cotton mill. The invention of new technologies was of course of great significance. But the process of change was much wider than that. The whole society was shaken up. New forms of wealth allowed an emerging commercial and industrial elite to compete with the old landed one. The organisation of jobs, time, homes, rights, family and community lives altered fundamentally. Nor did the process stop at the shores of the British Isles. Through colonialism the re-structuring of ways of life continued even the other side of the world.

In terms of economic growth, there is no doubt that the industrial revolution represents development. But for many of the people who lived through it, this process involved anything but progress or improvement. The historian E P Thompson (1980) points out that in the late eighteenth and early nineteenth centuries in particular, the writings of working people show that many felt their living standards were in decline. The livelihoods of skilled craftworkers were threatened by mass production, agricultural workers were thrown off the land and customary rights to grazing and secure tenure were taken away. Many were unemployed or struggled to scrape together a marginal living. Those who did gain work in the new factories often had to labour for longer hours with less autonomy and in worse conditions than their grandparents or great grandparents had ever known.

These views 'from below' show that the costs and benefits of economic development are not shared equally. It is not enough to know the overall growth in national income, or even the rise in 'average' wages. We need to ask how that income is spread. What is the range of wage rates, and what kinds of people (old or young, men or women, skilled or unskilled) are employed at what levels? What forms of 'off the books' earnings may people have lost, when they had to leave their own homes and gardens for factory jobs? What is happening to the cost of living for different sectors of the population? This means bringing out the *politics* of the process to ask: development *for whom?* Who participates, how and on whose terms? Who gains and who loses what and why?

A second set of questions can be summed up as: Development *by What (and Whose) Standards?* Important though levels of income and consumption are, quality of life cannot be read off from economic indicators alone. At least as significant are the relationships within which people live their lives. It was these which most often provoked working people in early nineteenth century England to voice public protest (Thompson, 1980:221-2). They felt bitterly the growing social and economic distance between employers and workers, the erosion of traditional rights and obligations, the tedium and loss of independence of new working practices, and the way they were reduced to mere instruments of production. The key issue here is not material goods, but values. What was at stake was not just their economic standard of living, but who they felt themselves to be. Although not expressed in religious language, these are *spiritual* concerns. They point, once again, to the interdependence of theology and development. And most importantly, they do so not from the perspective of the rich, but of the poor.

The final point that comes out from this is that *there are alternatives*. In their writings and political meetings, working people showed that they had different ideas to the bosses about how development should be organised. That the industrial revolution took the form it did, that the costs and benefits were distributed in the way they were, was due not to the steam engine, but to the values and interests of those in power. The voice proclaiming development as economic growth at any price may be the loudest, but this does not mean it is the only view. Amongst the poor, and even amongst the non-poor, there are also other speakers, with very different ideas, plans and strategies. The challenge of doing development is to let those voices be heard.

Doing Theology and Development

In the last two sections we have tried to separate out what we mean by 'theology', and what we mean by 'development'. Putting these two together we can come up with a more concise statement of what we mean by 'theology and development'.

Doing theology and development means to engage in the cycle of experience, analysis, reflection and action in the context of our relationship to God, and to one another as poor and non-poor.

This reflects the conviction that growing in God should make a difference to how we relate to one another, and that how we understand and act towards one another will shape our experience of God.

Within this very general definition, theology and development can take many forms. We have already seen one in the shape of Michael Portillo's speech. His underlying conviction regarding individual responsibility shapes both his political strategy and his reading of Christian tradition. Both reflect the New Right of radical economic liberalism which has dominated British politics since Margaret Thatcher became Prime Minister in 1979. We explore this further, along with a number of other approaches, in Chapter Three. Here we outline only our own starting points, as we consider what doing theology and development means for us.

As we talked this through, we realised that we both saw a common pattern. It is Romy's experience that reflects this most clearly, but none-theless it is something we had both come to quite independently. The pattern concerns how we as non-poor relate to those who are poor. it involves the movement from working for, to working with, to being with. We can express this best by telling part of Romy's story.

Romy:

While I was in seminary, I helped in training for the government co-operative programme, in which the Church was involved. There were credit unions, consumer co-operatives and grains marketing co-operatives for the farmers. The aim was to cut out the middle traders who were taking most of the profits. This was *working for.* We went into co-operatives because the Germans and Americans said so. Most of them collapsed. It was a foreign model. They were not touching the lives of the very poor. Farmers left the credit unions and consumer co-operatives because they felt they had no say in the making of policies or management. The members were farmers but the leaders professionals. It was mainly the professionals who benefited. For example, in the credit unions the rule was that people could borrow up to two times their capital share. In one case the daughter of the President had a share of 2000 pesos and had taken a business loan for 4000 pesos. That took up all the contributions of the small farmers. There was nothing left for them to borrow.

When I went to the parish, I wanted first just to be there. Even though I had not left my country, I had become a foreigner. I had been so long away in Manila, living a life very different from the farmers'. For one month I just listened to the local radio to re-learn the local idioms. My talk had become too abstract. I could no longer read the local language on sight.

As I went around listening to the farmers I understood why they did not join the government programmes. They were not responding to their own questions. They did not need loans for high yielding seeds or fertilisers because they were working on virgin land which was very fertile. What they needed were working animals. And there was no programme for that.

In the second year we made a project proposal, organising groups for sharing water buffalos which would be collectively owned. Eventually we got funding for it from Christian Aid. This was *working with*. Although there was growing government repression, I could consider myself untouchable as a priest. I was very privileged in respect and influence. Maybe I ate similar food to the poor, and lived with a similar degree of comfort, but I did not share their experience politically or socially. I always had security, and they did not.

Then while I was still a priest I decided with a group of farmers to move to a new area and set up a communal farm. We borrowed a tent and between twenty of us in three days built two houses. I remember our reflection at the Eucharist – how together we could do so much. I wanted to stay as one of them but they refused. They said I could be an honorary member but not a full one like they were. They could do the physical work better than I could and it was a waste for me to stay with them, when I could use my education to go and help other groups like them. I had to leave. In the end, they could not stay there either. A year later the anti-government forces took over the whole mountain range as a hideout. After only one harvest the farmers had to leave. They decided to do what they could at home and to stop dreaming of migration.

It was after I gave up being a priest that I came more to share the experience of the poor. It was not socially acceptable. I lost my privileges, my old contacts, my security. I felt very vulnerable. I used to wake in the night afraid that I would get sick and have no money to pay a doctor. Or if I was taken in by the military I could expect no institutional back-up. I had forfeited all sympathy. Priests left either because of a woman or because they had lost their faith and become Communist. But again, I could not share fully with the farmers what I was going through. I could be one *with* them but not one *of* them.

It is relatively easy to *work for* the poor. This is what 'doing development' generally means. In the twentieth century, development has been planned by governments, beginning with the Soviet Union in the 1920s, and then almost everywhere. In the late 1940s the first international development agencies were established, originally to work for relief and reconstruction after the Second World War. Early assumptions that development would 'trickle down' to the poor from economic growth at the national level have come to be questioned. As we saw in the case of the industrial revolution in Britain, the development process is always uneven and contradictory. Some people gain more and some less, while others lose out altogether. In view of this, development agencies now draw up special programmes and projects 'with a poverty focus'. The poor become the 'target group' of interventions from outside. They still have little influence over the kind of development that takes place. And they are kept at a safe distance. They are 'the problem', and we the ones who can solve it. Any relationship between poor and non-poor is at (at least) one remove. We need to *know about poverty*, but we do not need to *know the poor*.

Working with the poor is a lot more difficult. This means recognising that being poor is not just about lacking income, but also being excluded from positions of power. Working with the poor means waiting for poor people themselves to define what their needs are, and to support them in the action they decide to take to change things. It involves entering into a relationship with poor people, and so surrendering some of one's own autonomy and sense of power in being able to identify what needs to be done and take steps to make a difference. It means offering what one has and is for their use.

Being with the poor is more difficult still. It means experiencing in one's own life what it is to be poor and oppressed, to be disempowered. To set aside one's plans and strategies for change, and simply feel with the poor the pain of their situation. It involves seeing the implications poverty and development have for people's sense of themselves and their connections with one another, not only their material well-being. This spells the end to an easy view of poverty as romantic, or the poor as simple and virtuous. It means to see the tensions and contradictions within and between the poor and the non-poor, and to recognise through this that all of us are a part of the problem. Poverty is not just out there, but also within us, whoever we are. We need to understand the connections between internal poverty and emptiness and material poverty, between the drive to have more and the fact that others have less.

Like experience-analysis-reflection-action, this pattern is a cycle, there is no simple progression in a straight line from one end to the other. It is perhaps best thought of as a spiral, as the level of understanding deepens (hopefully) each time that it revolves. Each of the stages in the process has its own value. It is clearly important to *work for* the poor, for example in lobbying for fairer trading relationships between North and South. It is also necessary to *work with* the poor, and to seek to establish alternative structures and strategies which create space for their active involvement at all levels in doing theology and development. We do not mean to suggest that the final object of our commitment to theology and development is to enter into some kind of mystical empathy with the poor, which requires no further action. Rather, the point is that it should be out of this experience of *being with* the poor that our action comes. We cannot work effectively for or with the poor if we do not know who they are.

This orientation gives us the questions with which we come to our religious tradition. We do not see our relationship with God as separate from, but a part of this process. As we have already outlined, we do not view 'the spiritual' as a special realm that can be divided off from the rest of life. Our understanding of the fundamental Christian insight as love in the context of personal relationship, means that God comes to us in our encounters with one another. That love for our neighbour is impossible without justice means that God is revealed particularly in our encounters with those who have least. This is the theological foundation of making an option to *be with* the poor. Their experience emphasises the reality of the cross and shows that sin exists within us all as individuals, but also in the structures of society. Religious structures are not exempt from this. Being with the poor means reading religious texts from their standpoint, to find in them a message of liberation rather than one that justifies exploitation and legitimates the status quo.

We realise God in as much as we live in community. This means that our own well-being is intimately tied up with the well-being of others. *None* of us can realise Jesus' promise of 'life in all its fullness' while *some* of us suffer violence, hunger, homelessness, torture, poverty-linked illness, marginalisation or environmental degradation. But it is also in the struggle against oppression that we recognise our own poverty, our own longing for liberation. These needs are met, in turn, in community, and the love of others through which God comes.

CHAPTER TWO

Who are the Poor?

Introduction

What do we mean by poverty? The poor themselves don't need to ask: they live it daily from the inside. For the non-poor, though, this can be an abstract question, a concept to define and debate about. Poverty is something hidden, dirty, something that should not be seen. We shut the poor in council estates well away from the comfortable suburbs, in villages far from a tarmac road, in shanty towns or inner city ghettos, where respectable people are afraid to go. If we must think about poverty we do it from a distance. We draw up indicators to measure poverty, levels of income or calorie consumption. We romanticise the poor as hard-working and virtuous, or caricature them as feckless and criminal. If we do get closer, we want to keep it on our terms: 'don't give them my telephone number.' Because the poor are a threat. They disturb our sense of how the world is. All is not well. They make a claim on us so we feel guilty, embarrassed, ashamed, or afraid of losing what we have. We fear the poor, because they threaten our sense of who we are.

Things were much the same in Jesus' time. One of his best known stories, the Good Samaritan, turns on just this unease of the non-poor faced with the poor (Luke 10:25-37). The conventional response to poverty is shown by the religious leaders: on seeing the man in need, they passed by on the other side. But the Samaritan took the risk of acting differently. He looked at the man and was moved with compassion by what he saw. Instead of hurrying past he went over to where the man was, and set about caring for him.

The first step in doing theology and development is to overcome our hesitation, and to look squarely into the faces of the poor. We need, like the Good Samaritan, to look and be moved by what we see. This means opening ourselves to an encounter with poor people and being ready to listen to their stories. Taking time to share, if only through listening, some of poor people's experience, is vital if we are to understand better what being poor means. In the first part of the chapter we therefore present the stories of some of the poor people we have known. This is the basis for the second part of the chapter, in which we move from experience to analysis. Here we try to see what these stories tell us about being poor, the things that are in common and the reasons that some people may be more vulnerable to poverty than others.

The Faces of the Poor

In the early years of their marriage Julian and Teresa had been quite comfortably off. Julian was a fisherman and Teresa used to sell the fish he caught in the market. Also, their family was one of 40 who were tenants of a 240-acre coconut plantation. They took care of the trees on a six-acre plot. They were not paid wages but could keep one third of the harvest. In addition, they grew a maize crop under the trees and were allowed to keep all of it for their own use.

Then a road was built to the area. For the first time, lorries could come in to transport the fish to the big cities. Rich people bought trawlers and the stocks of fish near the coast began to fall rapidly. Local fisher-folk like Julian and Teresa were put out of business: the only remaining fish were out in the deep waters, where their paddle boats could not go.

The end of their fishing business hit Julian and Teresa badly, but with the income from the coconut trees and the cereal crop, they were still able to feed and clothe their seven children. Then a drought hit the area. Production was less than half the usual level and they could not harvest any grain. Even the banana plants could not produce any fruit. Their root crops were destroyed by the lack of rain. The local merchant refused to extend them any credit because he was also losing money. Neither could they get a loan from their neighbours. No one had anything to spare. Julian and Teresa were at their wits end. They didn't see how their family could survive. Only one option seemed open to them: they would have to sell two of their children.

★ ★ ★

Like the other people in his village, Fernando had first come to the area looking for a place to settle after a multi-national had bought up all the land where he grew up. The first years had been hard but gradually they had cleared land for planting and cut down some trees to make houses for themselves. Other families had joined them and the village had begun to feel like a community.

But the forest was attractive also to the armed underground forces. It gave them an ideal hiding place so they moved into the area, beginning to organise the villagers to supply them with food and to recruit the young men to join them. Whether they sympathised with them or not, the villagers were frightened into compliance. The guerillas spoke strongly against the corruption which riddled society up to and including the government. It was only the revolutionary forces, they claimed, who could impose justice and order.

The underground forces singled out two men to demonstrate their commitment to justice. One, they claimed, was an informer. He had been picked up by the military and tortured until he had told the little he knew about the underground's operations in the area. The other was accused of stealing wooden posts meant for a school building. He had admitted his guilt and asked for time to repay. Both were shot dead.

The terror from the underground was met by terror from the government military forces. Unable to trace the guerillas, the military came and took four leaders of the community and charged them with murder. Fernando was one of them. He had done nothing but be a community leader and a member of the board for the local co-operative store. He could neither write nor read. But he was gifted with a sharp analytical mind and a good memory. He could remember what he had learnt in seminars even years later. That they were not responsible for the killings made no difference. With no money to hire a lawyer to defend them, the four men were held for more than a year until a group of their farmer friends got together to mortgage their land to raise funds to release them on bail.

★ ★ ★

Sam and Jackie were desperate when they came to the advice centre. They felt caught in a trap which they did not know how to get out of. It had all started a year ago, when their daughter had an accident and had to go into hospital. At the same time, Jackie lost her job. With less money coming in and their worries for their daughter, they got behind on their loan repayments. They had bought some things on credit and soon the finance company was sending them threatening letters, saying they would be taken to court if they did not send the money they owed. The interest on these loans was more than 25%. If Sam and Jackie had gone to court the interest would have been frozen instead of continuing to mount up, but they didn't know this. Because of the intimidating tone of the letters they felt they must repay the finance company, and so fell behind on their mortgage payments.

In a few months the building society was threatening them with repossession of their home. The mortgage was high because they had taken it on when Jackie had her job and Sam was getting overtime. Not seeing any way to make the payments, they sold the house at a loss. Sam's wages were too high for them to qualify for housing benefit, but too low to afford rented accommodation, so they moved into a caravan. Then the caravan was damaged in violent storms. They became homeless, so the council re-housed them in bed and break-fast in a room over a pub. The noise disturbed their eighteen month old baby and the council said they would have to pay £80 a week rent. The council never pushed for this but they were afraid of it, so they moved back to a caravan.

The building society was demanding that they pay the costs involved in the house sale, otherwise it would take them to court. At the same time Sam's hours had been cut, so they had even less to live on than before. They could just have afforded mortgage payments on a small house, but because of the court order against them no building society would lend them the money. Now the council was threatening to take their baby into care saying the caravan wasn't a proper home for him.

★ ★ ★

A village was scheduled for re-settlement. Its inhabitants were Higa-onons, members of an indigenous Filipino ethnic group. This village was the home they inherited from their forebears. As far as they could remember, their ancestors had never been anywhere else. Their burial grounds and the fruit trees they planted after they cleared the forests to settle down as farmers bore testimony to the years that they had lived in the area. They did not apply to get titles for their farms because for them the land, the water, the trees, the air could only belong to the *Magbabaya,* the Creator. But they believed that they had the right to settle on their farms to support their families.

But the Government wanted the country to progress. The press-ing need was for more investment and new production to earn the foreign exchange vital for buying the modern imports the country required. The Higa-onons' land was fertile. It was wasted on them, using it only to meet their own subsistence needs. Foreign investors would find it an attractive location to set up a sugar plantation. So far away in the capital, the decision was made. Without warning, houses and corn fields were bulldozed. The Higa-onons were loaded into dump trucks together with whatever belongings they could salvage and relocated to hillside areas along the fringe of the forest. What *they* wanted was of no consequence. The country needed to develop and they were backward people with no statutory rights, obstacles in the path of change.

* * *

Felisa was only twenty years old. She had a two-year old son and was heavily pregnant with a second child. The family lived in a village which was three hours by small wooden boat to the nearest doctor. Throughout her pregnancy, she did not see a doctor because they needed whatever money they had for other things. Health care was mostly in the hands of private doctors and government health services were virtually non-existent in the remote rural areas.

Even when she was in labour they had no money to call a doctor, so she was attended only by an old village woman. After twenty four hours in pain, her family, friends and neighbours clubbed together to hire a boat to take Felisa to the hospital. They carried her on a stretcher to the sea-shore. But it was too late. As they lowered her into the bed that they had prepared for her in the boat, she let out a loud sigh. It was her last breath.

* * *

Like many other farmers in the village, Loreta was desperate for a loan. School graduation always coincided with the lean period, a few weeks or a month before harvest.

Loreta was a widow with three children. They were old enough to help her in the farm, but she would only ask them to help her when they were free from school. Somehow she had managed to feed, shelter, clothe and send them to school. But as the years went on, the productivity of the farm went down. One of the children was graduating from high school and she needed some cash. She had none. She had no land title so she could not go to the bank. Besides, it was ninety kilometres away and five hours ride by bus.

If only graduation had been four weeks later! Her maize crop would be ready for harvest in three weeks. If she borrowed from the local merchant, she could get the money she needed without interest. But she would then have to sell her whole harvest at the price the trader was willing to pay. And it was customary for traders to deduct two to ten centavos for every kilo from the current market price. She could barely afford this loss. But her only other alternative was to go to money lenders who demanded 17 kilos of grain for every fifty pesos they lent. This would mean paying 30% interest in four weeks!

★   ★   ★

Greg was unusually quiet when he first came to the night shelter for homeless young people. He had been on the road for only a few weeks. He still had a lot to learn. When the meal was prepared he ate hungrily. It was only toast and baked beans, but he hadn't eaten all day. He could not get income support because he was only 17, and anyway had no address to register with the Department of Social Security. He had come down south looking for work as there were no jobs in his home town. But work was hard to find. As his clothes got dirtier and his face more desperate, it didn't get any easier to find places to take him on. He no longer had the money to get home, and anyway there was no welcome for him there. If he didn't get work soon he would have no option but to beg on the streets. He was afraid. One night in the shelter for adult homeless had appalled him at the violence and filth. He didn't want that to be his life. But as the days passed it was harder and harder to see an alternative. There were so many people just like him.

★   ★   ★

For several years Asha had faced the fear that they would go hungry. As it was, there were times of the year when they had only rice and salt to eat. Her father was old and lame and could no longer manage the farming properly. He couldn't bend, so for weeding he had to go down on his hands and knees. It was a pitiful sight. He couldn't produce the same harvest that other farmers did. So this year they had been given only half the amount of land to sharecrop that they had before. They were lucky in having a kind patron, otherwise they would have had nothing at all. But they had only just managed to make ends meet with the crop from the land that they used to farm before.

The house needed re-thatching and they all needed new clothes. But as a woman, there were hardly any opportunities for Asha to get work. Though very bright, she had no education and work in richer households brought only her meals as a wage. The culture prohibited women from farming or going to market; in fact even if there had been chances for her to work outside the home, this would just lay them all open to gossip and criticism. If they had land of their own they could have hired workers and been assured of an income. But as it was the future looked bleak. Next year, perhaps, her father would not be able to work the land at all. They were already dependent on handouts from wealthy people in the community at festival times.

Asha felt ashamed and frustrated that her father in his condition should still have to work so hard. But she couldn't see any way that she could earn enough to support herself, let alone her parents.

How are Poor People poor?

These are some of the faces of the poor. There are many others. Everyone can think of poor people they have known, who would have some things in common with the people in these stories, but whose situation in other ways would be quite different. These stories raise two questions for us in trying to understand poverty. First, the faces of the poor are quite different. The problems facing Greg are very different from those which faced Felisa, the difficulties of Julian and Teresa very different from those of the Higa-onons. What is it that these people have in common, across such varied situations, that makes us able to recognise them all as poor?

The second question is linked to this. Even in a single person, being poor has many different faces. The faces of the poor are like our faces: they are the faces of men or of women, of young or of old, of members of majority or minority ethnic groups. Poverty has many different sides to it. What then are the different elements that can go into making people poor, and keeping them so? In this section we will focus on these two questions as we try and understand more of what it means to be poor.

The most obvious thing that poor people have in common is low income in comparison with those around them. That is, poverty is an economic problem. To say 'low income' alone is not enough, because levels of income and living standards vary so much in different social settings. Even if he manages to sign on for income support, Greg will be poor in the context of the UK. But in Bangladesh, the money he gets might make him relatively well off. Direct comparisons of poverty levels across different countries can therefore be misleading. A friend from the UK went to the West Indies and was shocked by the poverty he saw there. In comparison, he felt, there is no poverty in Britain, so whereas before he had been sympathetic to the claims of the disadvantaged in the UK, he was now much less ready to listen. But was this the appropriate response?

The World Bank (1990:26) defines poverty in terms of consumption levels. Consumption is a more appropriate indicator than income, because households with free access to public services can survive much better at a relatively low income than those without. The World Bank recognises two components in measuring consumption. First, the ability to secure a basket of 'basic needs': sufficient food, clothing, shelter, access to health care and education; and second, the cost 'of participating in the everyday life of society'. If you adjust for price differences, the first of these is relatively standard across countries. The second, however, varies according to locally defined perceptions of 'necessity' and 'luxury'. The level of income necessary to supply these needs is the 'poverty line' in a given country. The number of people below this line is expressed as the 'headcount index', which shows the proportion of the population in poverty. The 'poverty gap' calculates how far the poor fall below this line. As national prosperity increases, so the poverty line will rise, though the 'headcount index' and 'poverty gap' may not fall, or even increase.

Even in quantitative terms, these measures are quite limited. For example, they cannot show the distribution of poverty – they do not recognise transfers *between* the poor in which the income of one declines and the other rises. Also it can be very difficult to establish what 'basic needs' really are. People themselves have different ideas about what count as necessities, and what luxuries. Also, people often find it easier to define basic needs at a minimum level when it is other people's needs they are talking about. When it comes to themselves, the list of essentials tends to grow.

Aside from these 'technical' difficulties, there is a more serious underlying problem to this approach. This is, that it takes no account of how people experience themselves as poor. Most of us have had the experience of feeling fine about ourselves until we go into a room of well-dressed people, and suddenly feeling under-dressed and ashamed. Or of feeling that we would not like to invite people to our houses when we have visited them in theirs and found the quality of the furnishings and the food we were given so much higher than what we can provide. In a similar way, a boy from a remote village never thought of his family as poor until he went to the big city and saw the high buildings, the tarmac roads, the streetlights and was suddenly made aware of the mud houses, dirt tracks, and lack of electricity at home. The experience of poverty, then, is *relative*. To comprehend more fully what poverty means, we need to bring inequality into the picture.

To understand what we see in the faces of the poor, it is necessary also to look into the faces of the rich. This brings us to ask what the relationship is between the rich and poor: are the poor poor because the rich are rich? We consider this question further in the next two chapters. Here, the point to recognise is that when we talk about people being poor, we also assume that some people are not poor. In this sense, the concept of poverty itself is relative by definition – just as we cannot understand light without darkness, or good without bad. When we see that central to the idea of poverty is inequality, this draws out the social and political aspects of being poor. Economic considerations are only the starting point for understanding what being poor means.

Poor in Power

When we look more closely at what low income means, we can see that there are two main dimensions to it: access and control. In urban settings, access to income is primarily through employment – either working for others, or self-employment in a small business. In rural settings, assets may be more important, particularly land, but also other 'capital' – draught animals, tractors, or other inputs necessary to produce a crop. Access to either assets or employment may depend on access to other benefits such as health care, education, or information. But access does not necessarily give control.

Asha's family, for example, has access to land for sharecropping, but they do not own it, so they have no control over whether they will receive it the following year. People may know their legal rights, but not be in a position actually to achieve them. A woman may have access to employment, but not control the income she earns, because her husband or father takes it from her. In understanding the different dimensions of poverty it is therefore important to consider not only what access people have to key resources, but also the terms on which they have that access. Is the access full or conditional? How far does it confer control?

Looking into the faces of the poor the importance of control becomes very clear. What they all share, apart from economic need, is a sense of powerlessness. Perhaps most centrally, poverty is about the absence of options. What options there are, are desperate ones: selling their children, for Julian and Teresa; or taking very high interest credit which could ruin her in the longer term, for Loreta. The Higa-onons had simply no say in the decisions which were to affect their whole livelihood and way of life: because they had no land-titles they were outside the system and it was in no one's interest to recognise their claims. For Sam and Jackie the experience of becoming poor had also been one of losing control: they were made helpless and afraid by the many threats of the finance company, the building society, and finally the social services.

Being aware of the sense of powerlessness involved in being poor makes clear how it is not enough simply to consider the poor a 'low income group'. Looked at from a distance, poverty may be seen as a state, a category into which a certain number of people fit. But through the individual stories it becomes clear that poverty is rather a process, a process with a dynamic of its own. It is like a slippery pole: once you get on it, it is very easy to slide further down, very difficult to climb back up. But unlike a pole, poverty has many different dimensions. It is not just a matter just of falling income, but that opens people up to many other kinds of vulnerability: losing their homes, health, access to interest at normal rates, sources of livelihood, and perhaps even their families and freedom. As in the parable of the talents in the New Testament, it seems to be the rule that 'to all those who have, more will be given; but from those who have nothing, even what they have will be taken away' (Luke 19:26).

Poor in People

Feeling powerless also commonly means feeling alone. Some have suggested the term 'poor in people' to capture this aspect of poverty. This again is a common experience, well expressed in the words of the song: 'Nobody knows you when you're down and out' (Nina Simone). In the first instance, a household may be 'poor in people' because it has few members who are able to earn an income, relative to the number of mouths to feed. Households maintained by women alone are particularly likely to be in this position. This may also be a phase that a household goes through when the children are young, which passes when they become old enough to go out to work and may return if they marry away and the elderly parents are left alone.

But another side of being poor in people is having a shortage of links with others outside the household itself. Asha's case shows the importance of wider relationships as the family is totally dependent on having a kind patron. Even so, as she looks hopelessly for alternative ways of making a living, Asha shares with many of the poor a sense of isolation, of being alone with her problems. A common experience of those on low incomes in the UK is that they have little or no social life: they simply cannot afford to go out any more. This is compounded in the case of single parents on low incomes. Single parents are, first, more likely to be poor in income, because caring for children alone restricts job opportunities, and they have no income from a partner to help out. This, along with having no one to leave the children with, may make them virtual prisoners within their own homes. Because he is homeless and literally alone, Greg is the clearest example of poverty involving being poor in people, but it is true to a greater or lesser extent with all the people whose stories we have presented.

There is a paradox here. It is those with few material resources who are most in need of the non-material support of friendships and relationships. These may bring some practical help such as a no interest loan to tide Loreta over until her maize could be harvested. They are also important to affirm poor people's sense of value and self-worth against a system which measures these things mainly in terms of wealth and prestige. But it is often the better off who have the personal links to smooth their way through more difficult times. It is they who know people who can put in a word for them when there is a job going. Or who have friends or family in administration who can advise them on their statutory rights and how best to claim them. Or who can gain credit at special low rates of interest because of the promise of a favour in return.

Whatever the official rhetoric, personal bonds are still important in every country for gaining access to the information and opportunities people need to advance their own interests. Poor people are less likely to know their rights and less likely to know their way around the official system so as to be able to claim them. Even at a personal level poor people can be more alone than the better off: in general, bonds between people require some kind of exchange, and the poor may not be well placed to offer anything much in return.

These three related dimensions – poor in income, poor in power, poor in people – enable us to see how people whose situations may appear very different in fact have much in common. At the same time, however, it is important to take seriously the variety of faces of the poor, and so to consider the second question we raised above: What are the different elements that can go into making people poor, and keeping them so? Poverty is a social and economic problem, but it is also experienced in a highly personal way. It takes a different form depending on who it is that is poor, as lack of income can intensify other sorts of inequality in society.

Poor by Gender, Ethnicity, Age, Disability

The constraints that Asha faces, for example, are not simply due to her family being poor, but also because she is a woman. The culture which frowns on women working outside the home makes it particularly difficult for her to take any action that would relieve her family's poverty. As a result her family is poorer than it would be if Asha were a man. For other women childcare and domestic responsibilities make it difficult to take full time paid work. So they are confined to home-based working, often on piece rates, which is notoriously poorly paid. Or they are restricted to part-time employment, which typically has less security and fewer benefits than full-time work. And more often than not, the work that women do within the home goes unrecognised either by the family or by society at large. They get the blame when domestic work is not done, but no particular thanks when it is.

The form poverty takes is therefore affected by gender: whether the poor person is a man or a woman. This is explored more fully in Chapter Six. In a similar way, members of a minority ethnic group may experience poverty particularly sharply. In addition to low income, they have to face racial prejudice and cultural misunderstanding which may significantly cut down their opportunities for changing their situation.

The Higa-onons, for example, were vulnerable not simply as poor farmers, but also as indigenous people. They were packed into lorries as if they were cattle. Driven away from the ancestral home they believed the Magbabaya had given them, they were brought to marginal land in less accessible areas. They were stereotyped as backward and primitive. Their way of living in harmony with nature was ridiculed. Instead of being seen as something of value to learn from, it left them more open to exploitation.

In Europe also, members of ethnic minorities have typically to compete on very unequal terms with people of the majority community. This is borne out by the unemployment rates in the UK. Even by Government figures, which are generally agreed to be low, unemployment amongst whites in 1990 was 7%, while that of West Indians and Guyanese was 11%, and that of Pakistanis and Bangladeshis 17% (HMSO, 1992). Even where they do find jobs, the type of work people do is often 'colour coded' along racial lines. In the UK, for example, it is striking how people of South Asian origin predominate in certain types of work: in corner shops, restaurants, taxi businesses, the health service and the rag trade.

Age can also be a factor in making people poor. The very old and very young are both more vulnerable to poverty than those in the middle period of life. The similarity between old and young is reflected in the way that old age is often described as a second childhood. Older people are more likely to have health problems which cost money to treat and leave them unable to work and so poor in income. The situation of old and frail people in nursing homes in Europe and the USA gives a very extreme example of people who are poor in power. Like children, they are usually physically weaker and often weaker in understanding than the people on whom they depend.

Older people may find control of their money passes out of their hands, and even the pattern of their day is organised by others. Their sense of isolation, of being poor in people, people who are theirs, may be very strong, even if they have to spend most of their time surrounded by others. Older people may be better off in countries of the south where they are respected and looked after in the family. But as poverty increases this form of security can break down, especially when other changes – such as migration for work – are happening. This can leave old people with nothing to do but beg when there is not even a minimum state pension to support them.

Ill-health or disability also plays a part in making poor people poor. In a study of urban slums in Bangladesh, Jane Pryer (1989) found that the main breadwinner getting ill was the main factor in families' rapid decline into extreme poverty. In some cultures, babies with a disability are seen as having been born 'wanting to die', and are given enough care only to keep them quiet. In Bangladesh it is quite common even for older children to die from 'failure to thrive' once they go home from hospital after a seriously disabling accident. They have become a burden, a liability, to their families who may already be struggling to make ends meet, and simply lose the will to live. In the UK levels of compensation awarded after accidents are rarely enough to support full rehabilitation to the original standard of living. Whatever their own capacities and potentials, disabled people also have to suffer the profound handicap of living in a society where able-bodied people regard them as incompetent and inferior, and are unwilling to give them the opportunity to prove themselves otherwise.

Seeing the differences between men and women, between ethnic groups, by age and disability, in the ways people experience poverty, draws attention to a very important point. This is, that although the poor may be seen as a common category by outsiders, they do not necessarily see themselves in this way. There are two aspects to this. First, poor people recognise differences among themselves according to degrees of poverty. An example of this is given by Nancy Scheper-Hughes (1992:85), quoting a poor woman in a Brazilian shanty town. The woman divides her community into three sub-classes. First there are the hardworking 'respectable poor', who have built their own homes and have regular employment, a 'self-respecting class with a social conscience'. Then there are the 'truly poor', with no security or stability, seasonal and temporary workers who rent rather than own their hovels and are buried in paupers' graves when they die. Finally there are the 'truly wretched' ones who have nothing, living from hand to mouth, sometimes having to resort to begging to feed themselves. Similar divisions between the 'managing', 'very' and 'absolutely' poor are also drawn in rural Bangladesh.

Alongside these 'vertical' divisions according to degrees of poverty, there are 'horizontal' divisions between men and women, different racial or ethnic communities, old and young and so on. These other aspects of their identities may prevent poor people from developing a 'we-feeling' of sharing common problems, or being a group with common interests. Poor people are also often competing with each other for access to scarce resources of land, state benefits, employment, or wealthy patrons. As we will see again and again, solidarity amongst oppressed people has to be struggled for, it cannot be assumed. And once achieved, there is an on-going battle for it to be maintained.

Regional Differences

So far, we have looked at poverty as an individual, or at most a community problem. Does it also make sense to talk about poor countries? We commonly do, as the variation in standards of living between countries is so great. According to the 1996 World Bank Development Report, the lowest national income per head was $80 (Rwanda), the highest $37,930 (Switzerland). There are some exceptions, but in general these differences in income are also reflected in other ways, such as life expectancy, infant mortality, levels of education and the availability of health care, food and fuel consumption. Figure 2.1 gives as an example the contrasts between the Bangladesh, the Philippines, the United Kingdom and the United States in these areas (figures relate to 1993 and 1994).

Figure 2.1   International Differences in Welfare and Consumption

Variable	Bangladesh	Philippines	United Kingdom	United States
Life expectancy at birth	57	65	76	77
Infant Mortality (per 1000 live births)	81	40	6	8
% Girls of school age in Secondary education	12	74+	94	97
Commercial energy use*	65	364	3754	7905

*   per capita in kilogram oil equivalent
+   1992 figure for boys and girls

As well as differences between countries, there may also be great variation in standards of living between regions of the same country.

Typically, for example, rural areas are less well served with transport, electricity, health services and schools than urban areas are. Rural areas that are irrigated may be much better off than those where agriculture still depends only on rainfall. Similarly, in regions where the soil is very fertile, or where there are natural resources like valuable minerals, people are less likely to be poor than in others. As with individuals, so with geographical areas: being well placed in one way tends also to lead to advantages in others.

Comparing locations in this way does not mean that everyone in poor countries and regions is poor, nor everyone in rich ones rich. But it does have two advantages. First, it draws attention to the way that the wider social setting makes poverty more or less likely for a larger number of people: if you live in a Bangladeshi village you are more likely to be poor than if you live in an English suburb. Second, it allows us to ask similar questions about countries and regions as we have asked about people: What is the relationship between rich and poor? Are some countries and regions poor because others are rich? This subject is taken up in the next chapter.

Conclusion

In this chapter we have tried to understand something of what it means to be poor. The most important way in which we can do this is to be with the poor. In looking into some of the faces of the poor we have made a step towards this, we have been with them in our imaginations, trying to see the world the way they do.

In reflecting on the situation of the poor we have seen that there are three key dimensions: poor in income, poor in power, poor in people. The experience of poverty and the options open to the poor also vary according to who they are – whether they are old or young, men or women, able-bodied or disabled and what ethnic group they belong to – and where they are, the region or country where they live.

Asking who are the poor is the first move, because it makes us critical of our own prejudices and assumptions. In the next chapter we follow this up by asking the question: Why are the poor poor? But we close this chapter with one more character, who throws the question of who is poor back to us.

Eric

You live it
What we just haltingly dream of:
Detachment.
A shout, as I go to buy stamps
'Good morning, my lovely, how're you doing?'
'OK,' I say, 'And you?'
'Fine,' you say, 'Fine'.

'I'd swap a bottle o' wine for a cup o' tea,' you say
I laugh: 'I'll bring you some tea'.

An old man, propped against a brick wall on a frosty
February morning.
You are what should not be seen:
Homeless
Unwashed
What people turn from as they hurry on their way
But you claim attention
Shout for it,
Randomly accosting people as they pass
Not for money, but for a little warmth
A greeting given and received
A smile shared.

'People are good,' you say, 'look how they talk to you!
Since I come here only one bad thing happened
I had a sleeping bag and it got stolen
But I told this woman and see these blankets? she gave them me
So many!
And yesterday, believe it or believe it not
I was short of 20 pence for a bottle of wine
I said to this bloke, I'm sorry to ask you, but could you spare 20 pence?
He asked what I wanted it for, so I told him, and he give me 75 pounds!'

'You'd better keep that carefully,' I said.
You laughed: 'It's almost gone already!'

'People give me things,' you said. 'See here these clothes?
A lady came and give them me yesterday
Good stuff!
But don't reckon I can take them along

Don't like to carry things, you see.'

As I sat there with you, drinking tea,
You offered me beer, wine, clothes and sweets
Your hands, like your eyes, were open
Open to accept and freely give again.

'Ten years ago my wife died,' you said
'That's when I left. Couldn't stay there any more.
Couldn't live with the memories.'

You shook your head.
'Left the key with a neighbour,' you said
'Told her to give it to my daughters.
I've got two daughters, 31 and 32, older than you!
Tell them, I said, to do what they like with the house.
Give them the key when they come.'
'They'd be worried' I said 'to find you gone.'
'I phone them,' you said 'every now and then.
Tell them I'm working and doing alright.
They'd worry if they knew I's on the street.'

'What did you do before?' I asked.
'What haven't I done!' you said,
'Been in the army, worked on a building site
Was even a miner for a while
Look at these hands: they're hands that've worked.
No one could say I haven't worked,' you said.

'I must go,' I said
'Go and do some work.'
'I must go and do some work too,' you said
'Find myself somewhere to pee!'

I went back to the house
As I came out, you called again
'Come and talk to me tonight!'
'I will,' I said 'I will'.
But that night you'd gone.

CHAPTER THREE

Why are the Poor poor?
Four Paradigms

Introduction

Poverty, like suffering, needs to be explained. We look to a God to have decreed rich and poor; a former life to set our fate in this one; an after-life to put all wrongs to right. We blame the empire, or the immigrants, human folly, or human greed. We call for economic growth, or redistri-bution, a change of government, a change of heart. We need to find a reason, whatever form it takes. Because poverty is an offence, something disturbing, something that should not be. Poor people feel this and try to hide it; saving a good sari or a smart pair of shoes to disguise the poverty they are made to feel is their shame, not ours. We need an explanation to restore our view of the world. Because seeing people poor challenges our sense of what is right.

In the second chapter we looked into the faces of some poor people to try to feel with the poor something of what poverty means. In this chapter and the next we aim to build on this as we ask: 'Why are the poor poor?' The reason for this question is quite practical: we need to under-stand what makes poor people poor, in order to work out what we should do about it. We begin with the views of a group of poor people in the Philippines. They give a range of responses which reflect very different beliefs and values about how the world is and should be. Based on this we distinguish four different types, or paradigms, of theology and development. The definition of these is very broad, and each contains many different approaches. There are also many viewpoints which do not fall neatly within one or another. Nonetheless, we feel it is useful to identify some very basic differences of outlook, before we go on to develop our own.

The purpose of this chapter is to set out these paradigms in a little more.detail. Starting from their explanation of poverty, we consider how each paradigm sees our relationship to God, and to one another. We sketch their core values, their views of society and the role of the Church, their understanding of Biblical teachings on wealth and poverty, and the

33

social and development policies they lead to. This takes us into a brief history of development approaches, as we explore how each of the paradigms has influenced development policy and practice. Finally, we ask how well the 'answers' the paradigms give to poverty measure up to the experience of poor people.

Reasoning it out

Romy:

Danny was a village boy who 'made good'. He was one of nine children. His father owned three acres of land which provided their foodgrain needs. For cash, he relied mainly on fishing. He never earned enough to send his children to college. Except Danny. He won a scholarship and studied in Manila. After graduation he went to work in Davao City. His parents and other brothers and sisters still lived on the small island of Samal. During vacations he always went back to visit his relatives and friends. One summer Danny invited me to come along.

It was a very slow trip. The motorised wooden boat stopped in several seaside villages. At the end of the five-hour journey my face and arms were sun-burnt and sore.

Danny was a village boy again. The airs of city life completely vanished. He was truly one of them. No wonder everyone was glad to see him again. When evening came, they built a bonfire and fishermen came bringing some of their catch for everyone to have a meal. Hardly anyone came to visit their village and my presence was something special. But I felt it was not for me that they came together. They wanted me to see their regard for Danny. They were proud of him. Though Danny had gone to college and had a permanent job in the city, he never forgot them. He was different, and yet, he was the same Danny who grew up with them.

After the meal, a couple of young men brought out their guitars. It was a good mixture of lively and sad songs. Though it was only 8:30 in the evening, the night seemed to be very late. We had no light except for three kerosene lamps made out of empty rum bottles. But before the group broke up, they wanted me to say a few words. I had not prepared a speech. I did not know what to say. I did not really know them. So I asked if I could put some questions to them instead. They agreed.

'Are you rich? Or are you poor?' I asked. 'We're poor,' they answered in a chorus. 'Why are you poor?' I proceeded. 'We're lazy,' a voice spontaneously erupted. 'We're ignorant,' another added. 'It is written on the palms of our hands,' still another suggested. An old man said, 'See my fingers. Some are fatter than others. They are also of different lengths. Some are long, others are short. God did not create us equals. Some are rich, others are poor. It's our fate to be poor'. And then silence fell.

'The night is still young,' I said, 'but you said that you must go to sleep soon. What time do you get up?' 'Four o'clock,' some said. 'We do not know the exact time. We have no watches or clocks. But we wake up a couple of hours before sunrise.' Still others said, 'When the cock crows'. 'But why do you have to get up so early?' I countered.

The responses were varied. 'We have to feed and water our water-buffaloes and start ploughing before the sun gets hot.' 'We have to climb the coconut trees to gather the coconut wine.' 'We have to prepare the food for the day, for the men to carry with them.' 'We have to boil water for coffee and feed the pigs and chickens.' 'We have to leave early so that we are out at sea soon after sunrise. We only have paddles to move our wooden boats.' Again I asked, 'Who built your houses?' 'We did.' 'Who built your wooden boats?' I continued. 'We did.'

'You wake up very early and you know how to do all these things. And yet you say that you are poor because you are lazy and ignorant. I do not understand. I also wonder if you are poor because God wants it so.' There was a long pause. They looked at each other. I sat and waited for a response.

Finally a woman stood up and said, 'I take back my agreement to the reasons given why we are poor. We are poor because our maize, copra, coconut wine, fish and other products are bought by the traders at low prices. And yet we pay high prices for the things they sell to us. We are poor because others are rich. It is not God's will but the will of human beings'.

This story indicates a whole range of answers to the question 'Why are the poor poor?' None of them is simply descriptive – all of them have moral, and we might say spiritual, elements to them. The first response is to blame the poor: 'We are poor because we are lazy.' Of course, it is not only the poor who see it like this. The non-poor also argue along these lines. The poor are blamed not only for what they do not do – work hard enough, educate themselves – but also for what they do. Instead of making the most of what they have, they drink, smoke, or gamble it away. No wonder they cannot make ends meet! And then they try to get other people, or the state, to pick up the tab for their indulgence! There is something very comfortable about this view of the world.

Everyone gets what he or she deserves. Things may not start out absolutely equal, but if you work hard and have a bit of luck you can get on. After all, Danny started from where they are, and he 'made good'. The people who stay poor are too lazy, self-indulgent, or simply too stupid to better themselves.

In the second place, poverty is put down to fate: 'Look at my fingers ... some are long, some are short .... God did not create us equals.' Poverty is just 'there', it is no one's fault. It is to be accepted. This view is reflected in an old verse of the hymn, 'All Things Bright and Beautiful':

> The rich man in his castle,
> The poor man at his gate,
> He made them high and lowly
> And ordered their estate.

Society is built on a natural order, in which everyone has his or her rightful place. The 'rich man in his castle' may throw some pennies to 'the poor man at his gate' to help ease his situation. What he will not – and should not – do, is to invite the poor man into the castle with him. To do so would mean upsetting the established order. And far more to be feared than poverty, is social unrest.

A third voice identifies poverty with backwardness: 'We're poor because we're ignorant.' In this view, Danny's community is poor because they have been 'left out' of development. Their fishing and farming methods are primitive, and so low in productivity. Poor transport and communications mean their village is remote. This shuts them off from wider markets, the spread of new ideas and technologies, and programmes for welfare, education, or training in new skills. Poverty, therefore, is a technical problem. Poor people should not be blamed for their poverty, their 'backwardness' is not their own fault. They need to be helped to overcome their 'traditional attitudes' of fatalism, and given access to the skills and resources that will lead them into the modern world. Poverty can be eradicated: it is a hangover from an earlier, less technologically advanced world order.

The final response is rather different: 'We are poor because the rich are rich.' This is the only view which puts the *relationship* between poor and non-poor clearly in the picture. More than this, the mechanisms which produce poverty are identified: here, the unequal pricing system between the villagers and the traders. What distinguishes this from the other answers is not just the analysis of causes, but also the action that it leads to. The first two responses lead either to non-action, or to action on an individual basis. The third view of poverty recommends action by the state or other development agencies to bring the poor into the broader movement towards progress. It is only this last response which suggests that how society is organised must itself be changed. That the way out is not individual escape, charity or fuller incorporation into the existing system, but group action to transform the structures that generate poverty in the first place.

Each of these explanations of poverty points to a broader framework of meaning by which people interpret the world and 'make sense' of what they see about them. As Danny's community shows, elements of all of these exist alongside each other. Looked at historically, however, we can also see that different types of world-view have tended to dominate at different times. In the next sections, therefore, we consider the first three paradigms in the order in which they have appeared. The 'traditional' view we label the *conservative paradigm*. This is the one that sees poverty as part of the natural order: 'It is written on the palms of our hands.' In reaction to this, the liberal approach developed. Founded in a belief in progress, this sees poverty as due to ignorance, which could be solved by development. More recently, this optimism has been challenged by the *New Right*. Here, poverty is traced not to the natural order or the 'stage of development' of the community, but to individual responsibility: 'We [or they] are lazy.' The final paradigm we call the *liberational*. Historically, this developed in reaction to the liberal world-view, and was a trigger to the authoritarian backlash of the New Right. Since the liberational paradigm sets the overall framework for our own analysis, however, we set it apart to be discussed in more depth in the following chapter.

The Conservative Paradigm:
The Poor are always with You

In the conservative world-view, poverty is just there. It is regrettable but unavoidable, something to be accepted, lived with. Society is made up of some who are poor and others who are rich, some who are meant to lead and others to follow. The relationship of rich and poor is a personal one of mutual rights and obligations, which are ordained by tradition. The responsibilities of the rich towards the poor are to behave with fairness, forbearance and compassion. The responsibilities of the poor are to accept their place in life humbly, being hardworking, law-abiding, loyal and grateful for the charity of the rich. This overall framework is called in social science a 'moral economy' and is very common in peasant and tribal societies. The core values are social stability, adjustment to circumstances, respect for tradition and behaving properly according to one's station in life.

In terms of its view of how the world is, or should be, this is essentially a consensus model. Men and women, rich and poor, all have their proper place in society. Personalities are important, but people are seen as part of a community, rather than as self-contained individuals. If they fulfil their given role faithfully, this will be to the social and spiritual benefit of all. As in the case of Danny's community, it is this response which most commonly brings God into it. This is no coincidence. The social order is seen as a moral order, with no clear distinction between the sacred and the secular. Religion provides the 'social cement' which binds the society together. Religious texts are interpreted according to established tradition, with relatively little scope for contemporary innovation.

The existence of traditional rights and obligations between rich and poor in the moral economy should not be over-romanticised. It does not mean that once there were simple, egalitarian communities in which everyone fitted to make up a harmonious whole. There have always been tensions between personal and community interests, and people who refused to honour their responsibilities. The core of the moral economy is not the sense that it is wrong for some to have more and others less. Rather, it is the view that everyone should have a certain minimum, that none should be left destitute. The conservative world-view is widely held amongst ordinary people, across all societies. This sometimes takes the malign form of belief in 'natural difference' where women, black people, and/or the poor, are seen as 'naturally inferior' to men, white people, and the wealthy. But more positively, it also appears as the conviction that there should be some baseline rights, a minimum standard of living beneath which people should not fall.

Since society is seen to be built on personal bonds which are governed by tradition, the conservative world-view does not have a social or development policy as such. Nonetheless, it does imply that there should be certain basic mechanisms to protect those at the margins – the widows, the orphans. In development, this is reflected in relief programmes to ease immediate hardship and in welfare approaches concerned with meeting 'basic needs'. More broadly, it is seen in institutions such as the 'poor relief' at the parish level. As in this case, the provision of such support is often seen as an important part of the role of the Church.

In the context of a conventional moral economy, everyone knows everyone else. The fact of being poor itself establishes your rights to help. The moral economy approach is much more difficult to apply in an urban industrial society, where people move to find work and communities have to be built up, rather than simply existing because people live close together. Nonetheless, within families and between neighbours or friends, a lot of informal helping out does take place. In addition, some notion of the moral economy is reflected in the commitment to provision of essential public services funded through taxation, and in giving to charity.

The Moral Economy and Religion

As already noted, the moral economy is very often expressed in religious terms, and the society of Ancient Israel is no exception. Abuses of traditional obligations angered the great prophets of Israel, who echo again and again that it offends Yahweh to see the rich take advantage of the poor, the orphans and the widows. Righteousness is seen as something that must be achieved at a community level. Piety divorced from the struggle for justice is condemned as offensive to God. The following passage from Isaiah 1:11-17 gives one of many examples of this:

'What to me is the multitude of your sacrifices?'
says the Lord;
'I have had enough of burnt offerings of rams
and the fat of fed beasts;
I do not delight in the blood of bulls,
or of lambs, or of goats.

'When you come to appear before me,
who asked this from your hand?
Trample my courts no more;
bringing offerings is futile;
incense is an abomination to me ....

'When you stretch out your hands,
I will hide my eyes from you;
even though you make many prayers,
I will not listen;
your hands are full of blood,
Wash yourselves; make yourselves clean;
remove the evil of your doings
from before my eyes;
cease to do evil,
learn to do good;
seek justice,
rescue the oppressed,
defend the orphan,
plead for the widow.'

It is important not to misunderstand this by translating it too quickly into the present. Giving to the poor was certainly a means to earn spiritual merit, but it was not a purely private, individual action. Seeing society as a moral economy means that caring for the poor is actually built into the political framework. It is the responsibility of the community to ensure that the vulnerable ones are looked after.

In itself, such a call for people to honour their traditional responsibilities does not entail any programme for radical redistribution. The social vision of ancient Israel, however, went considerably beyond this. Hebrew law set clear limits to accumulation by individuals. Restrictions were placed on what should be taken from the fields at harvest, to ensure something would be left for the outsiders and the poor. Every seventh year should be a jubilee, when slaves would be set free and debts be pardoned, and the dispossessed allowed to return to their homes. Social justice was not just a concern at the margins of Hebrew society. The law actually set structural mechanisms to limit the gap that could grow between rich and poor.

In practice this vision of social justice has rarely been achieved. As passages like the one above show, people repeatedly fell short of the moral economy ideal, and had to be reminded of their duties in no uncertain terms. Religious institutions were as likely as any others to go astray. Instead of affirming the claims of the poor, the conservative worldview is all too often used to sanctify the domination and accumulation of the rich.

The role of religion as social cement is thus ambiguous. The core vision is that society should be founded in God's justice, which should hold together rich and poor in a way that is sustaining for all. There is, however, a persistent tendency for this to be twisted. The view that the social order *should be* a moral order can quite quickly slip into the claim the established order whatever its character has been ordained by God and so must be upheld. The guiding value becomes not love but (hierarchical) order; the great fear is chaos. The structure of the Church mirrors the political system, and religious leaders become closely allied with those in power. God is King, at the top of the hierarchy, with Mary, perhaps, as 'Queen of Heaven', and the human monarch the next step down. Princes, bishops and officials come next in the ranking, which continues on downwards until it reaches poor men, women and foreigners.

This has been the dominant trend in Church social practice. State ceremonials are celebrated by top representatives of the official Church. In the past in the United Kingdom, special areas in parish churches were reserved for the family of the local lord or squire, to preserve them from mixing with their social inferiors. In such a system, 'minding your manners' and 'keeping out of trouble' become the foundations of morality for the lower classes. The social cement is not to bind society together in just relationships, but to sustain oppression by keeping the poor in their place.

The teachings of the Church can reinforce this tendency. Rewards in an after-life are promised to compensate for hardships in this one. Suffering is to be expected 'in this vale of tears'. In the Catholic tradition, this may be backed up by lingering images of the suffering Christ. Among Protestants, it more often takes the form of a strong emphasis on personal salvation as a passport to heaven. Complementing the promise of future rewards is the threat of punishment for misbehaviour. Here the emphasis is laid not on heaven, but on hell. Sin is seen as an individual matter, often with great emphasis on sexuality as a fertile breeding ground for introspective guilt. This is what some have called 'worm theology', where the main impact of Christian teaching seems to be to foster feelings of personal unworthiness and unfreedom. God and the bosses are emphatically on the same side.

The Liberal Paradigm: Poverty as Backwardness

In the conservative world-view, human nature is definitely fallen. Mechanisms of social control are necessary to ensure that the will to sin and self does not result in disorder and chaos. By contrast, the liberal approach brings a blast of optimism and faith in human capacities. Those who are poor or 'backward' should not be controlled, but enabled to reach their full potential. Poverty is the result not of the natural order, but of incomplete development. With the right policies, and the proper application of science and technology, it can and will be eradicated.

As this suggests, the liberal world-view is historically intertwined with modernity. Intellectually its roots lie in the 'Enlightenment', the name given to the diverse bubbling up of human self-confidence in Europe, dating from the sixteenth to the nineteenth century. The old attitudes of fear and reverence towards the unknown were no longer appropriate. Tradition was rejected as the basis of authority. Both natural and social worlds could be understood rationally, and explored empirically. Physical, social and political problems were puzzles that could be solved, and human inventiveness was quite adequate to the task. With the philosophy of Rene Descartes (1596-1650) and the experimental methods of Francis Bacon (1561-1620) and Isaac Newton (1642-1727), the foundations of modern science were laid. The hallmark of liberal thought, a critical attitude, was firmly stamped on society.

This early modern period saw tremendous social, economic and political upheaval. Competition between the European powers extended into their race to claim new territories and gain control over the valuable resources that these would bring. 'Voyages of discovery' re-drew the world map and subsequent colonisation decimated indigenous cultures. The enclosure movement in England and the Highland Clearances in eighteenth century Scotland tore away the rights to land that people had enjoyed for centuries. New agricultural methods and migration to work in nascent industries also contributed to the re-structuring of the natural environment and human beings' place within it. The printing press and rising literacy in Europe facilitated the spread of new ideas and the formation of nation-states. The French revolution of 1789 shook assumptions of political order and gave further boost to the new ideals of human rights, equality and the importance of the individual.

With so much change going on, the old fusion of social and moral order was inevitably called into question. The Protestant Reformation had broken the spiritual monopoly of the Catholic Church. The social and political scope of the Church was reduced further as many of its former functions in health care, social welfare, education and the law, came to be taken over by secular foundations or the state. The role of the Church was seen as encouraging lay people to become involved in these institutions, and so to ensure they were informed by Christian values, rather than actually providing them itself. Separation of Church and State became a core tenet of liberalism. This mirrors a much broader division between the public and the private sphere, the personal and professional. Economically this is seen in the replacement of the 'family farm' by the separation of work-place (factory) and home. Politically it is expressed in the rise of state structures staffed by bureaucrats, whose job is to deal impersonally with everyone alike, implementing a 'rational' system rather than one founded in personal preferences, such as family connections. Religion, like family, shifts firmly to the private sphere. While both may be important at a personal level, neither should be brought directly into the work-place.

Intellectually also, there was a tremendous shift. The division between public and private was expressed in a strong commitment to objectivity. In the liberal world-view, to call something 'subjective' is a criticism. It is the intrusion of the personal into the public sphere, which should be concerned solely with matters of fact, not feeling. The guarantee of authenticity comes not from within, but through publicly observable, demonstrable data, which is (in principle) equally available to all.

Like other forms of knowledge, the liberal approach opened up the sacred texts to the tools of reason and the individual's critical questioning. Religious understanding became much more personal and individual, with a high value placed on toleration towards others' beliefs. Less emphasis was placed on formal religious observance, and more on applying the values derived from religion, in 'living a good life'. For some, the whole package became irrelevant. Religion belonged to the 'childhood of humankind', whereas the Enlightenment represented 'humankind come of age'. For others, however, there was a shift in the kind of meanings that the texts embodied. In the liberal view, traditional interpretations become open to question, as the Bible is seen as a set of historical documents which reflect a particular context in need of de-coding to speak to today's world. Instead of the miracles being taken literally as magical events, for instance, natural explanations are proposed. A common example of this is the interpretation of the feeding of the five thousand (Mark 6:30-44). As it is written, Jesus takes five loaves and two fish, blesses and breaks them, and so provides enough to feed a crowd of five thousand who had been listening to him all day in a deserted place. A liberal reading of this would say that it does not mean that the laws of nature were suspended. The miracle lay, rather, in that one person's offering of the little they had led to everyone else being willing to share the food they had brought with them, and finding that instead of there being a shortage, there was actually more than enough.

In the conservative world-view, human society is caught up in a cyclical dance of rise and fall, development and decay. By contrast, the liberal belief in progress means that history is seen as a linear, evolutionary process, in which societies achieve ever higher levels of development over time. It is this 'modernisation' approach which has been dominant in international development. With regard to poverty, the emphasis shifts from the community to the individual. Instead of simply being born into their place in life, people should work to fulfil their potential. The world is not given and unchanging, but there to be won. At the same time, liberal approaches recognise that people cannot simply 'pull themselves up by their bootstraps'. Instead, social policy favours broad-ranging reform, with a strong role for education and training to enable people to overcome the disadvantages they are born into. While the rich – or the 'advanced' countries – should aid the poor, the relationship is not primarily personal, but mediated through official structures. The core vision is democratic rather than hierarchical. A secular state should act as a neutral arbiter for the good of all, providing law and welfare to temper the inequalities of civil society.

The liberal stress on the value of the individual finds a strong echo in the Biblical tradition. In the Gospels, Jesus is shown meeting people at the point of their need, being open to them and responding to them on a one to one basis. This is consistent with the whole Hebrew and Christian tradition, which is the deeply personal one of a covenant between God and God's people. The Bible is colourfully alive with characters, people with names, personalities, and stories. The liberal stress on historicity is also borne out by the way God is revealed not in philosophical abstractions, but in particular lives in particular places. In the Hebrew Bible the stories are often those of religious or political leaders, but they are tales not of heroes, but of flawed human people. Most of the characters in the Gospels are social and political nobodies, fisherfolk and farmers, local officials and teachers, soldiers of the occupying forces, village women, sick and disabled people and prostitutes. It is to these people that Jesus came, and to those who received him gave the power to become children of God (John 1:12).

It is important, however, not to emphasise *only* the value of the individual, or there is a risk of distorting the Biblical tradition. Jesus was not running an out-patients clinic for the sick and disturbed of first century Palestine. He was proclaiming the kingdom of God. His healing of individuals was the firstfruits of this kingdom, but the vision of the kingdom was a collective one, in which justice would reign. In responding with love to those who counted for little in his society, he confronted the religious leaders with their own lovelessness, concerned more with the small print of the law and their personal purity than caring for those in need. It was precisely this challenge to authority which infuriated those in power, and ultimately led to the cross. The story of the man with the crippled hand is typical (Luke 6:6-11).

> On another sabbath he entered the synagogue and taught, and there was a man there whose right hand was withered. The scribes and the Pharisees watched him to see whether he would cure on the sabbath, so that they might find an accusation against him. Even though he knew what they were thinking, he said to the man who had the withered hand, 'Come and stand here'. He got up and stood there. Then Jesus said to them, 'I ask you, is it lawful to do good or to do harm on the sabbath, to save life or to destroy it?' After looking around at all of them, he said to him, 'Stretch out your hand'. He did so, and his hand was restored. But they were filled with fury and discussed with one another what they might do to Jesus.

We have moral responsibility as individuals, to act with personal integrity and show love towards one another. But we also have a collective responsibility for the society in which we live. We cannot act justly as individuals, if the structures within which we live are unjust. The vision of Christianity is a corporate vision, shown in the practice of the early Church holding all possessions in common. The value of individuals is stressed, but as the value of different members together making up one body, not as self-contained beings, entirely independent of one another.

The Liberal Paradigm in Development: Modernisation

International recipes for combatting poverty have changed over time in line with trends in international economics and politics. The enterprise of international development as we know it today began around the end of World War II. The end of the war also saw the success of independence movements in a number of former colonies. The old power structures were disintegrating. A new model was needed for the relationship between North and South. The liberal paradigm provided that model, in the shape of modernisation theory.

In the modernisation view, development is understood as a matter of 'traditional societies' moving towards 'modernity'. Societies are all travelling along a single path called progress, but some are further behind while others were well in advance. The basic model was evolutionary, with 'modern man' of Western Europe and North America as the peak of human development. The main obstacles to development are lack of capital, skills, technology and modern political institutions. These are made worse by a 'traditional orientation', in which people work to cover their needs, rather than to produce a profit. This limits levels of production, since any surplus is simply consumed rather than reinvested.

National economic growth is seen as the answer to poverty. Contact between the North and South will bring benefits to both. Economically, the poorest countries have a 'comparative advantage' in cheap labour and primary products, but their 'backwardness' means they cannot make the most of these. Mines and plantations established by foreign companies allow extraction of the resources required by the North. At the same time they bring about the cultural and economic transfers which will speed up development in the South. There is also a political aspect to the modernisation approach. As part of their Cold War rivalry, both the United States and the USSR used their aid programmes as a way of extending their own power blocs.

Opposition to modernisation theory arose on two fronts. First, critics in the South, particularly in Latin America, pointed out that their countries had long been integrated in the world capitalist system, but had not seen the kind of development enjoyed by the North. Instead of working towards mutual advantage, continuing links between North and South resulted in the further development of the 'centre' countries of the North at the cost of continuing underdevelopment of the 'periphery' countries of the South. Little had really changed since colonial times. At their most radical, these 'dependency' theorists called, therefore, for 'de-linking' from the international system. They believed that only through political and economic autonomy could genuine development come to their countries. Others maintained that some development in the South was possible within the system as it stood, but that it was a 'dependent development', a capitalist breach-birth.

Forceful economic arguments supported these views. Evidence showed that foreign companies, rather than the countries in which they operated, took the lion's share of the profits, and reinvested them in operations elsewhere. Few 'backward or forward linkages' in the shape of broader industrialisation in the local economy were to be seen. Since much of the profit is made in manufacturing and processing, exporting primary products always brings a minimum return. In addition, the economists Hans Singer and Raul Prebisch analysed changes in terms of trade over time. They found that there is a tendency for the prices of primary products to decline, while those of capital goods and other finished products go up. Trading on the basis of different 'comparative advantages' could therefore never counteract inequalities. Instead, it would result in the poorer countries' market position getting worse and worse.

Second, the assumptions of modernisation theory were also criticised. There is no reason to believe that all societies must take an identical path towards a single model of modernity. Nor is it justified to see 'traditional' cultures as static, waiting 'penetration' from the West before they could 'develop'. All societies change and develop over time. The great empires of Babylon, Rome, Egypt, the Moghuls, the Aztecs, the Chinese Ming dynasty ... rise and fall. There is no single direction of change, but many contradictory ones. The evolutionary model also fails to see how societies develop in relation to one another, through trade, warfare or conquest. In particular it ignores colonialism, and the part it has played in shaping contemporary development and underdevelopment. A quite trivial example shows how important this is. What is the essentially British drink? Tea. And yet no tea is grown in the UK! Development in the UK was built on the extraction of resources from British colonies; it was not simply self-propelled. Similarly, we cannot understand the problems which countries in Africa face today without recognising the historical destruction of local ways of life through the slave trade and subsequent colonial intervention.

Overall, then, the opposition which modernisation theory sees between 'tradition' and 'modernity' is much too clear-cut. In the ideal of modernity, people achieve their position in society solely through merit. In practice, however, the 'traditional' rule that what you get depends on who you know, continues to operate in all societies. After being subordinated to broader national interests, ethnicity has reappeared in the 1980s and '90s as an important basis of political mobilisation. This makes an appeal to 'traditional loyalties' – but in the service of contemporary political interests. What counts as 'tradition' is not set, but varies over time, and is open to considerable manipulation. Rather than being in opposition to one another, the two are often complementary. 'Tradition' may serve the purposes of modernity, and modernity bolster tradition.

In order to combat what they saw as the structural inequalities in the capitalist system, much of Latin America, and some other countries such as India, followed a strategy of 'Import Substituting Industrialisation' (ISI). This involved restricting imports and trying to build up industries locally which could provide for their needs. Some of the achievements are impressive. Today, almost all the cars in India are made locally, making them cheaper and so available to a far broader group of consumers. This forms a striking contrast to Bangladesh, in which there is no intermediate option between Chinese made bicycles and Honda and Suzuki motor-cycles and cars. Overall, however, the results of ISI were mixed.

Concentrating on heavy industries meant the technology used was highly capital intensive. They were still heavily dependent on imports for materials and intermediate products for use in manufacturing. The absence of competition because of protectionism resulted in poor quality products and great inefficiencies. In many countries the internal market – in terms of those with sufficient money to purchase – was too limited to sustain a buoyant industry. The strategy had proved 'both concentrating and exclusive', with the main benefits going to a minority of capitalists. Instead of industrialisation spreading throughout the economy, it looked as though there was increasing dualism. A small highly mechanised 'modern sector' seemed to be pulling away an ever growing distance from the majority in subsistence activities.

By the 1970s it was recognised that many countries had failed to achieve the hoped-for economic growth, and that anyway growth did not necessarily bring benefits to the poor. The emphasis was changed to direct provision of health services, nutritional support and education: the so-called 'basic needs' approach, more characteristic of the conservative world-view. From the mid-1960s onwards there were also efforts to bring about a 'green revolution' in agriculture, through a package of high yield seeds, mechanical and chemical inputs. Underpinning these policies of state subsidies and expanded services lay a wider environment in which many banks in the developed countries were awash with petro-dollars. Actively seeking out borrowers, they were eager to give loans to Southern countries at low interest rates. Unfortunately for the debtors, when the time came for them to repay, the world economic climate had shifted from growth to recession, and New Right, rather than liberal assumptions, came to dominant the development scene.

In opening up the critical space for individuals to question the established orthodoxies, the liberal project contains within it the seeds of the liberational world-view. Its stress on liberty is of tremendous importance and can be a powerful weapon in the struggle against oppression. In addition, in economic terms, liberalism has been able to deliver considerable prosperity to the core capitalist countries of Europe and North America. It has been less successful, however, in extending this state of well-being to all, even within those nations. The major criticism of liberalism does not relate to the values in themselves, but doubt whether its vision is genuinely universal, encompassing the majority, rather than just the few. In practice, the liberal world-view tends to speak for a largely white, largely male, elite segment of the world's population. Evidence of this converges from a number of different points of view and is explored in later chapters. Numerous studies show the state, for example, not to be a neutral agent for the good of all, but captive to a number of (often contradictory) particular interests. Chapter Six indicates how the strong division between public and private spheres has served as an ideology which legitimates the exploitation of women to the structural advantage of men. Chapter Seven reports how environmental activists point out the desperate consequences for the natural world of the modernisation model of development. Chapter Eight shows the inadequacy of the liberal stance of academic disinterest when faced with the aggression of a totalitarian state.

The New Right Paradigm: Blame the Poor

The New Right approach draws on elements of conservative and liberal perspectives, but combines them to forge a radically new paradigm. This is introduced in Chapter One in the account of Michael Portillo's views. The economic commitment to liberty and individualism is taken from liberalism and put together with strongly authoritarian politics, more characteristic of the conservative world-view. Society is made up of a collection of individuals, each of whom is morally responsible for his or her own fate. Life is about choices and opportunity, and riches or poverty reflect individual merit and effort. The world is, or should be, an arena of perfect competition.

Although there are some social scientists of the New Right who would defend the view of people as autonomous individuals solely responsible for all that happens to them, the mainstream tradition does not support them. Social psychology points to the importance of childhood experiences and upbringing in shaping personalities. Sociology demonstrates 'how working class kids get working class jobs' (Willis, 1979) and how the elite acts to keep others out of positions of power (Mills, 1964). Anthropology shows the importance of culture to how people see the world and how personal identity is always forged in relation to others. This is not to say that people are *simply* the product of their environment. They clearly go on to take actions which themselves challenge or re-confirm the existing social system. This dynamic is summed up neatly in Karl Marx's famous words: 'People make history, but not in conditions of their own choosing.'

Against the liberal optimism about humanity, the New Right believe that people will behave badly if not subject to discipline and control. Religious texts provide the core of this, in an unchanging ethical code. This should be taught by the Church, schools, and the family.

Distorting the community orientation of the conservative world-view, morality is preached as a primarily personal responsibility. People are taught the 'civic virtues' of hard work, good money management, stable family commitments, sex within marriage, and respect for authority. God is a strict schoolmaster, insisting on discipline for our own good. This should also be reinforced by the use of law as punishment.

The New Right answer to 'Why are the poor, poor?' has three key aspects, which are closely related. The first of these is the diagnosis: that the reasons for poverty lie with individuals, and specifically in the *choices* they make. Poverty, that is, is seen as a matter of individual morality. The other two aspects build on this. They concern the prescription for combatting poverty – the political implications. In the second place, therefore, New Right social policy makes a critical distinction on moral grounds between the 'deserving' and the 'undeserving'. Third, the New Right believes the answer to poverty lies in individuals assuming the moral responsibility to provide for their own, and their families' needs.

The social and development policies of the New Right are a strong commitment to the free market. The state should have a minimum involvement in the economy since it is private enterprise and competition that lead to economic growth. Social welfare programmes should similarly be kept to absolute basics, as otherwise they will only encourage dependence. If people wish to do something for the poor, this should take the form of personal acts of charity. The remedy, like the problem, is an individual issue. Morality is a simple matter: if everyone is answerable for his or her own actions, we no longer need to look to social deprivation, for example, as part of the explanation for crime. The point is not to understand why people break the law, but to make sure they are punished. In turn, of course, this means there is no need for social policy to try to improve conditions for the poorest as a means of tackling social problems.

People will never gain self-respect unless they learn to stand on their own feet and meet their own needs. The responsibility of the state is to ensure the conditions for this to take place. This means that individuals should have – and be able to keep – the money in their pockets to choose health care, education, pension plans and so on. The maximum social benefit is the sum of all the gains that people make as individuals. In particular, this involves reducing taxation and a strong commitment to law and order. Paradoxically, the belief in freedom and choice leads to a strongly authoritarian state, often with a central role for the military.

Deserving and Undeserving

The division drawn between the 'deserving' and the 'undeserving' is of course nothing new. In terms of thinking what should be done for the poor, this distinction goes back at least as far as the Elizabethan Poor Law in sixteenth century England. Then, as now, its main purpose is to reduce the numbers of the poor who have the right to claim any help. On the one hand are the hardworking virtuous poor, or those who have an incontestable, usually physical, reason for being unable to work, such as serious illness, disability or age. On the other hand are the undeserving poor, the scroungers, the long-term unemployed, the welfare system 'cheats', the idle, the extravagant, the immigrants, the single mothers .... As the political commitment to cut welfare payments gathers pace, it becomes harder and harder to qualify as 'deserving', while the list of the undeserving seems to grow longer almost daily. Eventually, an almost perfect fit is achieved between those who are classed as socially undesirable and those who make any claim on state support.

In understanding this, it is helpful to draw on the sociological concept of 'labelling'. This describes the process by which groups of people are classified in ways that serve certain political interests. The 'label' that is given to people then determines the treatment they get. In the UK in the 1990s, for example, single mothers have been defined as 'undeserving' and this legitimates the withdrawal of their established rights to council housing and other forms of support. Ironically, at exactly the same time, within development circles the claims of single mothers are just beginning to be recognised. Labelled as ' female headed households' they constitute a new 'target group' for intervention: suffering particular social and economic hardship, they are seen to deserve special support in their struggle to care for their families.

What this shows is that the content of the label tells us less about the group itself, than the political context in which it is applied. The more general point, which we return to many times in the course of the book, is about *the politics of language*. This builds on the core insight of liberational perspectives, that knowledge is always from a particular point of view. Here we see that we need not only to ask 'who speaks?', but also how is the argument made, what is the context of the speech, and who is being spoken to?

The irony of the use of labelling by the New Right is that it undermines their core commitment to the centrality of individuals. Because labelling refuses to see people as individuals. Instead, it bundles people into a category which denies them personality and, ultimately, humanity. It says we know how to deal with 'these people' without having to listen to what they say. Above all, it shuts off any possibility of encounter.

This has a critical impact not only on the *kind* of services available, but also the way in which they are provided. Where health care, education and support in old age are available free to all, there is no stigma attached to 'dependence' on state services, and no need to distinguish the 'deserving' from the 'undeserving'. Paradoxically, the higher proportion of the population that 'depends' on the services, the better quality they are likely to be. Where wealthier people turn to private education and health care, the standard of public provision tends to go down, and inequalities are passed on into the next generation.

Where government rhetoric concerns human rights, individual freedom and self-reliance, it is ironic that its style of welfare provision means that state intrusion into the lives of the 'undeserving' is on the increase. This is the inevitable logic of means-tested benefits, which often seem designed to cause maximum discomfort to the applicant and so put people off. In a culture which sees those registered for state benefits as 'scroungers', policing benefits can easily become a higher priority than ensuring they reach those in need. The relationship of people to the state becomes no longer one of claiming rights but one of pleading favours. This becomes disempowering on the one hand, and incites people to fraud on the other. 'Self-reliance', in the shape of refusal to register for support, then becomes not a positive assertion but a reaction of hopelessness and alienation. Nor is rationing benefits necessarily 'cost-effective'. In the mid-1980s in the UK, grants to the poor for essential household items were replaced by discretionary, means-tested loans. *Forty-seven per cent* of the total expenditure on this 'Social Fund' was spent on administering the system (Platt, 1992).

The division between deserving and undeserving is radically rejected in the life and teaching of Jesus. Throughout his ministry, Jesus was concerned to overthrow the established distinctions between the upright and the sinners. As we saw above in the case of the man with the crippled hand, Jesus responded to the needs of the marginalised people, in a way that called into question the praxis of the 'righteous'. He did not accept the negative labels given to people in need, but turned the focus back onto the self-styled 'righteous', to dislodge their complacency. One of the most striking examples of this is found in John 8:3-11.

The scribes and the Pharisees brought a woman who had been caught in adultery; and making her stand before all of them, they said to [Jesus], 'Teacher, this woman has been caught in the very act of committing adultery. Now in the law Moses commanded us to stone such women. Now what do you say?' They said this to test him, so that they might have some charge to bring against him. Jesus bent down and wrote with his finger on the ground. When they kept on questioning him, he straightened up and said to them, 'Let anyone among you who is without sin be the first to throw a stone at her'. And once again he bent down and wrote on the ground. When they heard it, they went away, one by one, beginning with the elders, and Jesus was left alone with the woman standing before him. Jesus straightened up and said to her, 'Woman, where are they? Has no one condemned you?' She said, 'No one, sir'. And Jesus said, 'Neither do I condemn you. Go your way, and from now on do not sin again'.

A Prosperity Gospel?

The dualism between deserving and undeserving establishes an essential boundary. And boundaries always have two sides. Defining 'them' as undeserving, in turn identifies 'us' as deserving. Those people who behave in socially undesirable ways, are emphatically 'not like us'. The division between deserving and undeserving, then, does not only apply to the poor. Because implicit in this view is the notion – so fundamental that it is never even put into words – of the deserving *rich*.

In New Right language, the deserving rich appear as the 'wealth creators'. Just as the poor receive blame as individuals for their poverty, so the rich receive praise as individuals for their wealth. The contribution of ordinary workers becomes invisible, as do all the structural provisions of tax concessions, anti-union laws, state subsidies to the private sector, unequal access to markets, differential currency rates and so on, which help concentrate the fruits of wealth in the hands of a few people and countries. Here, we consider how justified is the New Right claim that individual accumulation of wealth is sanctioned by Christian tradition.

There are two parts to this argument. In the first place, in the words of the former UK Prime Minister, Margaret Thatcher: 'Abundance rather than poverty has a legitimacy which derives from the very nature of creation.' In the second place, it is recognised that love of money for its own sake is sin. But – and it's a big but – 'How could we respond to the many calls for help, or invest in the future, or support the wonderful artists and craftsmen whose work also glorifies Gods unless we had first worked hard and used our talents to create the necessary wealth?' (Thatcher, in Montefiore 1990:87–88).

It is certainly true that God's blessing in the Jewish and Christian tradition is seen as prosperity and not want. Creation is wonderful in its beauty and abundance. The children of Israel are promised a land 'flowing with milk and honey'. The Kingdom of God would be a kingdom of plenty:

> The time is surely coming, says the Lord,
> when the one who ploughs shall overtake the one who reaps,
> and the treader of grapes the one who sows the seed;
> the mountains shall drip sweet wine,
> and all the hills shall flow with it.
> I will restore the fortunes of my people Israel,
> and they shall rebuild the ruined cities and inhabit them;
> they shall plant vineyards and drink their wine,
> and they shall make gardens and eat their fruit.
> I will plant them upon their land,
> and they shall never again be plucked up
> out of the land that I have given them,
> says the Lord your God.   ~ Amos 9:13-15 ~

This vision of prosperity does not fit easily with the 'wealth creation' framework of the New Right. In the first place, the blessing of God is for the whole community, not just for certain individuals within it. This point comes through strongly in the prophecy from Isaiah and in the institution of the jubilee, noted above. In Christian tradition this has been continued in the institution of tithing, the free gift of one tenth of people's income, in recognition of responsibility towards others.

In the second place, the vision here is of holding in trust, not outright possession. This is true even of the parable of the talents, beloved of New Right theologians (Matthew 25:14-30). The talents were *given* to *stewards* to use wisely. They were not awarded because of the merit of the individuals, and they were given only for a time, to be later returned. In the Jewish and Christian tradition, God is the only 'wealth creator'. And the wealth that God wishes for us is far more than money. It is the wealth of the natural world, for us to care for and wonder at. It is the wealth of self-confidence and knowing all are free from want. It is the wealth of sharing the good gifts that we enjoy. It is the wealth of living in peace and safety. And above all, it is the wealth of loving and knowing ourselves loved by God and other people.

Third, far and away the most common context of these visions of plenty was a pledge to a people *in exile*. They were a promise to the dispossessed, of a new community of justice and peace. They were spoken to the poor, not to the rich. They were a protest *against* the established order, not a sanctification of it.

This leads us on to Margaret Thatcher's second point: that only if we are rich can we respond to the needs of others. She elaborates this in another speech, in which she claims that 'the whole point' of the story of the Good Samaritan was that he had money in his pocket. It was only because he was known to be creditworthy, that the innkeeper would look after the man who had been robbed, because he knew that the Samaritan would pay when he returned. But the difference between the Samaritan and the religious leaders that Jesus highlighted, did not lie in their ability to pay. As we saw in Chapter Two, it was the compassion, the capacity to feel with the needy man and enter into his suffering, which made the Samaritan different from those who passed on by. It is the generosity of spirit, not the generosity of the pocket, that matters. This is underlined by Jesus in his comments on the poor widow's gift:

> [Jesus] looked up and saw rich people putting their gifts into the treasury; he also saw a poor widow put in two small copper coins. He said, 'Truly I tell you, this poor widow has put in more than all of them; for all of them have contributed out of their abundance, but she out of her poverty has put in all she had to live on'.   ~ Luke 21: 1-4 ~

Taking Responsibility: The New Right in Development

As noted above, the New Right perspective has had a powerful impact on development policy since the 1980s. Its international dominance coincided with a world recession, which hit especially severely countries in the South that had borrowed heavily from international banks in the buoyant 1970s. Austerity was the new order of the day. Poor countries must 'adjust' to the negative external environment of world recession. Any country wishing to receive an International Monetary Fund (IMF) or World Bank loan must implement a fairly standardised package of austerity measures. Such a loan was seen like a certificate of creditworthiness; without it, few commercial creditors would be prepared to invest. The name given to this package was 'Structural Adjustment Programmes' (SAP). The basic formula was quite simple: 'Earn more and spend less.'

For the 1980s then, the (old-)new slogan for development was 'Export-led Growth'. Currencies were devalued to make exports cheaper and so more competitive on world markets. Of course, this also meant that poor countries had to sell much more in order to make the same returns. At the same time, this raised the price of imports. Intended to cut consumption of imports and so help the balance of payments, this often led to high inflation as imported goods became scarce and prices rocketed. Food production for local consumption became a lower priority than growing crops for export.

The 'spend less' part of the formula applied in particular to governments themselves. Rather than taxing income or assets, which might act as a disincentive on production, revenues were raised through indirect taxation on basic goods, commodities and services. On the other hand, subsidies for food, credit and agricultural inputs were removed. Wages, particularly for government employees, were frozen. Budgets for health, education, housing and other social services were slashed.

Some countries have seen substantial gains through export-led growth. In particular, these are those that began on this path earlier: Taiwan, South Korea, Malaysia and Indonesia. The numbers of people in poverty in these countries have declined, though there remain pockets of extreme deprivation. In line with the New Right paradigm, however, these success stories of 'free market' capitalism have been achieved by very strong, interventionist and authoritarian states. While other public expenditure is savagely cut, Southern governments' investment in arms has risen sharply in the 1980s and '90s. This military build-up is rarely to combat external enemies, but instead to put down internal dissent. Under the banner of 'national security', an atmosphere has been fostered in which 'criticism is sabotage and opposition is treason' (Jahangir, 1986:100). Marcos in the Philippines, Pinochet in Chile, Suharto in Indonesia, Thatcher in the UK, Reagan in the United States ... the 'champions' of the 'free market' are synonymous with the contraction of civil rights and often violent repression of their own people.

Even if the costs of widespread repression are held to be worth paying, it is doubtful that the same model can prove successful for all. Instead, the trend for many countries is to find themselves ever more deeply in debt. Rather than more money coming into the South, the rise in interest rates means the flow of financial resources has been reversed. Susan George (1992:xv) states that between 1982-90 in total $927 billion flowed from the North to the South in the shape of aid, trade credits and direct private investment and bank loans. Much of this represents new debt, which will further swell repayment demands in future. Over the same period, $1345 billion was remitted from the South to the North in debt service alone. At minimum there was therefore a net flow of $418 billion *out* of the South. This figure would be much greater if royalties, dividends and repatriated profits were figured in to the calculation.

Even the World Bank now concedes that the costs of Structural Adjustment fell most heavily on the poorest, calling the 1980s 'the lost decade' for development as real incomes of the poor fell in Latin America and Sub-Saharan Africa in particular. Others have put it still more starkly: the poor, and among them especially the women, became the 'shock absorbers' of the world economic recession. For many of the poorest countries, the much sought growth never came. And when governments save costs on basic services – transport, nurseries, health provision, welfare payments and education – the costs do not disappear, they are simply shifted out of view. What used to be provided by the state now has to be supplied within the family. Coupled with job cuts and the falling value of wages, this has caught many poor families in a scissor action where they find themselves earning less and having to spend – in time and money – much more.

In the 1990s, the tone of international development policy has changed once again. The scandal of the hardships which Structural Adjustment imposed on the poor has been finally recognised as unacceptable. From the late 1980s onwards, there have been calls for toning down some of the harshest aspects. The World Bank Development Report of 1990, dedicated to the subject of poverty, reflects this. While overall its reading of the international economy shows a hearty optimism, it proposes a new formula to promote an 'efficient, labour intensive pattern of development and investing more in the human capital of the poor' (p 3). Essentially this means investing in labour intensive industries and agriculture; basic social services; and providing some complementary targeted programmes to cushion the poorest against the inevitable economic 'shocks'.

Some things do not change, however. Occasional references are made to the responsibility of policies in the North for poverty – such as the need to ease trade barriers. But the crucial factor is identified as the commitment of poor countries' governments to a poverty-focused national economic policy. Aid should be concentrated on these governments, as the ones most likely to use it most effectively in reducing poverty. We are back to laying the blame at the door of government's mismanagement (blame the poor). The predominant tone is what has been called 'win-win' – everyone will gain from such a strategy, no one will lose. Poverty will only decline if there is national economic growth. Prospects for growth in the South are best served by healthy economies in the North, which can provide a market for southern products.

This boils down to a new answer to 'why are the poor poor?' – because the rich are poor! The problem with this view is that it assumes that the benefits and costs of changing economic climates are shared equally between the poor and rich countries. Like natural disasters, however, world recession hits hardest the already disadvantaged – loss of fat for the rich means malnutrition or starvation for the poor. Expansion in the North has some knock on effects in terms of benefits in the South.

But these are limited by structural inequalities in the international market, and the lack of capacity to take up new opportunities. As with people, the 'poorest of the poor' countries have multiple problems that keep them back even in the face of a general economic upturn.

Poverty: The Test of Experience

In the three sections above, we set out brief outlines of three of the paradigms which we believe structure the ways in which people see the world. Summaries of these are given in Appendix A. In the following chapter we set out the final paradigm – the liberational. First, we sum up the argument in this chapter as we ask how well the paradigms' explanations of poverty fit the experience of the people we met in Chapter Two.

Each of the explanations of poverty has something to be said for it. There is no doubt, for example, that the conservative explanation of poverty as fate rings true for many poor people. They are born poor, or become poor for reasons far beyond their control. Julian and Teresa seem an example of this, as they were hit by a natural disaster – drought. Fernando's imprisonment seems similarly random. Whatever the rights and wrongs on each side, he and his fellow villagers were simply the victims of others' conflict, caught in the cross-fire between the underground and the military. As they put it themselves: 'We are crushed in between two colliding boulders.'

The liberal view of the poor being poor because they have been 'left out' of development also fits some cases. If there had been a 'modern' health clinic providing cheap treatment near to Felisa's home, she might not have died. Asha's lack of options seem to be due at least in part to 'traditional attitudes' which frown on women going out to work – although as we see in Chapter Six, discrimination against women does not disappear with technological progress. Loreta could have escaped exploitation by the 'traditional' money-lenders if there had been a bank which would lend to her nearby.

Even blaming the poor for their poverty seems to make some sense. We have all known, or know of, people like Danny, who have started off poor and ended up wealthy. It is also true that some poor people drink, smoke and gamble. Many have less education than those who are better off. Some do lose hope of ever getting a job, so stop looking. Others do play both ends against the middle, registering for state benefits while they make some extra cash on the side. On the other hand, the structural constraints that face poor people trying to 'make good' point us towards the liberational approach. Was Greg responsible for the recession which forced him to leave his home and move south? Starting from another point, is it simply due to hard work that the children of middle class professionals tend to become doctors and lawyers themselves, while those whose parents are unemployed or manual workers tend to get lower grade jobs? What becomes clear when we try to understand wealth and poverty from the perspective of the poor is that it is their context, not their characters, which is mainly responsible for what people get in life. We saw in Chapter Two how poverty is a dynamic process. Different aspects of poverty are connected and one kind of disadvantage can easily lead into another. The pole gets more slippery the further down you are. It is no coincidence that there was one Danny, and many poor left at home. Individual success stories of escape from poverty are the exception, not the rule.

Looked at more closely, it is clear that while each of the explanations has something that can be said for it, it is the liberational approach that comes nearest to telling the whole story. There are, of course, random events like drought that push people into poverty. But the reason this hit Julian and Teresa so hard was that their other source of income, fishing, had been taken away. Even 'natural' disasters do not hit everyone equally. They hit hardest those who are weak, unwell, have no alternative sources of support, have flimsy housing, or have been pushed onto marginal land more prone to hazard.

The liberal explanation also needs to be questioned. It was, after all, 'development' in the shape of the expansion of fishing by higher technology trawlers that meant that Julian and Teresa's community had lost their customary fishing rights. Perhaps most brutally, the Higa-onons' environmental moral economy was swept aside in the race for 'progress' and 'development'. It was changing production organisation and techniques that led to unemployment in Greg's home town. And it was sophisticated weaponry in the hands of the underground and military forces that resulted in the sufferings of Fernando and his neighbours. The fruits of 'progress' are bitter-sweet.

This reflects on the conservative world-view, as well as on the liberal. Whatever was the case in the past, the stories in Chapter Two suggest that the integrity of the moral economy has broken down. The finance company and building society threatening Sam and Jackie, are operating as impersonal institutions, concerned only to protect their own profit margins. Remnants of the moral economy persist in people's sense of what they, and others, are entitled to. But it has ceased to provide the overall framework within which people live. Most critically, it can no longer be taken for granted. What it used to be about, providing a reliable safety net, is precisely what it now fails to do.

What of the New Right approach? It is clearly wrong to think of the poor as blameless, virtuous victims, but are their 'vices' the *reasons* for poverty? Do not wealthy people also drink, smoke and gamble? Are all the rich intelligent, hardworking, and full of ambition? Do not the non-poor also exaggerate when they claim expenses and evade tax by not declaring all their income, paying accountants to find the best ways to exploit all the legal loopholes? When it comes to the reasons for poverty and wealth, vice and virtue do not seem to have a lot to do with it.

In looking at experience, we need to separate out the *characteristics* of poor people from the reasons for poverty. One of the first lessons in social science is that 'correlation does not equal causation'. If all the people in hospital are ill, this does not mean that being in hospital makes you ill. Similarly poor education, for example, is more often an outcome of poverty than a reason for it. Even the so-called 'vices' of the poor may be understood in this way. Whatever the rich do, it clearly does not make sense to drink, smoke and gamble if you are on a very low income and need every penny to make ends meet. On the other hand, it may be for some people that it is *because* they are poor that they do these things as an escape. When you are very poor, there may not seem much point in saving for the future, rather than spending the little you have on making life a bit more bearable today. Gambling, in particular, may seem like a rational thing to do for people who see the odds in their daily lives so stacked against them that their only hope for change is some massive stroke of luck.

The experience of poor people also gives the New Right stress on individual choice a hollow ring. As we saw in Chapter Two, lacking choice is one of the fundamental characteristics of being poor. Poverty is not only about being poor in income, but also poor in power. And the two are very closely related. In practice, the 'freedom of choice' which the New Right believe in, is a freedom only for those with money in their pockets. In a 'free market' economy, the freedom to choose between purchases, school or colleges, careers or forms of medical treatment, depends critically on ability to pay. If Asha had been wealthy, she would have had many options – of hiring in labour to work their land; or training for a profession, which would bring her income and be sufficiently high status to overcome prejudices against women going out to work. It is precisely her lack of material resources that locks her into a situation with hardly any room for manoeuvre.

There is a further aspect to the 'freedom of choice' issue. This is that the lack of choice of the poor is directly related to the 'freedom' of the rich: they are simply two sides of the same coin. Effective minimum wage legislation would have meant that Asha's neighbours could not employ her for a full day and give her only her food as payment. She could have demanded a living wage, or even been able to build up some reserves so that she could broaden her options in future. Ensuring the rich have the freedom to choose how to use their money by low rates of income tax, results directly in the absence of choice in terms of access to health care, education and welfare services for the poor. While it poses as universal, the New Right's commitment to freedom of choice is actually quite restricted. In assessing its validity, we need to return to the core question of liberational perspectives: *whose* choices matter?

The stories of Loreta and Sam and Jackie point very clearly to the human basis of poverty. Their need for credit was a positive opportunity for others to make substantial profits. Poverty has to be seen in the context of inequality. The first step is to see that poverty is a relative term. As pointed out in Chapter Two, to describe one income as low makes sense only if another is high. But we need to go further than this. Poverty is not just 'there' – it is caused. And just as there are those who lose, so there are those who gain from this process.

How then do we reconcile the fact that many poor people genuinely believe that their fortune is already decided, that what will be will be? In some cases there is no doubt that this reflects the use of religion as 'social cement', teaching them to reconcile themselves to their place in life, not to make waves. But what it also reflects is their overwhelming sense of helplessness. Fernando and his friends know that the 'boulders' are not impersonal forces, but people making decisions, who could choose in other ways. In using that image, they express their feeling of being power-less. It is this that the liberational approach takes as its main challenge. If people can analyse the causes of poverty, what it is in themselves and their context that makes and keeps them poor, this is a vital step towards taking action against it.

Conclusion

In this chapter we have taken the question 'Why are the poor poor?' to introduce quite briefly four major types of world-view. In their response to poverty all of the paradigms capture a little of the truth. On the other hand, seeing how differently they view the world spurs us to re-examine our own fundamental assumptions, and to work out in a more coherent way what theology and development means for us. This is the challenge that we take up in the next chapter. At best, the conservative, liberal and New Right paradigms prescribe *working for* the poor. In making a categorical division between the poor and non-poor, they shut off opportunities for *working with* them, and even more for *being with* the poor. Instead of trying to tackle poverty at its roots, these approaches aim to manage poverty by keeping the poor at a distance.

At the level of words there is some agreement between all the four approaches. They would all maintain that it is right to try to meet the needs of others. Where they differ is in the way that they understand what these needs are. People's basic convictions, as we have already stressed, cannot be easily separated into 'religious' and 'secular'. If we blame poverty on the poor or the design of creation, then the needs we will see will not be ones for political change or public services. The great prophecies of Israel become anachronisms from a bygone age. Jesus' urgings of love in action, something for special days, particular acts of charity, not relevant to the mainstream of our economic and political life.

CHAPTER FOUR

Poverty and Riches

Introduction

Sarah:

It was already getting dark as Asha, her brother and I made our way across the fields to the little cluster of houses exposed on high land at the edge of the village. The people laid out mats for us to sit on and gathered round, the light and shadow from my lamp flickering on their faces and on the mud hearths where a few were still cooking. After some general talk we all fell silent as Bolai, one of the younger men, spoke:

'Listen, let me tell you something. It was the lean time, and we weren't getting work anywhere. I'd come back home and my kids were crying: Dad, I'm hungry; and I had nothing to give them to eat. So we went to Fazlur and asked if he had any work. He said he had some earth work that needed doing, how much would we take? So we thought: it's the lean time, there's no point in hustling and asking a lot. If we get six taka we can just about manage. So that's what we asked for.

'So he said: O, my son's just bought a Honda, six taka, how can I manage that! So there we are, listening to the tale of his woes. In the end he says: I'll give you three taka. Three taka for a day's work! So we thought and said, Give us one taka more, give us four. And he said: O, how can I manage that? I'll give you three and a half taka, take it or leave it, that's my last word. So we took it. What can we do? They know we have no choice.

'I tell you, if it weren't for the night times, the poor would have no happiness at all. You with your reading and writing, you can work on all night. But us, they can't make us work after daylight. That is our only comfort.'

(White, 1992:47-8)

For Bolai, the answer to 'Why are the poor poor?' is clear: we are poor because the rich are rich. In the wrangle over the wage, he and his employer act out the essential contradiction between rich and poor. In that year, the usual daily wage rate was ten taka plus food. Bolai wants a living wage to feed his children; Fazlur wants to cut it down, to offset his son's luxury purchase. The exchange between them is unequal, the personal encounter is overlaid by structural differences in power. Fazlur's work could wait until some other day; Bolai's children are crying for food now. As in dependency analyses, the interaction between rich and poor only reinforces poverty. As in liberation theology, the personal sin of Fazlur's lack of charity only reconfirms the structural sin of a system in which such exploitation can routinely occur.

In this chapter, we explore the implications of this understanding of theology and development. We begin by outlining the liberational approach, as we reviewed the other paradigms in Chapter Three. We consider how liberation theology works as praxis, and the challenge it presents to the Church. We then look at the resistance that it has encountered from outside, and also potential areas of weakness within it. In considering how widely the liberational paradigm is relevant, we ask, 'Are the non-poor also poor?' To help trace the connection between internal or 'spiritual' poverty and material deprivation and oppression, we then introduce the notion of 'poverty of being'. We see how this is linked to external structures, and yet cannot simply be reduced to them. Finally, we return to our original question of 'Who are the poor?' as we review how poverty has figured in Christian tradition and consider what this might mean for us.

The Liberational Paradigm: Because the Rich are Rich

In the liberational world-view, poverty is not 'just there', part of the natural order, a hangover from the past, or the result of individuals' failures. It is something that is caused by a system founded in injustice. The reasons for poverty lie in the relationship between poor and non-poor: the poverty of some and the wealth of others spring from the same source.

Drawing on Marxist analysis, the liberational paradigm sees society as based not in harmony, but conflict. There are sharp divisions between the 'haves' and the 'have-nots', and the interests of these two groups, like those of Fazlur and Bolai, are essentially opposed to each other. Where one gains, the other loses. Power is thus seen as fundamental to the constitution of society. People are viewed not as self-contained individuals, but as belonging in community. Social divisions mean, however, that the community is fragmented. Only when society is founded in justice and there is an end to oppression will that community be fully realised.

In both development and theology, the roots of the liberational paradigm lie in Latin America in the 1960s and '70s. The integral development expected by modernisation theory had not come. Instead there was jagged economic growth and spiralling inequality. Politics were similarly unstable, alternating between promises of wide-reaching reform, government sponsored mass organisations to harness popular support, and violent military repression. While levels of religious belief and practice were high, institutionally the (Catholic) Church was weak. Huge parishes served by small numbers of professionals, meant that poor people might not see a priest from one year's end to another. As David Lehmann (1990:102) remarks with irony, this institutional weakness may have meant that the Church hierarchy was less able to neutralise the potential radicalism of its own message. But even from within the hierarchy there were moves towards change. The early 1960s saw the global Catholic council, Vatican II. This marked a new openness, a vision of the Church as a 'pilgrim people' ready to re-think tradition and to question established patterns of authority. Intense political repression added urgency to these tendencies. In some countries, church buildings became virtually the only places that people could gather without risking arrest. As the state took on totalitarian form and human rights were routinely abused, the liberal division between spiritual and political, church and state, was thrown into question. Could the Church just stand by as her people suffered? What theology would serve as the oppressed took up arms against injustice?

In the liberal paradigm objectivity is seen to give validity. Liberational thinkers believe, by contrast, that neutrality is impossible in a world that is so divided. So-called objectivity is a mask for specific interests, knowledge is always from a particular point of view. Instead of being something to hide or apologise for, therefore, subjectivity is to be embraced. This makes clear the role of context in shaping views: 'where you stand depends on where you sit.' It also makes it possible for the poor to re-claim their role as subjects of their own destiny, rather than being objects of others' plans and policies. Rejecting the liberal stance of disinterested observer, the liberational paradigm urges the importance of 'making an option'. Its own is to start from the standpoint of the poor and the marginalised, to seek quite explicitly a view 'from below'. To make such an option is not open only to the poor, but also to the non-poor, as an act of solidarity. The stress on subjectivity, however, has led to a strong tendency for identities to become politicised. This means that theologies, for example, are described by who does them – such as Black, Dalit, Asian, or feminist theology – rather than impersonally – such as systematic, contextual, or fundamentalist.

In social and development policy and practice, the liberational paradigm leads to a strong emphasis on 'people power', and the sense that 'small is beautiful'. Action should come from below, with poor people analysing their own problems and formulating their own solutions. Authority should be de-centralised, with decision-making kept as local as possible. It is through experiencing that they can take control of their own lives that the poor will be genuinely empowered. Impact at the national and international level should be made through federations of people's organisations, who perceive common interests across their own specific causes. Ultimately, the challenge for development is not just to reform the existing structures, but to forge alternatives.

Liberation Theology as Praxis

A meeting of tenant farmers in the Philippines rumbled through their recurrent complaints. Time after time presidential candidates had promised land reform, but after the elections the tenants were left landless as before. They were fed up with the half-hearted attempts of the different administrations. Change from the top was too long in coming. They should get organised and take action into their own hands. At last an old man got up to speak. With the eloquence of a poet, he said:

> I am not a bird that flies in the air;
> nor a fish that swims in the water.
> I am a human being who stands on land.
> I need a piece of land to plough and to plant on.
> I need a piece of land to be buried in when I die.
> What does the Church have to say about my right to own land?

The old man continued, the anger trembling in his voice:

> If the Church has something to say only about my gambling and drinking which happen on some Sundays, but nothing about my Monday till Saturday when I am with the land, then I don't want to have anything to do with such a Church that cares only about my Sunday and ignores all my other days!

This old man is one of millions of poor people who are demanding that the Church leave its old securities and make an option for the poor. In the Philippines, land provides an embodied symbol, for while the poor are insecure tenants the Catholic Church is itself a large landowner. All its pledges to coach the leaders and future leaders in Christian values so that they will correct injustice sound like the empty election promises of politicians. The land stays in the hands of the bosses and the multinationals – it is the poor who are moved on. And yet, in their Bibles, poor people like this old man read that God's chosen people were the dispossessed just like them. They see themselves in the longing for freedom of the Israelites in Egypt. They do not hear God asking them to suffer now because they will enjoy the blessings of heaven in the next life. Instead, they hear God's promise of liberation and prosperity. What they plant, they will harvest and consume. Their house will be their home and they will cease to be refugees in a foreign country. And the land, source and symbol of secure well-being, will be theirs.

Of all the different theological traditions, it is liberation theology that most emphasises that theology must be *done*. And it should be done not by isolated scholars in their ivory towers, but by poor people themselves, gathering together in groups to listen to what God is saying to their situation. Such groups are known as BECs (Base Ecclesial Communities) or BCCs (Basic Christian Communities). Although as a proportion of all Christians their total number is quite small, they now exist all over the world. Their form varies from place to place, but the basic methodology is simple. A Scripture passage is chosen and the people read it together. They then sing a song. Someone then poses the question: What is the message of this passage? And they discuss it together. After another song, they ask another question: Have you ever experienced something like this in your life? Again they talk this over. A third song leads on to the final question: What can we do to make sure that we experience this blessing, or cease to suffer this injustice, in our lives in the future?

Reading the Bible means, therefore, confronting text with context. The overall orientation is personal and practical. 'God's Word for us' is to be heard in the dialogue between Biblical text, its social-historical context, and one's own social context. The liberal approach of scientific distance is replaced by a stress on experience; God's promises are not relativised or spiritualised, but claimed as concrete pledges of change. The context out of which the Bible speaks and into which God's word comes is the life-world of the poor.

The central place given to the perspective of the poor gives the question 'Who are the poor?' a new urgency. The answer again lies in the dialectic between text and context. The textual side of this we review in the last section of this chapter. But what of the context? What do the poor say for themselves? In Danny's story we have already heard some voices of the poor. They contradict each other! Poor people do not have privileged access to the truth about society, any more than the rest of us. Like anyone else, they need tools of analysis to help them understand their situation. The aim of these is not to teach people something new, but to help them to see more clearly what they already know. Reviewing their situation in a more systematic way is a crucial step on the path to changing it.

Like the parables of Jesus, these 'tools of analysis' should be made up of materials lying close to hand. In a maize growing area, for example, tracing out its 'life story' provides a useful focus. Small groups of about six people sit together to discuss three basic questions:

1 What are the different stages in the life story of maize?

2 If maize brings wealth, at what stage(s) is it concentrated?

3 Who are the people involved at each stage?

People may identify many steps, but five phases usually stand out: production and harvesting, crop sale, processing, food sale, and consumption. Years of farming may have enabled them to buy corrugated iron sheets to roof their houses, send some of their children to high school and buy some things for the house. But in contrast they see the middletraders and owners of corn oil factories and mills buying more lorries, big houses, high-tech equipment, and sending their children to college. Clearly money is made in the three middle stages: precisely those in which the farmers are not involved. One farmer summed it up like this:

> No one gets rich through farming. You have to go into business to get rich. We don't have a say on the prices. We have different first names, but we share a common surname. We are Mr and Mrs *Pila* (Mr and Mrs How Much). Whether we sell our produce or buy goods from the traders' stores, we have to ask, 'How much?'

As well as theological reflection, the BCCs thus provide an opportunity for some basic political education and training in organisation. As they analyse their situation, people build community together and confidence in their own abilities to make changes. Over time, however, the limitations of small, local projects become clear. People may become disillusioned, or go on to develop new skills as they build networks and federations, to press their demands on a broader front. In this way, the BCCs become a kind of modernising force. Through them people can learn some essential skills for citizenship and enlarge the social space available, presenting a challenge to established patterns of authority in state and society.

This challenge is evident within the Church, as well as in secular politics. Simply by reclaiming their right to read their Bibles for themselves, poor people in the BCCs question the Church hierarchy's monop-oly'on interpreting the Christian message. And what they read threatens this further. For read from the standpoint of the poor and oppressed, the Bible shows that God has a bias to the poor. The individualism of liberal and New Right views is set aside. In its place, the conservative world-view's corporate vision of the social order founded in a moral order is reclaimed, but as a radical political demand. The divisions between material and spiritual, public and private, personal and political, are over-thrown. Personal spirituality makes no sense apart from social action. The Kingdom of God is not a pledge for the after-life, but a promise for the here and now. Sin has too long been seen as a private, individual matter. Now it is time to denounce the sin and injustice enshrined in the social structure. The Church's claim to be above politics is a hollow sham. To be true to the Biblical vision, it should declare a preferential option for the poor.

Such a radical vision of the Christian message has provoked tremen-dous reaction. For some it is nothing but Marxist ideology clothed in religious language. The Bible has become a political tract, emptied of spiritual meaning. The Kingdom of God is not some earthly utopia, but the promise of salvation, of individuals being brought into a right relationship with God. Personal conversion, not revolution, is the way to the Kingdom. Others do not go this far, but object that a bias to the poor would be exclusive. The Church is the Church for all. To claim a bias to the poor is unfaithful to this universal character. The Church should not take political stands between the rich and poor. To do so would undermine its proper role as mediator in the conflict, a bridge to bring together the two sides. The mission of the Church is to bring harmony and reconciliation. Others argue that the Church's business is salvation. Christ's ministry does show a preferential option for the poor. But the rich are also poor. They are spiritually poor and need the Church to minister to them.

This approach seems to contain the contradiction that 'big sins', such as those which the great prophets of Israel condemned, appear less important than the 'little sins' of individual people. If social, economic and political structures do result in poverty, it seems strange that these should not also be a target for conversion. On the other hand, it is certainly true that being poor is no guarantee of spiritual well-being. The choice is not to struggle for change *either* at the personal *or* at the social level, but to recognise that the one entails the other.

The claim that the Church is politically neutral is hard to sustain. Since the time of Emperor Constantine at least, the Church has been seen to consecrate the dominant social order. This is so taken for granted that it is no longer even noticed! The Church hierarchy models the hierarchy of the state, Church institutions primarily serve the rich, poor parishes are neglected while rich ones are staffed with many ministers. This itself reinforces the alignment of the Church with the rich. Since priests live in the town centres, they associate mainly with the better off. Educationally, they are also more in tune with them. It is impossible for them to get to know the poor who live in the villages. It is hard to take sides with the poor if one's friends are the non-poor.

In opting for the poor, it is not enough for the Church to campaign for justice in 'the world'. It has also to recognise the power relations enshrined in its own structures. The call to make an option for the poor is a call to the Church for repentance. As with any repentance, the first step is to acknowledge the sin. As with any repentance, this means to die a little, in letting go of the habits and structures in which we have grown to feel safe. To experience the anxiety of the loss of old certainties. To lose our way, to allow a new way to open before us.

Resistance

It would be a mistake to see all of the dynamic for change as coming from below. Many of the people with liberational vision are priests, and some bishops. Influential liberation theologians are professional academics, with tenured posts not so different from those whose standpoints they criticise! Some sceptics maintain that most of the momentum is actually generated by educated professionals, rather than the poor themselves. What is certain is that, from the beginning, there has been a struggle for definition and control of the movement.

Inevitably there have been anxieties that the 'people's church' might turn into a 'parallel church' which breaks away to set up its own institution. But the history in different countries has also been quite varied: in Brazil, for example, liberation theology has received great support from the Church hierarchy; in Colombia it was rejected out of hand.

Certainly Vatican II initiated a powerful movement for reform 'from above' in the Roman Catholic Church. There should be greater transparency in Church finances and operations, with the lay members taking a much more active role. The model of partnership was put forward, as an image of the relationship between the congregation and ministers of the Church. In some places this was put into practice resulting in a renewal of parish life. But there was also resistance, even to quite small changes.

In some cases, lay people wanted to be assured that they would have real power if they got more involved in the work of the parish, that they would not just be a rubber stamp for what the priest wanted to do. But the situation in other parishes was summed up by an older Filipino priest:

Partnership? Co-operation? We don't need any change in my parish. I do not understand this talk about new ministries. I have a harmonious relationship with my parishioners. I am the head. They are the hands and the feet. I plan. They do what I say. We are all very happy.

Nor did the resistance to change only come from priests. The commissioning of lay leaders to distribute Holy Communion was seen as an important step in broadening ideas of ministry. But on the first Sundays, while a double line queued in front of the priest, hardly anyone went to the lay leader on his left and right. The people voted with their feet. They wanted to receive the sacrament only from a properly ordained minister. That made it special. To receive it from people just like themselves would not be the same.

If changes in the organisation of services and responsibilities in the parish provoke resistance, any move of the Church to make an option for the poor is bound to meet greater opposition. This comes from governments and the business community, used to being able to rely on the Church's backing. Once they step out of line, Church personnel discover very quickly how substantial a support to the authorities their supposed neutrality in fact was. They may be verbally attacked for trespassing into politics, shifted to a less prominent position, or silenced more brutally by torture, 'going missing', or open murder. But opposition also comes from those within the Church, who have a genuine love for the Church as it currently is. To resist change may mean losing a limb or two, to accept change may threaten the whole body. In the Church of England for years the ordination of women was delayed and soft-pedalled. Many women left the Church in frustration and joined alternative feminist communities. But it was only with the acceptance of the ordination of women that the spectre of a divided Church was raised. Traditionalists simply could not accept the change that is proposed. The Church will no longer be the Church they knew. They would rather divide the Church of England in two, than accept the death of their idea of the Church, in faith that new life will come.

Even those sympathetic to the 'option for the poor' may resist change out of fear of dividing the Church against itself. The mask of Church political neutrality does not only protect the secular social order, but also imposes an appearance of unity within the Church. To forge solidarity with the poor and enter actively the political struggle for justice, would blow this unity sky-high. As in politics, so in theology, there has been a backlash from the right. Under Pope John Paul II many radical priests and bishops have been replaced by conservatives, control from the top is once more being tightened over doctrine and Church practice. Accepting the challenge of an option for the poor is too risky, both for the

Church's standing in the world and for its own internal structures. It was to shout down the cries for liberation that the New Right began to find its voice.

Keeping a Balance

In Chapter Three we saw how the conservative vision of the social as a moral order can slip into consecrating the established order, even if immoral; and how the liberal value of toleration towards other views can decline into abstraction and indifference. The liberational vision is to hold in tension the political and the personal; the textual and contextual; the structural and the individual. But just like the other paradigms, the balance can go awry. In this section we review a number of ways in which this can happen.

In some ways, the picture given above in 'the life story of maize' is quite accurate. On this basis, it is quite easy to paint the middletraders and business people as evil exploiters of innocent 'victims', the farmers. This may turn people to violence, as the only way to smash the oppressors. Or it may make them just feel helpless, that there is nothing they can do when 'the system' is against them. And yet in every town centre these traders exist and farmers go to their stores. Many small farmers regard them with respect. Others complain, but still sell their produce to the traders rather than to the government purchasing centres where the middle income farmers and large landowners go, because they offer higher prices during the harvest season. If the small farmers really want to have a say on the prices of their farm products and consumer goods, why do they not organise a co-operative store?

Another tool, called 'force field' analysis, helps to reveal the complexity of the situation. A chart is presented and explained. Each group then goes to fill it up. In this case, the discussion is an attempt to understand why they find it difficult to organise a cooperative store as an alternative to the middletraders' businesses. They are encouraged to be as detailed as possible in identifying forces in favour and against. The pros and cons are also subdivided into internal and external factors. Internal refers to the elements within each individual and the group for or against the venture. External points to the pressures outside them which encourage or hinder them. If the discussions are very thorough the strengths and weaknesses of the group will become evident. Each item can then be scrutinised and evaluated. The pros and cons can be weighed against each other and the group can decide whether or not it is possible for them to start a cooperative store. In some cases the project may not be viable. A sample chart is shown below.

Figure 4.1   Force Field Analysis

FORCES

	FOR	AGAINST
I N T E R N A L	– desire for fairer prices – common understanding of the grains marketing structure – growing sense of 'we feeling' – willingness to learn new skills – common desire for change – conviction that their poverty is not God's will	– lack of confidence to manage the co-operative venture – lack of trust of each other – dependence on middletraders as patrons – lack of experience in group-decision-making – 'to each his/her own' mentality
E X T E R N A L	– encouragement from the Church and NGOs – success of other co-operative ventures – no harassment of other non-government-initiated co-operatives	– threat from middletraders to withdraw emergency credit – failure of other co-operative ventures – suspicion of being subversives if they do not join the government-initiated co-operative network

Through the force field analysis the reason that poor farmers continue to sell their products to the middletraders becomes clear. The relationship is not simply a commercial one, the middletraders also provide the only form of 'social security' that the farmers have. This ties the farmers to the traders, and makes them fearful of alienating them. When a member of the family gets sick and needs hospital treatment, the farmers turn to the middletraders for help. When farmers need to buy agricultural inputs, it is the traders who give them a loan. If they have a daughter getting married, or their house needs repair, or their cattle die, it is to the middle-traders that farmers go for cash. The resilience of patron–client relation-ships all over the South is due to this contradictory character. On the one hand they are exploitative, and play an important part in keeping poor people poor. On the other hand, however, they do provide a safety net against crisis times. In the particular incident Bolai described, Fazlur's treatment of him was deeply abusive. But Bolai is not amongst the poorest in the village. He has also benefited through a relationship with a patron, which has given him regular work and access to land for sharecropping. As we saw in Chapter Two, being poor in people is a crucial aspect of poverty. For many, having a good relationship with a wealthier patron seems the only safeguard: the terms of exchange may be bad, but to be without would be worse.

Another side of this dependence on the traders is the farmers' lack of trust in one another. This was aggravated in the Philippines by the corruption of earlier rural co-operatives, which left farmers with a strong suspicion of the co-operative movement. As a result, in one village the farmers planned to set up a co-operative store, but none was willing to risk a capital share of more than five pesos (US $0.20)! As we saw in Chapter Two, poor people may have common problems, but this does not mean that they feel they have common interests. There is always a tension between the individual and the collective: at the very least deciding to work together means sacrificing some freedom and autonomy. The lack of confidence has a technical side too. Unused to formal budgeting, keeping records and the cash economy, they are unsure of how to manage their own small business. Habits of depending on leaders are so strong that making group decisions in a participative way can seem almost impossible.

Doing the force field analysis builds on from 'the life story of maize' in two very important ways. First, it shows that 'they' do not bear all of the blame for how things are. The farmers' own behaviour is in part responsible for maintaining the situation. This means that there is another alternative between violence and apathy. If the farmers want change, they need to start with themselves. Second, the force field analysis also makes clear that change costs. The current situation may be bad, but there is always something to be lost – if only that it is known and familiar. Seeing the positive side of present arrangements and so facing the risks involved in acting for change, is a crucial part of social analysis. Unless people recognise that change will bring loss, as well as possible gain, they will be poorly prepared for a sustained campaign.

Dependency

The liberational stress on the importance of recognising underlying structures and power relations means that it strongly identifies with dependency analysis in development. As Chapter Three indicates, the history of development shows that liberal, modernisation assumptions were optimistic, to say the least. For many poor countries, the dependency stress on the power relations between centre and periphery, such that the development of the one is the flip side of the under-development of the other, rings truer to their experience. Nonetheless, like the message of the life story of maize, the dependency approach needs some adjustment.

Mirroring the modernisation theory which it reacts against, dependency analysis has a strong tendency towards dualism. In modernisation, a sharp contrast is drawn between modernity and tradition; in dependency, it is between core and periphery. But will such a stark opposition really hold water? The evidence suggests things are not so simple. Colonialism, the centre-piece of dependency analysis, advanced largely through 'divide and rule'. In military conquest, the invaders turned disputes between local factions to their own advantage; the day-to-day running of colonial administrations was carried out largely by native people. Similarly in South Africa, the apartheid state built up hostility between different black groups, most notoriously through the establishment of 'homelands' which gave their chiefs a stake in the system which made black people subordinate overall. The spread of transnational companies also relies on some groups within the 'periphery' identifying themselves with foreign interests. Even within the local state there are split and contradictory groups and interests. Force field analysis would show that the dependency approach puts too much weight on external factors such as international aspects of economic exploitation and too little on the internal. In practice, alliances do not simply follow national boundaries. Neither core nor periphery is homogeneous. In each there are poor and rich, female and male, black and white, old and young, whose experiences differ widely. Emphasising only the opposition between them obscures the internal differences within each side, and the points they have in common.

Underplaying local responsibilities in underdevelopment ironically means that all the dynamism is seen on one side: modernity/the core initiates all action; tradition/periphery is inert, awaiting 'penetration' from outside. This makes the poor into simple victims, and seems to deny them any power to change the situation. In fact, as we see in Chapter Five, power relations are far more fluid and reciprocal than this suggests. The history of development also shows this openness: poor countries may have some negotiating power when they are in a strategically important location, or have resources which companies in the North require. Similarly, some countries of the South have managed to make substantial gains and significantly shift their position in world markets. While not denying the underlying power structures, it is important to remain alive to local opportunities for change. This is all the more so when the dependency approach can seem a counsel of despair. De-linking from the world's economy does not appear a real option, except perhaps for huge countries like China. Smaller countries simply cannot supply all their own needs, except at a very basic subsistence level which few would accept as desirable.

Further problems with dependency analysis as it stands are explored in later chapters. These come down to the fact that essentially it accepts the dominant model of development: the problem is that this development has not been seen in the South, rather than that it is undesirable. Like classic modernisation theory, dependency sees development largely in a male-biased way. Attention concentrates on areas of society and economy where men predominate, such as formal sector production, while women's work in domestic or subsistence activities is downplayed or ignored. Also, dependency theory, like modernisation, fails to recognise the environmental limits to growth. Finally, dependency analyses tend to be very large-scale, and rather theoretical. This means that they can gloss over the personal politics of poverty, failing to recognise that change needs to happen at a personal as well as political level.

Identity Politics

The stress in the liberational paradigm on 'where you stand depends on where you sit' can help people to recognise the limitations of their own vision. On the other hand, there is also the danger that it can descend into a form of labelling, which denies people's humanity. While all the white speakers at a campaign meeting in the UK have names and occupations, the one black person is billed as 'the voice from the South'. What he or she has to say is less important than the fact that s/he is seen to be there. For people committed to liberation, this is a highly ironic move. Because in it, whether consciously or not, such tokenism reproduces a fundamental characteristic of colonialism: the suppression of difference amongst the colonial populations. While the colonizers have names and faces, one 'native' may stand for all.

This labelling can operate in the other direction also. Accepting the general arguments about the domination of the South by the North makes white people feel they have no right to speak. White liberal guilt effectively disables whole swathes of sympathetic Europeans in the face of radical rhetoric from the South. From persons in a relationship, individuals are transformed into representatives of their peoples. In skilful hands, this guilt can be used to great personal advantage by a person from the South. What would never be accepted in another context passes without resistance. What is said feeds into the whites' own hang-ups, and the shame they feel gives the accusations the force of truth. They do not ask *whose* interests are being represented, or whether the priorities of the (almost always) relatively elite speaker reflect those of his or her country's poor. Such radical rhetoric can not only silence the North, but also other voices from the South. When something is made an issue of colour loyalty, others from Africa, Asia, or Latin America can feel that they must fall into line. If this happens amongst those who are represented in North-South forums, it is all the more the case for the majority who never have the chance to be there. In the name of truth and justice, great injustice can be done.

As in any relationship, in the partnership between North and South there will always be a need to move on, to re-shape the relationship in new ways as new circumstances arise. There has been enough bad faith. It is crucial that people of goodwill from North and South should be able to work together, not with caricatures of one another or with slogans that obscure, but with a genuine commitment to increasing understanding. Facing up to what divides them should enable people to celebrate the different gifts with which they come, and to share and strengthen these to serve better a genuine movement for change.

The danger of labelling appears also in a very different way. A number of studies are now questioning how far the liberational rhetoric adds up to liberation in practice. John Burdick (1992:172) draws on his research near Rio de Janeiro to point out that the BCCs provide only one of a number of religious and ideological alternatives facing the poor. Comparing the local BCC and Pentecostal Church in a shanty town, he found that there were not only three times as many active members in the Pentecostal Church, but that they were also on average poorer and blacker than the BCC members. The BCC stress on literacy for social analysis and commitment to projects beyond church attendance discouraged people who could not read, or who, because of child-care or low-grade jobs, had little control over their time. While the Pentecostal Church emphasised personal and domestic problems, in the BCC these were seen as less important than conventionally political ones. A woman bringing to the group her problems with an abusive husband, for example, would get very different responses from the two communities. From the Pentecostals she could gain the authority of a strong condemnation of such behaviour, to enable her to confront her husband with his sin and promise the power to change. The BCC, by contrast, would tend to turn her concrete problem into an abstract one, urging her to set her husband's abuse in the context of his unemployment, and that in the context of structural problems in the economy, and that in the context of North-South exploitation …. Instead of her tangible experience being validated and given a practical response, in effect it would be denied.

The Pentecostal doctrine of the separation of 'church' and 'world' was also something that black people in particular could use to their advantage. Being 'born again' meant leaving behind the old, stigmatised social identity and being able to take on a new status as saved, as especially open to the Spirit. The Catholic denial of 'in a flash' conversion, and the liberational stress on continuities between the religious and social worlds, did not offer this same opportunity for transformation. Finally, Burdick questions how deeply liberation theology has really affected people's consciousness. Even many BCC members, he suggests, still interpret their world in conventional conservative Catholic terms. For them, liberation means personal salvation, and the claims of the poor are to be met by charity, rather than politics (*ibid:*181).

Studies like John Burdick's provide a useful caution against the temptation to take *any* rhetoric, including the liberational, simply at face value. The textual and contextual need always to be held in tension. When what is experienced in one context is seen to have wider implications, it may be translated itself into a new 'text', either literally, by being written up, or metaphorically, by becoming a pattern others try to follow. If this becomes encrusted as orthodoxy, then, whatever its origins, it can come to serve established patterns of power rather than being an opportunity for challenge. How an approach is *used* can never simply be read off from what it *says*. This is explored in more detail in the next chapter, where we look at the politics of participation. Here, we illustrate this briefly through a quite different example: the New Right commitment to the free market.

Like religion, the ideology of the free market can operate to gain people's commitment to the existing social system. But it also carries within it the potential for radical change. The basis of this openness lies in its character as an ideal. The free choice it preaches is not a practical reality. As we have seen, in practice there are all kinds of factors which limit the options that people have. While the rich may have considerable room for manoeuvre, the poor have much less. If we view society as a 'market', we can see that it is no more a free one than is the market of international economic relations, dominated by international finance institutions, transnational companies and the superior military and economic power of the countries of the north.

So long as the reality differs from the ideal, the ideal can be turned around as a judgement on the system, a call for its overthrow, instead of encouraging conformity. If choices are not free, then the ideology of free choice can be used to argue for change to remove structural inequalities. Ideals of human rights, which developed within an individualist framework, can be mobilised to point out how human rights are denied *collectively* to groups of people on grounds of gender, religious or political conviction, disability, ethnicity or class. The fortress of 'free market' capitalism is not impregnable: it contains within it the seeds of its own transformation.

In this section we have looked at the limitations of the liberational paradigm, and the ways in which it can go astray. The final point we need to raise again relates to the commitment to the contextual. The liberational paradigm developed in response to the experience of the poor in the South. What possible relevance can it have to those whose personal context is quite different? It is this challenge that we take up in the rest of this chapter.

Are the Non-poor Poor?

Even as she answered the phone, you could hear the tension in Janet's voice. 'It would be good to see you,' she said, 'I just don't know when I can find the time.' She talked for 15 minutes about all the pressures on her, all she had to do. All the things she had done in the past few months since we were last in touch. 'I hardly have time even to be with the kids any more.' She said, 'I know it's not right, but there is so much to get done. They grow up so fast and in a few years they'll be gone, and I know I'll regret not being closer to them now. I should say no to more things, so that I could have more time quietly at home. But I have waited years to get to this point when people actually ask me to work with them, I don't want to pass up the chances now. And it's also good for the firm if my name gets better known, and of course the more I do the better pleased the boss is with me. I tell myself that after the next three weeks things will be better. I've got a number of assignments to finish just now, but I should get them done by the end of the month. Though I know I've said that before. Am always saying it, in fact.' She rang off, apologising for being so busy, already anxious about the time she'd lost in talking. Next month, when she was freer, she'd get back to me and we'd fix a time to meet.

★   ★   ★

Pedro and Anita had six children. Anita did not want to have any more. The pregnancies had taken a heavy toll on her health. And nursing and caring for the children fell mainly to her. They were already struggling to provide for the family. But Pedro wouldn't listen. The children were all girls. No one would carry on his name. He would not be satisfied until he got a son. Anita became pregnant again, and at last a boy was born. But still Pedro was not content. If there were two boys there would be some security, that one at least would live long enough to have a son of his own. Only through his sons and grandsons could Pedro 'live on'. Anita was his wife and it was her duty to follow his wishes. Only through the dream that his sons would be a success could Pedro find meaning for the hardships he had suffered in life.

For others it is not enough to have children who will put flowers and light candles on their graves. They want more than to live on in the memory of their children. That may do for ordinary people. But they want to be remembered by the nation; to be famous and to have a place in history. While Marcos was president of the Philippines, he had a bust of himself, hundreds of feet high, carved out of a mountain. He had murals of himself and his wife, Imelda, painted on government buildings. Some seek fame to become larger than life.

★ ★ ★

When Rohin was at college, he knew what he wanted in life. By the age of 35 he would have a beautiful wife and two children, a house in a prosperous neighbourhood, an executive job, a healthy savings account, a Mercedes Benz, and opportunities to travel abroad. It was a long list. But he was lucky. By his mid-thirties he had achieved everything he had wished for. But the quest was not over. Somehow Rohin still felt empty inside. He didn't seem to be able to reach out to his wife any more, he had become like a stranger to her. The children seemed to be interested in him only for what he could buy them. Rising so quickly up the ladder at work had made him few friends. He was sick of hotel rooms, which, in whatever country they were, seemed all to look the same. He knew that others were envious of him, for being so well known, having such wealth and power. But he felt a kind of bitterness. Getting what he had longed for had not quenched his hunger and thirst for them. Instead, the desire for more and more became more intense and compelling.

★ ★ ★

Clara held the cup tightly in her hands. 'Since the children have gone,' she said, 'it just doesn't seem worth going on. It used to give me such happiness, them just being around. I never wanted anything else. To be married, to have a family .... Even when I was a little girl, I played with dolls and looked forward to when I grew up and could have real babies of my own. And now ... do you know, sometimes I don't even feel I exist any more? People say, "You're free now. The kids are off your hands. Get out, enjoy yourself!" But I don't know what this "self" is. I've spent my life fitting in, filling the gaps,

79

making myself into what others seemed to want. Trying to please. I know the children took advantage of me at times. And my husband too, especially lately. Sometimes I think he'll really leave, like he's threatened, because there is no one there to keep him home. He despises me, I can see it in his eyes. Gets furious when I can't make up my mind. But how can I? Suppose I get it wrong? It was so easy before, when I could see what was needed, and just do it.'

★ ★ ★

In the local bar, Saul boasted about his latest conquest. She had been so beautiful! She'd tried to resist him at first, but in the end he'd won. And when he'd got her home, she'd been so hot for him. All her earlier coolness was gone. It had been an amazing night! When he got up to go she had begged him to stay.

The other men in the bar listened with amusement. They were used to Saul's stories. Every other night, it seemed, he'd be in there bursting to tell them about the latest woman he had had. Some of them felt envious. Others just felt sad. If these women were all so wonderful, how come Saul could never settle with any of them? What did he think he'd achieve, wandering like this from bed to bed, no longer able even to remember the number of women, let alone their names? They had tried to reason it out with Saul, but they had long given up. He was looking for something, but he couldn't tell them what it was. And it seemed to get worse, not better. With each bed that he left, he just felt himself more alone.

Poverty of Being

By the standards in their own societies, none of these people is materially poor – all but Pedro and Anita are in fact rather well off. But they all experience an inner emptiness, a sense of being driven, a sense that there is something more, something just beyond their grasp, that would set their striving at rest. Theologians have called this inner emptiness 'ontological poverty', the poverty of being. It is profoundly personal, and yet at the same time common to all people, across space and time, part of being human. It concerns the experience of self, and yet, because we belong in society, it is shaped by the broader culture.

For some people, poverty of being is felt in the limits to options. Every choice we make shuts off other choices. With every door we walk through, others close behind us. When we take a particular job, or marry a particular person, we say 'yes' to one possibility at the price of saying 'no' to others. Sometimes we make options even though the choices are not very clear. Or what seems to be the right thing to do at a given moment becomes questionable later on. And as we grow older we find that at a deeper level also, this is true. We do learn more, we come to understand new things. But we also lose some of the old certainties, find that life is much more complicated than we thought, things are not so black and white. Some of us react to this with denial; we insist on holding on to a particular view of the world, become less tolerant and less flexible. We define ourselves against others, we assert ourselves by refusing to see the world as they do. But, for others of us, the response is quite different. We see that our boundaries become less clear, we can no longer state, definitively, what we are. We see ourselves no longer as the centre of our own worlds, but simply one part in a large whole.

Others experience poverty of being in terms of lack of control. Our happiness depends at least as much on the external environment as on ourselves. In a recession people find themselves out of a job through no fault of their own. Suddenly the mortgage payments that were manageable become impossible to meet. In Bosnia, Rwanda, Yemen, Ethiopia, the Sudan, Mozambique ... war destroys homes and lives in a few moments, and in the longer term condemns millions of people to famine. Accidents and illness can turn all our plans and expectations upside down. Even in 'normal' times, people feel helpless to affect the policy decisions that make a great difference to their lives. Wealthy people may have more control, be better able to protect themselves against the unexpected, but this is never absolute. Being human means being vulnerable. To a greater or lesser degree, all of us experience ourselves as poor in power.

One of the sharpest ways in which we are out of control is in our need for others. This can take people in two different ways. Some, like Clara, may try to lose themselves in relationships, be so much defined in terms of others that they no longer know who they themselves are. Others respond by wanting to be self-reliant and needing no one: to stand on their own two feet against the world. Having to rely on others feels unsafe: they will let us down, or perhaps we will disappoint them. It seems easier to make our own way, to owe nothing and have nothing owed to us. But the paradox is that we need others to grow; it is only through others that we come to know ourselves. One of the most profound forms of torture is to leave a person in a bare room, utterly alone. There is something very terrible about loneliness. 'All you need is love' may be too easy a slogan, but is also contains a truth. Part of being human is the need for one another. We cannot simply stand alone. And yet nor can we enter a relationship if we have no self to share. To be a person means to know oneself in relationship. Interdependence rather than absolute self-sufficiency is part of the human condition.

A third aspect of the poverty of being is death. For some, death is a consolation. For most of us it brings fear. It is the ultimate evidence of our limitedness. It is the ultimate experience of our being alone. Paradoxically, coming close to death can also bring reaffirmation of life. In being so absolute, it can cause us to re-evaluate our priorities, to recognise how little of what worries us really matters. It can show up the poverty of our being, and fill us with a new freedom and peace. Diane, who developed cancer in her late twenties, put it like this:

> Perhaps the worst thing about dying is not death but is the loss of life, the rejection of potential, the things you will never do – all those things we keep putting off till tomorrow. I'm determined not to die, because I think I am finally learning something about life.

Poverty of being is a given of human living. But we can choose how we respond to it. Like Diane, we can welcome it and find in it our liberation. Or like Janet, Pedro, Marcos, Rohin, Clara and Saul, we can run from it. Trying to fill our emptiness with activity, with children, with fame, possessions or sexual conquests to prove our worth.

Poverty of Being and Economic Culture

When we extend our understanding of poverty to include poverty of being, it is clear that the non-poor can also be poor. Poverty of being is experienced as an inner emptiness that craves to be filled. Human beings need some achievements in order to feel good about themselves. The basic wishes of Janet and the others – to feel that you are doing a good job; to have children; to have the recognition of others; to have material comfort; to have a partner to love – these are not bad things. But they impoverish us when these desires become an obsession, when other people, and even ourselves, become only means to these ends. To some extent, how we respond to the poverty of being is a matter of personal choice. But there is also a wider, structural aspect to this. For different economic and political cultures treat the poverty of being very differently. Some set brakes on it, others actively emphasise it. Where people are in the social structure is also significant. Men and women, black and white, rich and poor, will experience the poverty of being in quite different ways. This is explored further through the case of gender in Chapter Six.

In arguing down the wage rate with Bolai, the excuse that Fazlur gave was that his son had bought a motorbike, he had no money to spare. It is difficult to believe that this would have left him so short of money that he could not afford the few taka extra that Bolai was asking. Nevertheless, it does point to an important connection: experience of the poverty of being for some can result directly in material poverty for others.

The economic culture of capitalism actually maximises people's experience of the poverty of being, harnessing it as its engine of growth. The form this takes has varied over time. According to Max Weber, one of the founding fathers of sociology, religion originally played an important part. What was distinctive about early capitalism was its orientation towards profit, not consumption. This meant that any surplus could be reinvested in production. The development of this economic culture was vitally linked, Max Weber believed, to the emergence of Calvinism in Christianity. This was an ascetic Protestant tradition, which held that only a small number of 'the elect' had been chosen by God for salvation. Following strict business ethics and despising accumulation of material wealth were seen as important signs of belonging to this group. Paradoxically, this meant that Calvinists tended to do very well in business, since they ploughed all their profits back into their companies, keeping very little for their personal use. More machinery was bought, and more people employed, leading to ever greater output. The productive potential of such a system was remarkable. Also, more people achieved higher standards of living than ever before.

As capitalism has become established, however, its underlying culture has shifted. The 'Protestant ethic' of hard work and high saving remains in the tendency to value people in terms of the work they do. But the drive for profit means cutting jobs, as new technology can produce more cheaply and efficiently than human labour. High levels of unemployment are therefore built into the system, resulting in a vicious downward spiral of poverty, self-doubt and depression. A second tendency turns the screws even tighter. While those on the margins still struggle to make ends meet, the non-poor are encouraged to acquire ever more comforts and luxuries. To keep the market buoyant the 'work hard' of the Protestant ethic is complemented by the new 'play hard' of the 'consumer ethic' urging instant gratification with the slogan 'buy now, pay later'.

Fashion in clothes is an obvious example of this. If one 'can't wear' the styles of last season because they have become outmoded, there is a pressure to buy again long before the clothes are worn out. High technology consumer goods are another. When most people have record players, the market expands into cassettes. When the potential for sales of cassette players falls off, the only way to listen to music is on compact disc.

Perhaps the fastest turnover of all is in computers, where it appears that new models come on to the market almost daily, ever faster, ever more compact. What amazed and delighted us yesterday becomes not worth buying today. This has no real relation to needs. Our 'needs' change and develop with the marketing of high performance models to meet them.

It is not difficult to see how the logic of such a system can contribute to poverty of being. The whole dynamic is to produce more, to expand, never to be satisfied but to push on further. Competition, not co-operation, is the rule of the game. People get caught up in the race to get on. It is not what they are, but what they do and what they have, that matters. This form of poverty is very much self-sustaining: people are running too fast to stop to ask why. And this is not limited to those in the vanguard, the same logic is perpetuated throughout the whole society. Because for businesses to prosper, it is not enough for them to manufacture, they must also be able to sell their output. Where production so far exceeds the needs of reproduction, needs must be created in order to generate markets for the goods. If people become satisfied with what they have, they may stop buying.

The fuel that runs contemporary capitalism, in both production and consumption, is dissatisfaction. For those with the jobs that allow initiative and the capacity to buy expensive goods, achievements at work offset self-doubt and a series of new purchases provides moments of enjoyment. But what of the others? Those who the same drive for profit has put out of work or consigned to insecure, dead-end jobs, with incomes far too low to buy into the consumer society.

For these people, experience of the poverty of being is particularly intense. They too are shaped by the wider culture, which measures what people are by what they do and what they have. But they do not have the opportunity of people like Rohin to discover the emptiness of 'the good life'. They are caught in a trap of high expectations that can never be realised. While in strict material terms they may have the means of survival, the relative deprivation that they suffer is acute. The price of buying consumer goods is getting into debt, often at punishingly high interest. They feel that they are failures in relation to their children as they cannot provide what they want. The media presents them as a burden on society; they are marginal and stigmatised. What work is available offers little pay and less security. They suffer in a very profound way the sense of being helpless and out of control. Contact with the state is degrading, serving only to underscore their feelings of worthlessness.

The combination of liberal culture and capitalism has delivered greater material prosperity and individual liberty to more people than has any other. The vision of socialism remains powerful, but so far it has failed to match this in practice. Despite their egalitarian rhetoric, the collapse of the Communist parties in Eastern Europe revealed tremendous power, wealth and privileges concentrated at the top of the political and military bureaucracy. For those lower down the scale, both material goods and personal freedom were in short supply. Although under state control, essentially the same model of technology-centred, industry-led growth was pursued in the East as in the West. The centrality of the state meant bureaucracy became massive, invasive, inefficient and corrupt. Competition in the market was replaced by manoeuvring in practical and ideological politics: those better at playing the game won out over others. Wherever possible, people tried to 'beat the system'. Work for the collective was resented, while people happily discounted the labour on their own private plots (Humphrey, 1983:188). The clear principles for administration were not so much 'acted on', as 'acted out' (*ibid:* 102).

It is easier to see the shortcomings of the market than to see what more effective mechanism could replace it as the medium of production and distribution. But it is clear that an alternative to the rampant 'free market' of the New Right must be sought. As we review in Chapter Seven, the environmental costs of the present system make it unsustainable. The human costs of making capital out of the poverty of being make it self-defeating and immoral.

Poverty of the Spirit

If the method of liberation theology lies in the interaction between text and context, what then do Christian texts have to say about its central focus, of poverty and the poor? This is the question we pose in the final section of this chapter. Returning to our core question, we ask who are the poor in the Bible and Church tradition, and how can this guide us in our response to both material poverty and the poverty of being?

The Christian tradition distinguishes two kinds of poverty – material and spiritual. Each of these is further broken down into voluntary (positive) and involuntary (negative) dimensions. These are shown in Figure 4.2 below (page 86). The rest of this section sets out their meaning in greater detail.

Figure 4.2   Poverty in the Christian Tradition

	NEGATIVE (involuntary)	POSITIVE (voluntary)
M A T E R I A L	'material poverty' – commonsense usage injustice, evil, offence against God's laws	'evangelical poverty' – asceticism self-denial living simply
S P I R I T U A L	'spiritually poor' – those attached to things of the 'world'; blind to their need of God	'poor in spirit' – detachment those who know their need of God

Involuntary Poverty

Reading from the top left-hand corner, the first meaning of poverty is the commonsense one: involuntary material poverty. How this is seen in the Bible is shown in the various terms that are used to refer to poor people:

ebyon:	the one who desires; the beggar
dal:	the weak one; the frail
ani:	the bent over one; the humiliated
anaw:	the one humble before God

The images are vivid. Even in the way they hold themselves, the poor show their poverty. They do not stand up straight, but are bent over under the burden of their need. They lower their heads as their standing is low in society. They have no power or status, no option but to beg for pity. In the final term, *anaw*, poverty is given a spiritual dimension. Having no worldly wealth or security, the poor are in a unique way dependent on God.

Such presentations of poverty are not the picture of a dispassionate observer. As the Liberation Theologian Gustavo Gutierrez (1974:165) says,

Indigent, weak, bent over, wretched are terms which well express a degrading human situation. These terms already insinuate a protest. They are not limited to a description; they take a stand.

As we saw in Chapter Three, prosperity, not shortage and hardship, is God's promise for God's people. That anyone should be in want is an offence against the law of Yahweh. This gives us the first part of our response to poverty: to raise our voices against injustice. In doing this we join the great Hebrew tradition of protest from the time of the exodus onwards. As we saw in Chapter Three, this is taken up by the great prophets of Israel, but it comes first from the ordinary people who cry out as they suffer oppression. Out of the burning bush God says to Moses:

I have observed the misery of my people who are in Egypt; I have heard their cry on account of their taskmasters. Indeed, I know their sufferings, and I have come down to deliver them from the Egyptians, and to bring them up out of that land to a good and broad land, a land flowing with milk and honey ....

~ Exodus 3: 7-8 ~

This is no isolated case, but a recurring pattern. Following the lead of Erhart Gerstenberger, Brueggemann (1978:21) points out that

... it is characteristic of Israel to complain rather than lament; that is, Israel does not voice resignation, but instead expresses a militant sense of being wronged with the powerful expectation that it will be heard and answered.

The cry of protest is the embryonic political act. It is the first step in refusing to accept an unjust system as legitimate. What is intriguing, is that this elemental political action is at one and the same time the primal cry of religion. The relationship between the people's cry and God's response is an intensely intimate one. The one seems a part of the other, just as a child sucking at her breast causes the mother's milk to flow. God is in the cry of the oppressed, as well as in the action to save them. Although the Bible begins with the story of creation, Biblical scholars say it was as their saviour, not creator, that the Israelites knew God first.

If the cry of the poor for deliverance is the elemental religious response, it is not surprising that the Bible contains strong warnings against the dangers of material wealth. While shared prosperity is God's blessing, individual riches can engender a second kind of poverty: the spiritual poverty of those who are blind to their need of God. Jesus' parable of the rich fool puts the message starkly:

> The land of a rich man produced abundantly. And he thought to himself, 'What shall I do, for I have no place to store my crops?' Then he said, 'I will do this: I will pull down my barns, and build larger ones; and there I will store all my grain and my goods. And I will say to my soul, "Soul, you have ample goods laid up for many years; relax, eat, drink, be merry".' But God said to him, 'You fool! This very night your life is demanded of you. And the things you have prepared, whose will they be?' So it is with those who store up treasures for themselves but are not rich toward God.
>
> ~ Luke 12: 16-21 ~

Passages like this suggest the second element in our response to poverty: to take seriously the personal and spiritual and not lose them in the economic and political. This applies both to those who enjoy wealth and power, and to those who are struggling for them to be more equally shared. It is not only material wealth that can blind us to our need of God. The failure of Rohin, Janet, Clara and the others to face the poverty of being give alternative examples of this form of spiritual poverty.

Voluntary Poverty

Following on from the dangers of wealth, some passages seem to advocate material poverty as a spiritual option. Luke 18: 18-27 gives an example:

> A certain ruler asked him, 'Good Teacher, what must I do to inherit eternal life?' Jesus said to him, 'Why do you call me good? No one is good but God alone. You know the commandments: "You shall not commit adultery; You shall not murder; You shall not steal; You shall not bear false witness; Honour your father and mother".' He replied, 'I have kept all these since my youth'. When Jesus heard this, he said to him, 'There is still one thing lacking. Sell all that you own and distribute the money to the poor, and you will have treasure in heaven; then come, follow me'. But when he heard this, he became sad, for he was very rich. Jesus looked at him and said, 'How hard it is for those who have wealth to enter the kingdom of God! Indeed, it is easier for a camel to go through the eye of a needle than for someone who is rich to enter the kingdom of God'.

Those who heard it said, 'Then who can be saved?' He replied, 'What is impossible for mortals is possible for God'.

This is only one of several so-called hard sayings of Jesus. It turned on its head the assumption that since prosperity was the sign of God's blessing, the wealthy were best placed to enter the Kingdom of God. Instead, Jesus' warnings against wealth are loud and clear. Poverty is presented as an ideal to be embraced.

This points us to the third part of our response to poverty: to choose against the cultural pressures towards conspicuous consumption and achievement at others' expense. Making a commitment to living simply has long been seen as a means of clearing away the clutter of the world and allowing one's mind to concentrate more fully on God. In the Catholic tradition this is termed 'evangelical poverty', and is usually reserved for a select few who have the vocation to join religious orders such as monks and nuns. The problem is that while they might own nothing as individuals, the communities to which they belonged were often very rich. This limited their capacity to be with the poor, as they might not suffer any material hardship or insecurity. Compounding this, the institutions might even be orientated towards the rich, providing medical care or schools for the top families, while their lands were worked by the poor at exploitative rates. This is very far from the ideal of poverty that Jesus envisaged!

Others make a more radical option, choosing to live amongst the poor and share fully in the circumstances of their lives. They may not be politically active, but their lives proclaim a living question against the choice to have more at the cost of others having less. Others still embark on a critical search for a way of living 'in the world' which strikes a balance between meeting their own needs and recognising the claims of others. Either way, to opt for less is a battle. The external environment is not neutral, but exerts strong pressures to go for more. The struggle against this will be ongoing, dynamic and continuous.

The final element in our response to poverty complements and expands on this. It is the interior orientation of being poor in spirit. The emphasis here is not on *material* poverty, but on an inner attitude of detachment from wealth and success, to guard against being possessed by our possessions or driven by our drive to achieve. Paul's letter to the Philippians provides a lead in this:

Not that I am referring to being in need; for I have learned to be content with whatever I have. I know what it is to have little, and I know what it is to have plenty. In any and all circumstances I have learned the secret of being well-fed and of going hungry, of having plenty and of being in need. I can do all things through him who strengthens me.

~ Philippians 4: 11-13 ~

The importance of this internal orientation being embodied in an external commitment to combat poverty cannot be too highly stressed. Taken alone, the social consequences of a stress on cultivating detachment can be very conservative. Poverty is 'spiritualised', its material reality is ignored. The rich are restored to spiritual good health, but the poor are left in want.

To draw together these four elements in our response to poverty, we return to the advice Jesus gave to the rich young man. There were three parts to it: sell what you have; give it to the poor; follow me. What does it mean to follow Jesus in his poverty?

The fundamental way in which Jesus was poor is captured in the last term we mentioned above as those used in the Bible for the poor. This is *anawim,* those humble before God. The *anawim* accept themselves as poor in response to the poverty of being. As they face their inner emptiness they look to God as their rock, their refuge and their shield. They surrender themselves to total dependence on God. As Albert Gelin (1964) quoted by Gutierrez (1974:169) puts it, this is ' ... the ability to welcome God, an openness to God, a willingness to be used by God, a humility before God'.

People who have this quality are the 'poor in spirit' whom Jesus calls happy or blessed in the Sermon on the Mount (Matthew 5: 3). The New English Bible makes this clear in its translation of this verse: 'How blest are those who know their need of God!'

This does not come automatically to either rich or poor. Both wealth and deprivation can provide a focus that blocks out all else. Even for Jesus, it was a struggle. Aloysius Pieris (1988:16) points out that Jesus experienced real humiliation. He suffered recurrent conflicts and temptations. He had to face that his mission as he had seen it had failed. The tide of his early popularity changed and instead forces were gathering against him. His following was falling away. In Jerusalem awaited him not triumph, but a cross. Only by being himself the bloody victim of the unjust social order could God's new order dawn.

Jesus took on poverty and suffered the injustice of the cross not to glorify it, but to overcome it. Poverty for Jesus was an option he chose, not as a passive state, but as a struggle *for the poor.* This shows up the importance of the second part of Jesus' advice to the rich young man. When he had sold what he had, he was to give it to the poor. The point of becoming poor is to reduce the poverty of others. The meaning of interior poverty is only fulfilled if it also has an exterior orientation.

For Pieris (1988:21), the struggle to be poor must aim

> ... to *follow Jesus* who *was* poor then and to *serve* Christ who *is* in the poor now.

To be poor is to stand in solidarity with the poor, and to protest against the forces that sustain poverty. This may mean questioning one's 'rights' over time, activities, the people we love, and autonomy, as well as goods and property. Above all, it means a willingness to let go.

From this perspective, we can return to detachment. But it is detachment given a new, positive meaning. It is detachment *for*, not just detachment *from*. Detachment needs an accompanying orientation. 'My soul is restless, and it shall remain restless until it rests in You, O God,' cried Augustine of Hippo. In his *Spiritual Exercises*, Ignatius of Loyola, the founder of the Jesuit Order, proposes that detachment should be the fundamental attitude of a Christian. He recognises the danger of people being owned by what they own. For him a Christian can only be committed to Christ – to the 'Greater Glory of God' (*Ad Majorem Dei Gloriam*). The value of all things depends on whether or not they serve this end (Ignatius [1963: 80]):

> So that, as far as we are concerned, we do not set our hearts on good health as against bad health, prosperity as against poverty, a good reputation as against a bad one, a long life as against a short one, and so on.
>
> The one thing we desire, the one thing we choose is what is more likely to achieve the purpose of our creating.

The precise path that individuals will choose cannot be prescribed in advance. To struggle to be poor is to walk an uncharted road. In one way or another, opting to follow Jesus in his poverty is to refuse to have more than enough, when others have less than enough. It is not to deny that prosperity is God's blessing, but to insist that God's blessing is to be shared. Though this may seem life-denying, it is in fact the opposite. To be the *anawim,* those happy because they know their need of God, is precisely what it means to 'choose life', as Moses urged on the Israelites shortly before he died (Deuteronomy 30:19). The Christian faith is a faith of paradox, that it is in giving that we receive, in dying that we know re-birth. It is only when we unclench the fist raised against the poverty of being, that our hands can open to the greater good that God would offer us. As Pieris (1988:20) says, bread eaten when others go hungry is an evil; but bread shared becomes a sacrament.

Conclusion

A group of Filipino farmers had gathered together to make a joint assessment of the development project they had been involved in. Most listed economic benefits, but when Andot's turn to speak came he said:

> I am not a scarecrow.
> Though I am poor and lowly,
> my thoughts and feelings have value.
> I am a human being.

This expresses the core of the liberational vision: the embodiment of the spiritual in the material; the complementarity of interior and exterior. Like the other farmers, Andot had gained economically from the project. But what he chose to emphasise was that he had learned to recognise his own value.

In this chapter we have introduced in outline the liberational paradigm, to complete the four understandings of why the poor are poor that we encountered in Chapter Three. We have considered it as practice, not only theory, and not only its strength, but also the ways in which it can go astray. This shows the importance of holding in tension the structural and the individual; the political and the personal. In the second part of the chapter we have seen that poverty is a challenge for the non-poor as well as for the poor, as we have traced out some connections between material poverty and the experience of the poverty of being.

In Chapter One we set out what we mean by doing theology and development:

Doing theology and development means to engage in the cycle of experience, analysis, reflection and action in the context of our relationship to God, and to one another as poor and non-poor.

In Chapters Two to Four we have laid down the core of our understanding of this relationship through exploring the questions 'Who are the poor?' and 'Why are the poor poor?' In the remaining chapters we consider in more detail four themes that we hold critical in pressing the analysis further. These are respectively power and participation, gender, the environment and violence and non-violence.

CHAPTER FIVE

Power
and the People

Introduction

'Lend me your freedom and I will give you bread!' – so Marcos promised when he declared Martial Law. But as the months and years passed it seemed to more and more people that he had taken away both their freedom and their bread. Changing the system became a matter of urgency. At the end of one conference on social change, a prominent politician appealed to the community organisers to join him:

'These three days have revealed that we share the same vision. But your strategy is very slow. If you join our party we will have a better chance of taking power. And when we are in power we can change the economy and political system, so that cultural and social transformation will surely follow.'

The response of the community organisers was a resounding 'No'. They did want to change the structures of society. They agreed with much of what the politician stood for. But they did not want to be the 'saviours' of the people. They wanted to enable the people to help themselves. If people wanted their freedom and bread back, they would have to win them for themselves.

For the politician the people would provide the mass support needed to take his party to power. And the community organisers were the means to win that support. But for the community workers the people had the potential to become the subjects and authors of change. People should not only follow the politicians. They could also provide the lead.

In this chapter we set out the first of the four core perspectives in our own theology and development approach: the understanding of power. Power is central to the liberational view of how the world is and should be, but just what this means is not always very clearly set out. We begin, therefore, by asking, 'What is power?' Drawing on both theology and political science, we see how it is something provisional and precarious, not a 'thing' that people 'have', which can be grasped and held, weighed and measured. It is something that belongs in relationships, but also acts deep within us, forming our view of the world and our own place in it.

In the second section we look at empowerment. We see how power can be a positive force 'power to' – rather than being used for domination or control over others. We follow this by considering the main mechanism for achieving empowerment in development: the active participation of the poor. This is now advocated by agencies right across the spectrum, from the huge multi-laterals to the smallest people's organisations. The inclusion of at least some 'participatory' element in programmes applying for funding is now a requirement amongst many donor agencies. But of itself, participation in a programme does not guarantee empowerment. We consider first the practical implications. If development is something to be achieved *by* the poor, not delivered to them, what does this mean for institutional structures, patterns of leadership, and the role of outsiders in development programmes? We then look more closely at the various forms and functions of 'participation', to explore the politics of the interests it can serve.

These issues are followed through in the final part, as we consider a key passage in the Gospels which sets out the paradox of Jesus' teaching on power, and how it up-ends ordinary understandings.

What is Power?

Then they took Jesus from Caiaphas to Pilate's headquarters. It was early in the morning .... Pilate went out to them and said, 'What accusation do you bring against this man?' They answered, 'If he were not a criminal, we would not have handed him over to you'. Pilate said to them, 'Take him yourselves and judge him according to your law'. The Jews replied, 'We are not permitted to put anyone to death .... '

Then Pilate entered the headquarters again, summoned Jesus, and asked him, 'Are you the King of the Jews?' Jesus answered, 'Do you ask this on your own, or did others tell you about me?' Pilate replied, 'I am not a Jew, am I? Your own nation and the chief priests have handed you over to me. What have you done?' Jesus answered, 'My kingdom is not from this world .... ' Pilate asked him, 'So you are a king?' Jesus answered, 'You say that I am a king. For this I was born, and for this I came into the world, to testify to the truth. Everyone who belongs to the truth listens to my voice'. Pilate asked him, 'What is truth?'

After he had said this, he went out to the Jews again and told them, 'I find no case against him. But you have a custom that I release someone for you at the Passover. Do you want me to release for you the King of the Jews?' They shouted in reply, 'Not this man, but Barabbas!' Now Barabbas was a bandit.

Then Pilate took Jesus and had him flogged …. Pilate went out again and said to them, 'Look, I am bringing him out to you to let you know that I find no case against him'. So Jesus came out, wearing the crown of thorns and the purple robe. Pilate said to them, 'Here is the man!' When the chief priests and the police saw him, they shouted, 'Crucify him! Crucify him!' Pilate said to them, 'Take him yourselves and crucify him; I find no case against him'. The Jews answered him, 'We have a law, and according to that law he ought to die because he has claimed to be the Son of God'.

Now when Pilate heard this, he was more afraid than ever. He entered his headquarters again and asked Jesus, 'Where are you from?' But Jesus gave him no answer. Pilate therefore said to him, 'Do you refuse to speak to me? Do you not know that I have power to release you, and power to crucify you?' Jesus answered him, 'You would have no power over me unless it had been given you from above; therefore the one who handed me over to you is guilty of a greater sin'. From then on Pilate tried to release him, but the Jews cried out, 'If you release this man, you are no friend of the emperor. Everyone who claims to be a king sets himself against the emperor'.

When Pilate heard these words, he brought Jesus outside …. Now it was the day of Preparation for the Passover; and it was about noon. He said to the Jews, 'Here is your King!' They cried out, 'Away with him! Away with him! Crucify him!' Pilate asked them, 'Shall I crucify your King?' The chief priests answered, 'We have no king but the emperor'. Then he handed him over to them to be crucified.

So they took Jesus; and carrying the cross by himself, he went out to what is called The Place of the Skull, which in Hebrew is called Golgotha. There they crucified him …. Pilate also had an inscription written and put on the cross. It read, 'Jesus of Nazareth, the King of the Jews'. Many of the Jews read this inscription, because the place where Jesus was crucified was near the city; and it was written in Hebrew, in Latin, and in Greek. Then the chief priests of the Jews said to Pilate, 'Do not write "The King of the Jews", but "This man said, I am King of the Jews".' Pilate answered, 'What I have written I have written'.

~ John 18: 28-19: 22 ~

As the local representative of Rome, the colonial power, Pilate was a force to be reckoned with in first century Palestine. He had, as he threatened Jesus, the power of life and death over the local subjects. But this story does not present the picture of a powerful man. Instead it shows someone deeply ill at ease, manipulated by others, desperately seeking and yet failing to find a way to break out of the trap he finds himself in.

In ordinary speech, we often talk about people 'having' power. The rich 'have power' over the poor, or men 'have power' over women. But the example of Pilate shows that things are much more complex. Power does not only come from 'above', it also comes from 'below'. Although formally subordinate to Pilate, the chief priests were able to manoeuvre him into doing just what they wanted. Even Jesus, having stayed quiet, responds not to Pilate's power but to his weakness, his fear, as he reassures him: 'The one who handed me over to you is guilty of a greater sin'. Pilate's last attempt at escape is to go over the heads of the Jewish leaders to appeal to the people themselves. But there too he finds no support. Despite the formal authority he commands, Pilate is caught. It is not only those at the top who have power, but those at the bottom have some power also. This is the first important thing to recognise if we want to understand power. Power is always (at least) two-way.

The next step is to question the description of power as something people 'have'. As the chief priests resist his attempts to evade responsibility, as Jesus responds to him not with fear but compassion, as the people throw back in his face his last-ditch appeal, where is Pilate's power? Power is not a commodity, the property of an individual. It does not exist 'out there'. Instead, power is something that belongs *to relationships*. The colonial relationship of Rome to Palestine means that Pilate can command some sanctions. It is, after all, at his say-so that Jesus is flogged, taunted, and eventually killed. More positively, he expresses this power in the inscription he has written, and his refusal to adjust it to suit the chief priests. But in the practical politics of the chief priests' manoeuvres, Pilate finds that it is precisely this formal power that is used against him. Power does not belong to one party, but appears in interaction. Power is exercised, it is expressed, it is not 'possessed'. It has no existence outside of relationships.

To say this is not to down-play the reality of power. Power is a part of *every* relationship, we cannot begin to understand development unless we take power into account. But power is always conditional. It cannot exist in a vacuum. Power always involves a response.

Power and Conflict

It is easiest to see power at work when there is open conflict. It is plain, for example, in the exchange when Pilate's inept appeal to national pride: 'Shall I crucify your king?', is countered deftly by the chief priests' loyal response, 'We have no king but the emperor'. This underlines their earlier threat to go over his head: 'If you release this man, you are no friend of the emperor.' Pilate knows he is check-mated.

Measuring power by observing conflict is what Stephen Lukes (1974) calls the 'one-dimensional' view of power. A 'two-dimensional' view would take account also of the 'off-stage' manoeuvres that determine the outcome of formal decision-making processes. It is well known, for example, that decisions in practice often owe more to lobbying in the bar than to formal discussions in the meetings that follow. Alternatively, meetings may be called at very short notice or set at inconvenient times or places to exclude undesirable members. Pilate's appeal to the people was doomed, because the crowd had already been worked on, or even 'packed' by supporters of the temple authorities, who would not want to risk a repeat of the popular acclaim of Jesus' entry to Jerusalem, just a week before.

Taking account of how power is exercised behind the scenes also goes beyond looking at who wins (by whatever means) over a particular issue, to looking at how something becomes an 'issue' in the first place. Pilate seems to sense this, as he tries to shift the terms of the debate from what Jesus had *claimed* to any wrong that he had actually *done*. His opponents resist this. They were too cunning not to know that the most effective way of exercising power is to set the agenda for discussion, so that the fundamental points are conceded without ever coming to debate.

One important way in which this is achieved in development is through the process of co-option. This commonly occurs when a radical challenge has led to an apparent shift in the dominant agenda. The language of the critique is taken on, but somehow the meaning of the words changes. The process was analysed in an influential early study of participation, Philip Selznick's *TVA and the Grass Roots*. The Tennessee Valley Authority (TVA) was created in 1933 as a semi-autonomous regional authority for managing a power and conservation project. Its express commitment was to be 'close to the people', to fulfil the functions of integrated regional planning 'within the framework of democratic values' (Selznick, 1966:12). The practical outcomes of the 'grass roots' doctrine, however, were very different from the rhetoric. What resulted were two patterns of co-option.

In the first, local institutions were co-opted to 'participate' in ways that served the interests of the TVA, rather than the people themselves. They had no real influence within the Authority, but were used by the TVA administratively as a channel to mobilise people or communicate information, and politically, to claim the legitimacy of popular support. In the second, the TVA itself was co-opted, as it was captured by a right-wing faction, who used it to promote their own ideologies and interests. Keeping well behind the scenes, this group managed to manoeuvre the TVA into acting in direct contradiction to its original vision.

In co-option, the form of a radical challenge may be retained, but the sting is removed. What was wild and threatening and shut outside, may come eventually to find a place within the house. But the price to be paid is domestication. The creature is no longer what it was. This is the hazard faced by any new critique – whether on the grounds of people's participation, gender, or the environment – when it succeeds in becoming an item on the mainstream development agenda. Incorporation, rather than exclusion, is often the best means of control.

Lukes takes the understanding of power still further, to propose a 'three-dimensional view'. This recognises that when power is exercised most effectively there is no visible conflict at all. If Pilate had been a stronger governor, the Jewish leaders would never have sought to push him about as they did. But the point goes deeper than this. When most effective, power does not only prevent people from *expressing* interests that challenge the system, but means that they actually identify with the system themselves. We saw this in Danny's story, where some of the people blamed themselves for their poverty: 'We are lazy, we are ignorant.' In Chapter Six we see how the ideology that women's subordination is 'natural' helps keep them in their place, and even reproduce the system by policing the action of other women. People disadvantaged by the existing system can so internalise its values that they even resist moves to liberate them, because they feel they are somehow 'not good enough'. The following story gives an example of this.

Romy:

Eighteen years have passed. But I can still see the wrinkles in his face, his balding head and his hunched back. Over the previous weeks, I had announced that Holy Communion would no longer be given with people kneeling along the altar rail with the host placed in their mouths. As if on pilgrimage, I asked them to form a queue and I would place the consecrated host in their hands. The day to implement the change finally arrived. Communicants formed a double line. As each one came, I raised the host and said 'The Body of Christ' and laid the host in their outstretched hands. His turn came. He did not kneel down. Like the others he stood up. But he clasped his hands behind his back, closed his eyes and opened his mouth. I looked at him in silence waiting for his eyes to open. After a short while, he opened his eyes.

Softly I said, 'I'd like to put the host into your hands'. 'No, Father. You should not. I am ashamed of my hands,' he responded. 'Why?' I asked. 'My hands are used to grasping the handle of a machete and a plough. They are too stiff to hold something as thin as the host. Besides, they are calloused, scarred and stained with the soil. I am ashamed to receive the host with my hands.' 'Why are your hands calloused, scarred and stained with the soil?' I asked again. 'I am a farmer, Father. I work with my hands,' he answered. 'Why do you work?' I responded. 'I have a family. I have to feed, clothe, educate – to provide for my wife and my children.' 'But why do you have to provide for them?' I continued.

He hesitated a bit, as if embarrassed to give an answer. Then he said, 'Because I love them'. I answered quietly, 'Your calloused, scarred and dirty hands are a witness to your love for your wife and children. I don't think you should be ashamed of them. Please, receive the host with your hands. Christ will not mind'.

I saw the callouses, the scars and the stains as I laid the host into his shaking hands. They were beautiful hands. They were hands which spoke of love.

Power and Empowerment

In the discussion so far, power has been understood in a largely negative way. It has been seen in terms of people having 'power over' others, of being able to make them do what they would not otherwise do. This is the power of domination, manipulation, of more or less subtle coercion. But there is power also in creativity, in healing, in the resolution of conflict. Power is the capacity to make a difference and this can be positive, as well as negative. The exercise of power may empower others. This dimension of power is very important in development, where 'empowerment' of the poor has become part of the rhetoric. In this section, therefore, we explore the understanding of power implicit in 'empowerment'.

If power is found in relationships, how does it work? There are basically two models for this. In the first, the 'zero-sum', or 'power over' model, as one party gains power the other loses it. This goes back to the view of power as a commodity: there is a fixed amount of power to be shared out. In the second, the 'positive-sum', or 'power to' model, one party may gain power with no loss to the other, and even both may gain in power at once. An example of this is found in Caroline Moser's (1989:1815) description of empowerment as a women in development policy approach. This does not entail conflict, that men will lose power as women gain it. Rather, empowerment is seen 'in the capacity of women to increase their own self-reliance and internal strength'.

It is easy to understand the attraction of this view of empowerment to development agencies who are shy of politics and confrontation. But will it stand up to examination? Again, we look to a story to ground our analysis.

Encouraged by a community organiser, 25 hillside families in Mabuhay, Bukidnon, decided to form a consumers' co-operative. Prices at the local store were 50% higher than those in the town, but the town was four hours' walk away. They took some training on co-operative management from the local NGO, and gradually devised their own constitution, by-laws, roles and responsibilities. As their confidence grew, they decided to take on a number of other projects. Then a presidential election was called. The local Mayor and some other officials visited the area. They had only one message: 'Vote for Marcos.' They had no time to listen to the villagers' questions or enter into discussion with them. After the Mayor left, the villagers decided to boycott the election.

When the election came, all 398 villagers spoiled their ballot papers. The community organiser visited them two days later. The election was widely expected to be rigged but she had never discussed it with them, so was surprised and impressed by what they had done. She asked them for their reasons. One of the farmers explained:

'In the co-operative, we discuss problems. We look at them from different angles. When we think that we have understood the situation, we try to come to a consensus. We avoid voting as much as possible. When the government officials came, we asked for an explanation why we were given other than what we asked for. We asked for a school, teachers and a road. The Mayor sent us the army, guns and bullets. He refused to answer our questions. He just told us to vote for Marcos. We want the government to be run the way we manage our co-operative store.'

In the course of two years, the community had organised three co-operatives, for consumption, marketing and production. This is empowerment according to the positive-sum model. They developed the power to identify their needs and plan how to meet them. They took training in the skills they needed to implement the projects, monitor and evaluate them. As the first one succeeded they grew in confidence to go on to the next. They began to feel that they were in control.

But the action they took did not only affect themselves. It also had implications for others. By forming their co-operatives, the villagers were able to undercut the prices and avoid paying the margins of the local traders. As they began to take responsibility for themselves they became better informed about local and national political issues. They may not have gained power over anyone, but they certainly resisted the power over them that their relationships with the traders had formerly involved. When the officials visited they were no longer ready, as they would once have been, simply to listen respectfully and do what they were told. They wanted their voice to be heard. When the officials had no time to listen, they decided to express their views in another way. For the Marcos party looking for votes, the villagers' empowerment clearly had a zero sum aspect.

The predominant depiction of power in the Gospels conforms to the empowerment model. The emphasis on power in Jesus' ministry is positive, as he exercised power to heal, to release, to forgive, to convince, to restore. As in the interchange with Pilate, this also involved resistance to others' power over him. While he did not explicitly deny Pilate's assertion of his power over life and death, he did undermine its force in two ways. First, by addressing Pilate's fear, Jesus brought out a very different dimension of power than the structural one which Pilate was asserting. Second, he reduced the scale of Pilate's authority, by stating that it was his only because it had been given from above. As throughout the Bible, power to do good is the other side of power over evil: sin, evil spirits, illness, death. Where Jesus' praxis differs from the earlier Jewish tradition, however, is that these forces to be overcome are not identified as hostile people or communities. Instead Jesus says famously, 'Love your enemies and do good to those who hate you' (Luke 6: 27).

The final dream of the empowerment process is that it will be positive sum. If more poor people gain the confidence and skill to resist economic and political exploitation, the end result will be a more whole and more just society, which will be in the ultimate interest of poor and non-poor alike. But this is a long way off. If it is to result in real change, the empowerment process will be a long struggle, in which deep conflicts of interest between the poor and non-poor have to be confronted. To claim otherwise is to fail to recognise how fundamentally the existing patterns of relationship are engraved in power.

Institutionalising Participation

It is under the banner of 'participation' that issues of power and empowerment have been incorporated into development programmes and policies. This has a sound economic as well as political basis. 'Top down' programmes, designed and implemented by outsiders, have resulted time and again in expensive white elephants, sophisticated answers to questions that no one was actually asking. All over the Philippines and Bangladesh you can see components for latrine construction lying about gathering weeds because people lack the money to install them, do not see them as a priority, or have no supply of water nearby to flush away the refuse and keep them clean. Even when projects do get up and running, there is no guarantee they will continue to operate once the 'experts' have packed their bags and gone home. The history of development is littered with stories of latest model technology standing idle for lack of maintenance, fuel or spare parts. Somewhat late in the day, development planners came to recognise that devising a technical solution was not enough. Unless what was on offer was appropriate to local needs; unless the resources to service and maintain it were easily available; unless, most importantly of all, the people themselves would 'own' the project – then there was little prospect of it being sustainable beyond the shortest of short terms.

The need for local people to be more involved in the identification of problems, planning of solutions, and the implementation, management and evaluation of programmes, is now widely accepted. As a result a new specialism has grown up in development – the 'experts' in participation! Tools of analysis like those introduced in Chapter Four are exported around the world under labels like 'Participatory Rural Appraisal' or 'Participatory Action Research'. These can undoubtedly feed into a more people-centred development approach. On the other hand, there is a danger that they are just absorbed into the existing system as the latest technical fix. Simply providing the *mechanisms* for participation does not, as the TVA experience shows, ensure that they provide genuine opportunities for poorer people to express their interests. In the end, issues of participation and whose interests it serves are not technical, but political ones. In this section and the next we review some of these. We begin by looking at common constraints to community-led development in institutional structures and what it means for patterns of leadership. We then follow up Selznick's work on co-option, to consider the many different purposes 'participation' can serve.

The People decide

A commitment to bottom-up development in which 'the people decide' is fundamental to the liberational paradigm. But the demands of development institutions can make it very difficult to put this into practice. If 'the people decide', an NGO applying for funding has to wait for concrete proposals to come from the communities themselves. But agencies need to be able to plan, to budget in advance. They need to know which programmes will require how much funds, not just in the next few months, but over the next few years. The project officers who make funding decisions need to be able to justify the budgets to their superiors, and give an account of the indicators whereby a project will measure its success. Ceilings on the proportion of a budget application that can be devoted to administration similarly militate against people-led development. In a community organising programme, the staff *are* the programme, and almost all expenses would count as administration. This kind of difficulty can make donor agencies refuse funding.

Time is another factor militating against programmes being 'community-led'. It takes months or even a year to get funds from funding agencies. NGOs which wait for the people to decide thus risk long delays between the decision and the availability of funds. In some cases, the waiting period strengthens the community as the members take on other activities that do not need outside funding while planning in detail what they will do when the funding finally comes. Others feel that they are wasting their time and lose the vision of taking action together. It is particularly hard for people to wait when there are other agencies in the area who are offering immediate money to attract members.

To get over this problem, some Southern NGOs make a calculated guess at what projects will be identified by the community and the funding they will require. This enables them to satisfy the donors' demands for exact figures on what is needed and how it will be spent. In some cases, the NGOs may guess right. In other cases, they may try to re-negotiate with the funders to use the money for other projects. There is a temptation not to bother. The NGOs' commitment to partnership with the poor can make them ready to compromise on their partnership with the funders. They know the situation best and go ahead with the changes and inform the donors only several months later. This can cause a lot of tensions. Project officers feel they have been misled and the NGOs resent any intervention as colonialist, trying to impose the North's ideas.

The danger of institutional demands overtaking the original vision is even stronger when Southern NGOs gain funding from official agencies, such as the UN or foreign aid programmes. NGOs are faced with a dilemma. Official agencies have much more money than Northern NGOs, and more money will enable the Southern NGOs to expand their work. But large bureaucracies require large amounts of paperwork as their staple diet. They often have their own procedures and styles of accounting to which they wish the NGOs to conform. Flexibility and responsiveness to the local situation are a frequent casualty.

The procedures involved in gaining funding are not the only factor pushing NGOs to take over more of the initiative than they may have originally intended. As NGOs grow there is also a natural process of institutionalisation, which it can be difficult to resist. They build up expertise in particular kinds of projects, and so encourage communities to opt for these. They have the experience, so can see more quickly than the community what their needs are. They grow impatient with the slow process of identifying priorities and forging strategies for action. Or they launch a particular programme, and organise groups expressly to join this. It is cheaper and simpler to administer a lot of groups undertaking the same kind of project, than to have them all involved in different activities.

Getting 'the people' to decide is not always easy, either. Communities are themselves divided, often by wealth and ethnicity, and always by (dis)ability, age and gender. A 'community meeting' often means a meeting primarily of the older, more powerful men. Even if others are present, they may be hesitant to speak. Solidarity is never automatic, it is forged in struggle. People have contradictory interests, some of which are dominant and some submerged in existing power relations. It takes a lot of time and effort to get those denied voice to voice their own priorities.

Even when 'the people' do speak, their vision may be very limited. It is common, for example, for women's groups to ask for sewing or handicraft projects, because that is their idea of the kinds of projects development agencies have to offer. People are often very obliging in telling 'the officers' what they think they want to hear. One women's development organisation told in all seriousness how 'the women had decided' on the project they would have. In one area they would all receive a goat each to raise, and in another, a sheep. It just so happened that the agency was itself committed to livestock raising.

A rather different kind of problem is that people may not actually want to take responsibility for themselves. This was the case in the following example.

In 1990, the NGOs in Bangladesh were talking a lot about sustainability. It was not in people's interests, they argued, to stay in one area too long. This only fostered dependence. People needed to learn to stand on their own two feet. After all, the NGOs were there to serve the people. They belonged to the people, not to their workers or funders. The groups started by the NGOs should become independent, building up 'apex' structures of their own, which could take over the NGO functions. The irony was, that very few of the NGO members actually wanted the NGOs to withdraw. They saw the NGOs as new patrons, who had stepped in to help them in their struggle to survive. Most of them had gained very little in economic terms from the projects they participated in. The small businesses the

NGOs had encouraged them to set up gave them very slight returns. If a crisis hit the family, the businesses could easily fold up altogether. But what they saw quite clearly was that in times of disaster like hazardous flooding it was NGO members who were the first to receive relief. The NGOs represented, perhaps more than anything else, a kind of social insurance.

More than that, the NGOs had only quite recently been talking of withdrawal. This actually reflected the donors' concerns, it was not generated internally. The groups had been formed for ease of administration; they had not built up a strong sense of solidarity. One of the people poised to become an apex leader had already managed to get another group member to take a loan for his use, rather than her own. He was looking forward to the day that the NGO would withdraw, and he would have that much more scope to consolidate his power. The rhetoric was that 'the people decide', but the reality was very different. Most of the people were against the move, and the groundwork had not been done to ensure that all 'the people' would have an equal say in the new structure.

Leadership

One of the most common dilemmas in NGOs relates to leadership. They are typically set up by men and women of extremely strong characters. They have to be, to get something going against often formidable odds. Personal leadership can give NGOs flexibility and enable them to avoid the bureaucracy which was identified as a problem above. As in the example above from Bangladesh, people may themselves prefer to be secure clients of a benevolent and well-resourced patron. But as time goes on, the very strength which was vital for the development of the organisation can turn into its greatest flaw. If an organisation is to out-live the active years of a particular individual, some sharing of power and responsibility must take place.

At the other extreme from domination by a single leader, the commitment to partnership and equality can make organisations hesitant to set up any hierarchical structure. But this can bring its own problems. A system with no provision for checks and balances is open to abuse. Agreeing to submit regular reports and share evaluations can instead ensure a transparency which promotes trust and shared learning.

Another kind of dilemma relates to the role of change agents. If development is genuinely to be from the 'bottom up', then why should outsiders have any part in the process? The following story tells how one group of the NGO workers resolved this issue.

After ten years' experience, about a hundred community organisers from all over the Philippines met for the first time. This was one dilemma which they had all had to face. Does starting where the people are and listening to them, mean that the NGOs must always agree with the community? 'Are we truly facilitating the empowerment of the poor? Or are we *manipulating* them towards our ideological options?' they asked.

Reflecting honestly to each other, the community organisers had to admit that the questions they asked and the reflections they shared did aim to *guide* the poor to see their situation differently. Their questions already *contained* answers. They did not conscientise the people. It was the exploitation in which they lived that did that. But they facilitated the emergence of a new consciousness. They did not advocate any particular political party. They left the poor to make a choice. They were not pure facilitators, but nor were they just manipulating the people. They coined a new term to describe themselves: *facipulators*.

On occasions, however, even facipulators are taken by surprise.

Six years before, the first farmers association in Kinapat had formed to terrace their land and halt soil erosion [see Chapter Seven]. Since then many more groups had been established, and they had formed themselves into a federation. Then an election was called. They knew all too well the bribery and promises that preceded elections, and the corruption and pay-offs to the well off that followed. So the farmers decided to put up their own candidates.

MuCARD, the NGO that had first helped them to organise themselves, was pushed up against the wall. They had always avoided ties with any political party. They wanted the people to make their own way, not to be used as a mass-base by others. But the federation turned the tables on them. *They* were now asking for *MuCARD's* support. The farmers took the lead. The organising team followed with a compromise. Each individual staff member committed himself or herself to support the candidates put up by the federation. Two community organisers even joined the ticket. But MuCARD as an agency could not make such a commitment. If elected into office, the community organisers would have to resign as staff members.

The Politics of Participation

For the Mabuhay villagers (p 100) the practical experience of being involved in considering options, making decisions, and taking collective action to fight injustice was itself *transformative*. It led on to greater consciousness of what was making and keeping them poor, and confidence in their own judgement and ability to make a difference. Their participation was therefore at one and the same time a means to empowerment and an *end* in itself, breaking down the division between means and ends. In another sense, of course, this process never comes to an end, but is an ongoing dynamic which transforms people's reality and their sense of it.

But the fact that participation in development can be empowering to the poor, does not mean that this is always the case. As already noted, it may be seen as a means to other ends, such as cost-effectiveness or sustainability. Its apparent transparency – appealing to 'the people' – makes it particularly vulnerable to co-option. What goes under the name of participation can take on multiple forms, and serve many different interests. As Selznick showed in the TVA study, sharing through participation does not necessarily mean sharing in power. In this section, therefore, we explore some of the diversity of form, function and interests within the catch-all term of participation.

These are set out in Figure 5.1, below. This distinguishes four major types of participation, and the characteristics each of these has. The first column shows the form of participation. The second column shows the interests in participation from the 'top down': the interests, that is, that those who design and implement development programmes have in the participation of others. The third column shows the perspective from the 'bottom up': how the participants themselves see their participation, and what they expect to get out of it. The fourth column characterises the overall function of each type of participation.

This framework is, of course, simply an analytical device. Rarely will any of these types appear in 'pure' form. In practice, the uses (and abuses) of participation may be very varied and any project will typically involve a mix of interests which change over time.

Figure 5.1   Interests in Participation

Form	Top Down	Bottom Up	Function
Nominal	Legitimation	Inclusion	Display
Instrumental	Efficiency	Cost	Means
Representative	Sustainability	Leverage	Voice
Transformative	Empowerment	Empowerment	Means/End

Nominal Participation

Samahang Nayon (SN), or 'Community Association', was the name given to the government sponsored co-operatives in the Philippines. Their aim was to revitalise the rural economy by enabling the poor to bypass the middle-traders. They promised credit, lower priced consumer stores and higher priced marketing outlets for agricultural produce. In addition, regular users of the store would receive a loyalty bonus in the form of a refund, and savers would receive dividends in proportion to their deposits. To clinch their appeal, new members were promised that they would become President Marcos' business partners, since the SN invested in the agricultural supplies company of which he was a major shareholder!

Under Martial Law, recruitment to the SN was stepped up. For the regime's *legitimacy,* it was crucial that it could show mass base support. For the farmers, it served their interests of *inclusion* to have their names on the books. This would make them eligible for access to future government programmes, and gave them a better chance of gaining fertiliser and agricultural loans. Also, some were threatened with reprisals if they refused to join.

In practice, things did not work out quite as promised. The SN were dominated by their wealthier members, who made all the major decisions without consulting the others. Some poorer members lost their savings as large loans were made to the rich, who then failed to repay. Management of the consumers and marketing co-operatives was inefficient and often corrupt, and there were soon no goods in the stores and no funds to buy the farmers' produce. Of the loyalty bonus or dividends, nothing was ever seen. In most cases, the poorer members' participation was *nominal,* and the co-ops mainly served the function of *display.*

Instrumental Participation

With Structural Adjustment Programmes (SAP), government funding for essential infrastructure and services in many countries has been sharply cut. People's participation may therefore be necessary to provide the labour for local infrastructure, such as roads. This serves the *efficiency* interests of outside funders. The people's labour is taken as 'local counterpart funds' which guarantee the people's commitment to the project. The funders' input can be limited to financing raw materials, and the programme can therefore be far more cost-effective.

For the local people, participation is seen as a *cost.* The time they spend building the road has to be taken away from paid employment, household work or leisure. But if they want the road, they see they have little option. Participation in this case is *instrumental,* rather than valued in itself. Its function is as a *means* to achieve cost-effectiveness on the one hand and a local facility on the other.

Representative Participation

When workers from the NGO first visited Mabuhay, they enrolled the villagers in a health education programme. After a year they invited the local people to make an evaluation of the programme. The people approved it, with one proviso. The problem, they said, was that it was their poverty that underlay their poor health. Having gone through the initial programme largely out of the interests of inclusion, they were able to use their participation in the evaluation to gain *leverage* in the future shape the project should take. From the NGO's side, allowing the community *voice* to express their needs avoided the danger of an inappropriate and dependent project and so helped ensure *sustainability.* Participation thus took on a *representative* form, being an effective instrument through which the people could express their own interests.

Transformative Participation

How participation can be transformative has already been described in the Mabuhay case, but one additional point needs to be noted. Empowerment is usually seen as an agenda 'from below'. This is because empowerment must involve action from below. However supportive, outsiders can only facilitate it, they cannot bring it about. Nonetheless, as shown in Figure 5.1, empowerment may also be identified as the interest in participation 'from above', when outsiders are working in solidarity with the poor. From Marx's analysis of alienation, to Paulo Freire's work on conscientisation, to the 'alternative visions' of the Third World Women's organisation DAWN (see Sen and Grown, 1987) it is in fact *not* usually those who are poor or disadvantaged themselves who identify empowerment as the key issue. They generally have far more immediate and tangible interests and goals. This case is therefore typical in that *empowerment* of the poor was initially the concern of the local NGO. It was only through their experience in the co-operative that the hillside families also came to see empowerment as being in their interests, and to surprise the workers with the extent to which they had thought through the implications of this.

109

Dynamics in Participation

In all of these cases, the examples are positive. There is a degree of match between the interests from 'top down' and 'bottom up'. This is because the stories are told as a way of clarifying the framework in Figure 5.1. They are snapshots, abstracted from their wider social context and even their own history as development programmes. Only one set of interests is focused on, and presented as though this were all there is to say. Figure 5.2 moves beyond this by injecting a sense of dynamic along four different dimensions.

Figure 5.2   The Politics of Participation

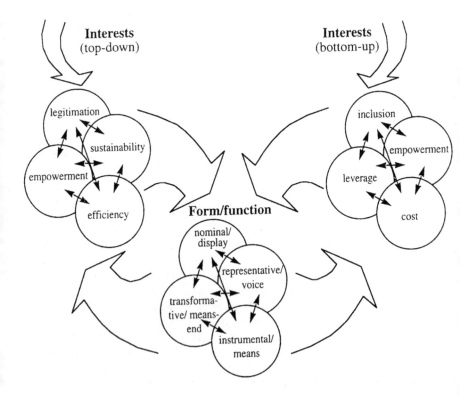

In Figure 5.2, clusters of circles show the interests from top down, bottom up and the forms and functions of participation. The tiny arrows between the circles indicate the first dynamic, that each of the clusters is internally diverse, and there is tension over which element – or combination of elements – will predominate at any one time. In particular, as seen already in the Mabuhay case, the character of participation typically changes over time. The second dynamic is shown by the arrows coming in to the form/function cluster from either side. These indicate that the form or function of participation is itself a site of conflict. The third pair of arrows comes out of the form/function cluster and into the interests clusters. These show that the outcomes of participation feed back into the constitution of interests. The final dynamic is indicated by the arrows feeding into the diagram from either side. These show that interests reflect power relations outside the project itself.

The Diversity of Interests

In all these cases, the villagers are presented as though they were homogeneous groups. In practice, of course, they are diverse, with differing interests and expectations of participation. This is clearest to see in the case of *Samahang Nayon*, where the co-ops were annexed by the wealthier members.

For outsiders, similarly, there is a mix of interests. The NGO in Mabuhay certainly gains legitimacy by having large numbers of group members. Their interests in efficiency and sustainability, as well as empowerment, are met by the hillside families developing and managing their own projects. In addition to this, there will be different interests amongst the local organisers and the NGO management. National leaders, for example, may talk more readily of empowerment than field workers who are aware of the dangers of reprisals from the local elite. The NGO may also 'package' the form and functions of participation differently to different 'markets'. In dealing with their radical Northern funders, they stress the transformative aspect. When engaging with the local elite and the national government, they may emphasise more the efficiency and sustainability dimensions. There is politics, therefore, not simply in the form and function of participation, but also in how this is *represented* in different quarters.

Changes in Participation over Time

The gradual increase in the level of people's participation in Mabuhay has already been noted. The opposite, however, is more often the case. There is a strong tendency for levels of participation to decline over time. Even those who did not lose their deposits eventually withdrew from the *Samahang Nayon* because they had better ways of spending their time than attending endless meetings. There is a tendency in participatory rhetoric to assume that it is always good for people to take an active part in everything. But people do have other interests and needs. One can grow tired of being an 'active citizen'!

Withdrawal from participation is not, however, always a positive choice. Women with heavy domestic responsibilities, for example, may find that they cannot sustain spending large amounts of time away from home. Also, even if power relations have been challenged by a successful exercise of participation, there is a danger that new patterns of domination will re-emerge over time. This is particularly the case where the project itself creates new positions, with some people being far more involved than others. The Mabuhay co-operatives have a relatively good chance of sustaining levels of participation, because all of the members are actively involved. In other projects which rely on the management of a few leaders, wider participation over time is likely to dwindle to nominal.

Participation as a Site of Conflict

In practice, the interests from top down and bottom up do not match neatly. Probably more often, the interests that one group identifies are *not* served by the participation that occurs. This was clearly the case with the *Samahang Nayon*. At first in whispers, and later more openly, the poorer members re-named their organisation *'samokang nayon'*, community menace; and the co-ops *'ko-ot'*, pick-pocket. The Mabuhay election boycott gives another instance of this mis-match of interests, though with a twist. Here, the interests of Marcos and his cronies in the nominal participation of the villagers is frustrated. The hill families see the visit of the Mayor as an opportunity for representative participation. When there is no opportunity for dialogue they simply refuse to play the game. This draws attention to another important point. It shows that participation is not always in the interests of the poor. Everything depends on the type of participation, and the terms on which it is offered. In cases like this one, exit may be the most empowering option.

Power and the Constitution of Interests

The episode of the farmer feeling unworthy to receive Holy Communion in his hands indicates how profoundly our sense of ourselves is affected by our position in society. It is important to remember this as we analyse development projects. However participatory a project is designed to be, it cannot escape the limitations on this process that derive from the power relations in wider society. That people do not *express* other interests, does not mean they do not have them. It simply means that they have no confidence that they can be achieved.

Some of the SN members genuinely believed that the programme would provide what they needed. Others joined out of fear of reprisals if they refused, or because they felt they had few other options. They had other potential interests, for example in using the co-ops actively to pressure government departments to provide real services to the rural areas. The fact that they did not express these interests – and may not even have recognised them – is not random, but reflects their low expectation of any change born out of a general sense of powerlessness or earlier disappointments. Their decision to opt for nominal inclusion in the SN, therefore, was not a *free* choice. To understand it, we have to set it against the backdrop of their wider social context. From the other side, Marcos' interest in legitimation came from his need to demonstrate 'popular support' to those backing him abroad. But at home, his interests lay more in keeping relations sweet with the local elites so it made sense for him to allow them to co-opt the programme, rather than insisting on real benefits being passed on to the poor.

Similarly, in the shadow of SAP, the local people's participation in building the road clearly shows their absence of other options. It is probable that those who *do* have alternatives (such as a relatively well paid job) are able to evade participating, perhaps by paying someone else to do their share. Whatever the collective rhetoric, it is well recognised that it is rare for the whole community to take part equally. Some will be excused for being too young or too old. But others will simply be able to call on their status: it is no coincidence that such 'community' labour projects in practice often fall to the women and poorer men. Wider power relations condition the interests of the outside agency too. Its concern for efficiency might indicate its limited budget. But it also clearly draws on the international supremacy of free market ideology, and the awareness that it could easily take the funds elsewhere if the local people do not co-operate.

That power shapes the constitution of interests is also shown in the way that experience of participation shapes what happens in future. One bad experience may lead people to avoid even nominal participation on another occasion. Alternatively, an apparent failure may sow the seeds of a wish to take action that comes to fruit later on. In his review of collective action projects in Latin America, for example, Albert Hirschmann (1984: 42) found that many of the people he visited had histories of involvement in other, often more radical, unsuccessful movements. He claims this shows a 'principle of conservation and mutation of social energy' which sounds a caution against too pessimistic a view of development 'failures'.

Perhaps the most radical re-working of interests occurs where transformative participation achieves empowerment. While outside agencies may genuinely desire the people's empowerment, they may find it rather uncomfortable when empowerment actually occurs. In the Philippines, for example, there is now considerable tension between some People's Organisations and the NGOs that fostered them. The People's Organisations now wish to communicate directly with the funders. The NGOs do not wish to lose control. Similarly, some Northern NGOs have found 'empowered' Southern partners rejecting as imperialist any demand for funding accountability. In some cases this may be legitimate; in others it is not. But if one takes seriously the fact that both parties have been shaped by unjust power relations, there is no particular reason to expect that the form empowerment takes will be benign. Former friends, rather than common enemies, may be the first and easiest point of attack. Top down commitment to others' empowerment is therefore highly contradictory. It is likely to lay bare power dimensions of the relationship that the dominant partner finds more comfortable left hidden. If it is genuine, the process must be transformative not only for the 'weaker' partner, but also for the donor agency and the relationship between them.

Participation: what counts and what doesn't

There is a final anomaly in the new pursuit of participation. Like the women in development agenda, it is founded on the assumption that those who have been excluded should be 'brought in' to the development process. It represents the people in the bad, non-participatory past, as passive objects of programmes and projects that were designed and implemented from outside. As the women in development literature now recognises, however, the people have *never* been excluded from development. They have been fundamentally affected by it. But more than this, people have also *always* participated in it, on as favourable terms as they can obtain. They have watched with a mixture of expectation and scepticism what the new agency which has come to their area is offering, and what it will want in return. They have opted in or out of projects as they judged it in their interests. At least some of what agencies see as project failure is the result of their being co-opted from below.

In Bangladesh, for example, an NGO introduced a hand tubewell programme for irrigation. The pumps were located in the fields to be used for vegetable production. The villagers, however, considered water for domestic use a higher priority. They therefore moved the pumps from the fields to their homes. Rather than recognising this as the expression of people's genuine interests, the NGO began to issue plastic pipes, which could not be relocated. Applications for the tubewells rapidly declined, and the programme was deemed a failure. This is by no means an isolated example. In the same area, shallow tubewell engines destined for irrigation were adapted by the local people to power rice mills and small boats. People have never simply been a blank sheet for development agencies to write on what they will.

There is of course need for more space for poorer people to participate in development programmes in representative and transformative ways. They should not need to resort to the 'weapons of the weak' of manipulation and covert resistance to express their interests (see Chapter Eight). Recognising that people have always used such tactics however, suggests that the problem is not simply 'enabling the people to participate', but ensuring that they participate *in the right ways.* This underlies, for example, at least some of official agencies' current enthusiasm for programmes in 'community based resource management'. These explicitly recognise that unless people are 'brought in' to the programme, they may actively sabotage it, by cutting trees or embankments, killing nature reserve animals, and so on. The fact that the way people have participated is so often classified as illegitimate, should lead us to question quite carefully: on whose terms is the current agenda, and whose interests are really at stake?

The Paradoxes of Power

As we have looked more closely in this chapter at what power means, we have seen time and again that rather than being strong and durable, power relations are fluid, unstable, constantly shifting. This is very much in line with the Biblical witness. The history of the children of Israel shows extreme reversals in fortunes, justice followed by injustice, oppression by foreign powers followed by liberation followed by oppression by the kings that they themselves had begged for. Solomon the wise was also Solomon the oppressor. The temple of Yahweh, Israel's saviour, was built by forced migrant labour (1 Kings 5: 13). The God whom the heavens could not contain (1 Kings 8: 27) ironically became a captive god of Solomon's empire. After Solomon's death, the people pleaded with his son Rehoboam to be easier on them, but he refused:

> My father made your yoke heavy, but I will add to your yoke; my father disciplined you with whips, but I will discipline you with scorpions.

> ~ 1 Kings 12: 14 ~

The people rebelled and the empire was split. The two parts fought with one another and within themselves. Like successive generations before and after them, as they strayed from the law of justice and compassion, they also turned to other gods. Before long a new prophet rose up, to give the ancient cry of protest voice.

At one level the Biblical record tells a very human story. It shows a cycle of a good person coming into power, subsequent corruption and abuse leading to decay, rebellion and the ascendence of a new leader. The deeper point that this underlines is that power is provisional. People enjoy power only, as it were, as God's delegates. Just as God is the source of all wealth, so God is the ground of all authority. All power is held in trust for God, who is its end and its beginning. This dependence on God, this reliance on God for all that is most precious, is emphasised over and over again. David sings of it, full of thanksgiving for being delivered from all his enemies:

> You delivered me from strife with the peoples;
> you kept me as the head of the nations ...
> The Lord lives! Blessed be my rock,
> and exalted be my God, the rock of my salvation ....

> ~ 2 Samuel 22: 44, 47 ~

He finishes with the vision of a ruler in the right relationship with God:

> The God of Israel has spoken,
> the Rock of Israel has said to me:
> One who rules over people justly,
> ruling in the fear of God,
> is like the light of morning,
> like the sun rising on a cloudless morning,
> gleaming from the rain on the grassy land.

> ~ 2 Samuel 93: 3-4 ~

In Chapter Four we saw how intimately involved God is in the cries of protest of God's people. Here we see again that the relationships within which power belongs include not just the people involved, but also God. What implications does this have for our understanding of power? What model do we have for how to exercise power in ways consistent with this insight?

To consider this we review two extraordinary chapters in Matthew's Gospel, which set out some of Jesus' core teachings on power. These show a deep sense of paradox, a kind of topsy-turvy world, in which commonsense understandings are called into question, and conventional values are radically reversed.

The two chapters in question are Matthew 19-20. They mark the culmination of the major part of Jesus' ministry, coming just before his final entry into Jerusalem. That placing cannot be coincidental. In too many ways that episode embodies all he has taught, cutting as he does a tragi-comic figure, acclaimed as Messiah and yet mounted on a donkey.

Matthew 19 begins with the Pharisees' question: 'Is it lawful for a man to divorce his wife for any cause?' Jesus' answer – 'What God has joined together, let no one separate' – has been written into the marriage service and quoted by contemporary opponents of divorce. But if we set it in its context, the meaning is quite different. As we see in Chapter Six, in many countries women are life-long minors, their only security lying in their relationships with men as fathers, husbands and sons. First century Palestine was no exception to this. Except in extreme cases of abuse, therefore, no woman would ever see divorce as in her interests. It meant shame, failure, destitution, returning to her parents to be a burden on their household. Meanwhile, however, men had created for themselves the legal loop-hole that if they provided a certificate of dismissal they could divorce their wives. In this context, to deny men this right meant a rejection of the dominant power relations. It was to guarantee women security in the relationships on which society made them dependent, to give them some structural back-up against the arbitrary action of their men.

The next episode shows a similar reversal. People are bringing children for Jesus to lay hands on and bless them. The disciples try to keep them away. Children were of no account; they were a diversion from the important matters at hand. But Jesus turned this on its head:

> Let the little children come to me, and do not stop them; for it is to such that the kingdom of heaven belongs.

The next encounter Jesus has is with the rich young man. As seen in Chapter Four, here again Jesus overturns conventions. Riches are not treated as a sign of God's favour, showing one particularly ready to enter God's kingdom, but as a shackle from which the young man needs release.

The disciples are anxious: they have left everything to follow Jesus, is their future secure? And Jesus reassures them, they will sit with him in judgement; like all who give up what is precious to follow him, they will receive eternal life. But even this has a sting in its tail: 'But the many who are first will be last, and the last first.'

Chapter 20 opens with a story to illustrate what he means. This again is deeply unsettling to accepted ideas of justice. Labourers are hired to work in a vineyard. Some start first thing, others are recruited only in mid-afternoon, and others still just before dark. But when the time comes for them to get their pay, everyone receives the same. Those who had been working all day grumble. But the landowner rebukes them. He had paid them what he had promised. If he gave over the odds to the others, what was that to them? And again the refrain comes, ringing like an echo: 'So the last will be first, and the first last.'

As if the point had not yet been made, the next episode clinches it. The mother of James and John goes to Jesus and asks a special favour: 'Declare that these two sons of mine will sit, one at your right hand and one at your left, in your kingdom.' Jesus answers with a question to James and John, containing a warning – Are you able to go through what I am about to go through? Not knowing what they are saying, they assure him, yes. And he answers them that they shall share his suffering, but the reward they seek is not in his gift to grant. As the other disciples get to know of the request, and are angered by it, Jesus tries once more to explain to them how wrong they have all got it:

> You know that the rulers of the Gentiles lord it over them, and their great ones are tyrants over them. It will not be so among you; but whoever wishes to be great among you must be your servant, and whoever wishes to be first among you must be your slave; just as the son of man came not to be served but to serve.
>
> ~ Matthew 20: 25-27 ~

The chapter finishes with a further encounter, in which Jesus lives the service he preaches. As Jesus was passing by, two blind men shouted out to him. The crowd sternly tried to quiet them, but the more the blind men shouted. Jesus stopped and asked them what they wanted him to do. They responded: 'Lord, let our eyes be opened.'

As in all these encounters, Jesus stopped. He was available to people, whoever they were – the educated elite Pharisees; little children; the rich young man; his disciples and their families; the blind beggar street people. And when he stopped, he listened. He listened to whatever there was to listen to. He heard the Pharisees trying to catch him out, but spoke instead for the vulnerable women who had no voice in legal debates. He listened as the parents whispered to him their prayers for their children, and touched the children in blessing with a listening hand. He listened to the question of the rich young man, and showed him how deeply he needed to be set free from the goods he owned. He listened to the ambitions of his disciples, and gently tried to re-direct them to a new understanding of power. And he listened to the blind men, asking that they speak out what they were wanting. In compassion he touched their eyes and they regained their sight. Further reinforcing his teaching, it is the outcast beggars, not the prosperous young man, who enter the Kingdom by following Jesus.

In John's Gospel this message is acted out even more graphically, as Jesus washes his disciples' feet during the Passover meal. When he has returned to the table, Jesus explains what he has done:

> You call me Teacher and Lord – and you are right, for that is what I am. So if I, your Lord and Teacher, have washed your feet, you also ought to wash one another's feet. For I have set you an example, that you also should do as I have done to you.

> ~ John 13: 13-15 ~

Conclusion

Taking power seriously means recognising that it plays a part in every relationship. It has both personal and structural aspects. Repressive structures can tend to disempower the poor, and participative structures may facilitate their empowerment, but power relations are plural and flexible, their key characteristic is their unpredictability. This reaches its peak in the praxis of Jesus. Here we see an understanding of power that is utterly transformative. No more is the vision just of changing positions, of the mighty brought low and the poor raised up in their place. Instead the whole understanding of power is shaken to its foundations. To be empowered is to be the better able to serve. When power is used for service, rather domination, the dualism between the powerful and the powerless, the strong and the weak, is overcome.

CHAPTER SIX

Gender

Introduction

As the Taliban student militia swept through Afghanistan in the early months of 1995, it imposed some law and order on the chaos and disorder left by the feuding warlords. An Islamic Fundamentalist movement, it acted swiftly against highway robbers and drug dealers. It also insisted women must withdraw from work outside their homes, and wear the veil. Amongst these women were development workers employed by NGOs. Their programmes had to be suspended until further notice.

In the United States the 1990s have seen a backlash against the feminist movement. This takes many forms, but one of the most visible is the highly organised campaign to outlaw abortion. 'A woman's right to choose' was a key rallying cry in the feminist movement of the 1960s and 70s, to try to halt the horror of mutilation and even death that women had to face on the back streets. Many of the campaigners claim that abortion offends against God's laws. On the strength of this, they terrorise women as they enter clinics, and in extreme cases have even killed doctors known to perform abortions.

An African male student gets angrily to his feet: 'All this stuff about women, about gender. We are sick of having you white people coming to our countries and telling us what to do. It's imperialism all over again. Feminism is a foreign import, it has no place in our African culture. You don't understand. Our women are quite happy. It's our tradition, our religion, and you've no place to interfere.' A country-woman of his smiles gently in reply. 'And your nice suit?' she says. 'And that smart car you are saving for? Are those in your African culture, your religion, your tradition?' She paused, 'Seems to me, brother, the issue's not *where* it's coming *from,* but whether you *like* what's coming'.

Gender is a controversial issue. It strikes at the roots of how we believe the world is and should be. 'Boy or girl?' is the first question when a child is born. Old or young, rich or poor, black or white ... we cannot imagine persons except as either male or female. What we see as the difference between them, and whether we put this down to 'nature' or 'culture', reveals our fundamental values. What we think it means to 'be a woman' or 'act like a man' affects our deepest sense of who we are and how we relate to those around us. Just how central it is, to both theology and development, is seen in the way that gender is the point at which religion is most often brought into development. Women provide a 'natural symbol' (see Douglas, 1970) through which communities assert their values and identities. As the examples above show, this makes gender the point at which religion and development most frequently and bitterly clash.

Gender is what society makes of the sexual differences between men and women. Along with age, it provides the oldest form of social structure known to humankind. Going far beyond biological differences in sexual function, gender orders who does what, and who has rights in and responsibilities for what. Where this prescribes male privilege and female subordination – as it does in virtually all known societies – it can be labelled 'patriarchy'. This affects virtually all areas of life: from property-holding, access to capital (money and technology), control over and returns on labour; through religious and political duties and authority; to sexuality, fertility, emotional expression and the use of violence. To talk of 'patriarchy' does not mean that gender difference takes the same form in every case. *How much* difference gender makes varies by context. In some societies, men and women are kept strictly separate, whereas in others there is scope for a larger degree of cross-over between them. The specifics of *how* gender makes a difference also vary. But *that* gender makes a difference is common across space and time.

In this chapter we explore how an awareness of gender makes a difference in doing theology and development. We begin with the initial question of gender analysis: 'Where are the women?' Where are the women in society and economy? Where are the women in the Church and the development agencies? Where are the women in Biblical texts and Church teachings; in development plans and projects?

Until the 1970s at least, the resounding answer was clear. Women were nowhere! Or if they were there, it was in 'special' roles, well down, or even outside the hierarchy. Priesthood was reserved for men. Even in those Churches that admit women ministers, the numbers in practice were few. Development professionals were overwhelmingly male, while women figured as 'support staff' or unpaid volunteers. Nor was the picture any better with respect to the key 'texts'. The major figures in the

Bible were male. Even God was spoken of almost entirely in male terms. Most development plans simply failed to mention women. Statistics that appeared gender neutral (that is, with no bias towards men or women) in fact were shown to take account of men's work only.

The first response to this was to try to overcome the 'invisibility' of women. This is where we begin this chapter. Drawing on a practical example of household responsibilities in the Philippines, we see how gender makes a difference not only to who does what, but also to how what is done is perceived. This throws into question the conventional models of work, household, and economy, which underlie the dominant development approaches. We follow this with a review of how development policy-makers have tried to overcome gender bias by 'counting women in' institutionally in development planning. We close the section with a reflection on the importance of imagery and symbolism to gender relations and the challenge this presents in doing theology.

Closer examination shows that the problem is not just that women are *excluded,* but that when they are included it is on male terms. In the next section we aim, therefore, to go deeper, to reveal how male dominance has biased not only what we see, but the tools of analysis themselves. We begin with development, showing the importance of looking at the problem in a way that places stress on relationships, rather than separate elements in isolation. We follow this by considering theology. Focusing particularly on the understanding of sin and the poverty of being, we ask how the teachings have been affected by being formed only by male minds, and what a more inclusive understanding might look like.

The absence or very partial presentation of women clearly throws doubt on the claims of both Theology and Development to offer a *universal* picture of how the world is and how it ought to be. The picture that has been taken for granted is shown up as limited. What posed as 'value-free', in fact contained a systematic bias. While gender begins as a 'women's issue, therefore, its implications spread far beyond this. The organisation of society by gender fundamentally structures the distribution of power. If issues of power are central to the liberational worldview, then so also must be issues of gender. In the final section we look to the future. How can we move beyond the dualism of male and female, so that power relations are not just reversed but transformed?

Where are the Women?

In Danny's story and in Chapter Four, we saw how questioning what 'everyone knows' can help to reveal how things are in a new way. When it comes to the nature of men and women, which 'everyone knows' about at such an intimate level, this process is even more necessary. This is shown clearly in the following example.

In the Philippines, an NGO was doing a study of household budgeting. Raul, a male group member, was asked about his household's finances. The income came to only half of the expenditure. Cautiously, the NGO worker suggested that perhaps his wife also earned some income. Raul was enraged: he was the man of the house, he was the sole provider. He was the only one with capital – water buffalos and coconut palms – with which to support the family. His wife, Anna, sitting nearby, signalled the NGO worker to let it go. A few days later, the worker returned. This time Raul was away, so Anna spoke to him. She had been thinking about how the family managed. Up to then, she also had believed that her husband provided most of the family income. But when they had done the accounts, she had seen it was not so.

Each morning, Anna said, she took on credit one kilo of flour and some sugar from the co-operative store. She made some cheap bread, *shakoys,* and took it to the school gates to sell. In the evening she returned the flour and sugar to the store, and kept the income for housekeeping. Twice a week, on market days, she took two kilos of flour, and sold the *shakoys* in the market place. She had no capital, so had not thought of the income as significant. Now she realised that in fact it came to more than her husband provided. It was she who bought what they needed day by day: the food, paraffin, soap and matches. None of the income from the coconut wine came to the housekeeping anyway; he kept that for his own gambling and cigarettes.

Pondering the NGO worker's questions made Anna see that things were rather different to what she had believed up until then. The 'official' story was that her husband was responsible for all the productive work which provided the income the family needed. As 'the man of the house', he was the sole supporter of the family. This is the kind of view that allows men everywhere to say 'my wife doesn't work', or women to apologise 'I'm only a housewife'. But when she counted up what she earned herself, Anna saw that this was a myth. Like women all over the world, the income she earned was crucial for the family's survival. In fact, when the hours worked by women and men are counted up, it often comes out that women spend more time working each day, and that the level of their work is more constant throughout the year, adding up to a much higher workload overall. Even when women do not earn income, the domestic work they do within the home is important economically, both to the household and to the society as a whole. The children could not have gone to school nor Raul work effectively if they did not have Anna to keep them fed, clothed and happy. It was not only her earning from the *shakoys,* but also her unpaid work in the home and skill in careful budgeting that kept the family afloat.

Although it was important to the family budget, the money that Anna earned from the *shakoys* was actually very little. But there were very few alternatives available. Although men and women both do 'productive' work, they enter the market on very different terms. A higher proportion of female than male workers are, like Anna, in the 'informal sector' of often marginal return, *ad hoc* micro-businesses or piece-work done at home. Even where they do have 'proper jobs', women rarely earn as much as men. Sometimes this is due to direct discrimination – a woman is paid less than a man for doing exactly the same work. This is again justified by the view that men are the 'bread-winners', while women's income is just supplementary, 'pin money'. But such direct discrimination is relatively rare. More often, women and men receive different wages because they are doing different work. For many reasons, men find it easier to climb the hierarchy than women do: even in 1995, in the UK the face of management is male, with women making up just 2.8 per cent of senior managers and 9.8 per cent of managers overall (*The Guardian,* 6.3.95). Women tend also to be concentrated in low wage areas of the economy; 'women's work' carries the low status of those who do it. In some cases, even the same task may be labelled 'skilled' when done by men, and 'unskilled' when taken over by women (see *eg* Humphrey, 1985).

A myth that goes along with the ideology of male breadwinners and female housewives is that the household is a unit and all members share the same interests. This sees an opposition between competition 'outside' in the market and an inner domain ruled by 'love not money'. The worker's questions showed this also to be misleading. The relationship between Raul and Anna was a power relationship. This was what made her afraid to speak while he was there. Part of this may have been because he earned more than she did. But if this had been the main issue, then she should have spoken out about the money she made, and so shifted the balance of power in her favour. Instead, she chose to hide it. Whatever the actual value of their economic contributions, she knew that she risked a beating or even desertion if she challenged him openly. Power relations in the household spread far beyond the individuals involved. They are heavily weighted by the patterns of male dominance in wider society.

It was not only Anna who learnt from this encounter. The worker too realised that he had been wrong in approaching Raul to speak for the household as a whole. He might not *know* what other members of the household did or thought, and even if he did know he might misrepresent them where his interests conflicted with theirs. Taking the (male) household head as representative of the whole household is a common mistake made by development agencies. A further problem with this is that it can exclude households without a male 'head'. Household maintained by women alone are important not only because of their numbers (30% of households in much of Latin America, and approaching 50% of households in some parts of the Caribbean), but also because they are particularly common amongst the very poor.

The influence of wider power relations on interaction within households underlies another important point, which was introduced in Chapter Two. This is that having access to resources does not guarantee *control* over them. Use of income is an obvious example of this. Anna kept control of her income by concealing it. In other cases, while women may go out to work and earn wages, it is their husbands or fathers who have the right to determine how the income is used. Just working 'outside', therefore, does not automatically increase women's voice within the household. Women's access to resources also often depends on other factors. Most significantly, it is often only through marriage that women gain rights to wealth and children, and they can lose both if their marriage breaks down. Of course, it is not only for women that having access to resources does not give absolute control. It is Western culture that makes an ideal of individual ownership, and other societies see property rights in very different ways. Nonetheless, it does seem that across many different cultures, men are *more often* in a position of *more control* over resources than women are.

Who manages the family budget is often seen as an index of power in the household. But it is important to see that this also varies considerably by context. In a wealthy family, 'holding the purse strings' may indicate real power, but where money is tight, things can look quite different. When an NGO in the Philippines was debating whether to take on gender in their programmes, a sharp exchange between the workers brought this out. It was begun by one of the men:

'We don't need "women's liberation" here! Women hold the purse. And whoever controls the money controls the family.'
The response from one of the women was quick and angry:
'You say that we are already free, that we make the decisions in the family. You are wrong! You lay a burden on us, while you go out to enjoy yourselves. Sure, you may give us your salary at the end of the month. But it is only when you have already taken what you want for your drink and cigarettes. What is left is less than we need to keep the family fed, clothed, and properly looked after. Aside from being

wives and mothers, you expect us to be magicians! You expect us to conjure enough from what is obviously too small a budget. You wash your hands of responsibility, while we break our heads to find a way to survive. Is this what you call our freedom?'

Reclaiming Women as Subject

Through reflecting on the worker's questions, Anna came to see her situation in a new way. She was not dependent on Raul, but the main earner supporting the family. Realising this did not make any immediate difference. She got on with her work, and Raul continued in his old ways. But quietly, to herself, Anna got to questioning more and more. If he was not the main breadwinner, then why should he treat her as he did? What was the basis of the authority he assumed as his right? Why was it that other women, just like her, put up with all they did?

As the months passed, Anna began, very gently, to raise some of these questions with her women neighbours. She was amazed to find how similar things were for them. So when workers from the NGO came back and said that they were thinking of setting up a women's programme, Anna and her neighbours were enthusiastic to join.

The basic approach of groups like Anna's is similar to that of the BCCs, described in Chapter Four. The starting point is for women to tell about their own experience, to find their own words to describe their lives, to say how things look from the inside out. This is more difficult than it seems. Because one of the key characteristics of patriarchy is that the world is defined in male terms. Women, as we have seen, are a 'natural symbol' to be interpreted by others. Men are the self that views, women the 'other' that is viewed. As for the poor, the challenge for women is to move out of being the objects of someone else's theory or policy, and to claim their heritage as subjects in their own right.

By coming together and sharing their experiences, women can own what has happened to them, and see that what they feel and do is valid and important. They are not just bit-players whose scripts have been written by someone else, but persons of value in themselves. Also, by reflecting on their experiences together, they realise that what they had seen as individual problems are shared, and begin to analyse the common structures they reveal.

So far, the process is parallel to the praxis of mainstream liberation theology. When women look to the Bible for answers, however, they face a lot more problems. There are no prophetic passages calling for the liberation of women, as there are of the poor. Instead, a whole host of texts either assume or explicitly prescribe women's subordination. Paul, who did so much to shape the early Church, sets down for example:

> But I want you to understand that Christ is the head of every man, and the husband is the head of his wife, and God is the head of Christ.
>
> ~ 1 Corinthians 11: 3 ~

As in this passage, the relationship of male to female is seen as a prototype of hierarchy: a recurring image is of God as male in covenant with the (weak and faithless) people as female. The whole of the book of Hosea, for example, is based on this motif.

The great stories of the Bible depict a drama between man and God, in which women figure largely in supporting roles. Men are in technicolour: as patriarchs, prophets, kings, fishermen, soldiers, disciples, tax collectors; strong, weak, wise, foolish, faithful and betraying. We follow at least the major figures through their lives, seeing them grow and develop, fail and repent. Women, by contrast, are either absent, well in the background, or fragmentary figures. Most Biblical scholars now maintain, for example, that perhaps the most colourful female character in the Gospels, Mary Magdalene, is a composite figure, made up by tradition out of dispersed references probably to several different women. Just at the level of numbers, the bias towards men is striking. Nicola Slee found in the parables in Mark's Gospel eighteen men and no women; in Matthew's eighty-five men and twelve women, ten of whom were bridesmaids; and in Luke's one hundred and eight men, and just nine women (quoted in Hampson, 1990:88). Even when women do appear in the Bible, it is almost invariably in sexual or family roles: as mothers, daughters, wives, widows, concubines, maidservants or prostitutes. Rarely does a woman stand for herself. Almost always she is defined by her relationship to someone else.

The picture worsens in subsequent Church history. Most of the time, women simply do not figure at all. All the key doctrines of creation, incarnation, atonement, sin and salvation were forged in male-only forums. Church law assumed and enshrined male rights in property and persons. Christianity took on the Greek dualism between (male, superior) mind and (female, inferior) body. This could lead to pathological depths of misogyny, as shown by the twelfth century theologian Thomas Aquinas' famous description of woman's nature as 'defective and misbegotten'. Christianity embraced, rather than resisted, the schizophrenia common to many cultures' views of women. The archetypal figures of goddess and whore were baptised in the characters of the pure and devoted Mary and the temptress Eve. Fear of women's sexuality was given religious sanction by the stress on Mary's virginity. Women who did not conform were persecuted in literal and metaphoric witch-hunts. Meanwhile, 'good' women were elevated as pure, spiritual creatures, needing protection from 'the world'. Woman's place was to be man's 'helpmate': gentle daughter, virgin mother and prudent housewife.

The first challenge for feminist theology is to disentangle the text from this patriarchal reading. There is a precedent for this in the widespread tendencies in popular culture to feminise the Christian tradition. As the male, priestly hierarchy distanced itself from the people, so the male figure of Jesus became less accessible. In his place, the gentler image of Mary the mother of Jesus became the focus for adoration in Spanish and Italian popular Catholicism. Fishing communities in South India similarly venerate Mary, stressing her motherhood, rather than her virginity (Ram, 1989). Radford Ruether (1991) records the recurrent emergence of new movements in European Christianity with female Messiah figures. The fourteenth century mystic Julian of Norwich's vision of Jesus as mother is a further example of the search for a greater wholeness in the Christian tradition through a recovery of the feminine. In relation to gender, as so much else, the Christian tradition is plural and contradictory. Its definition is not set, but forms a site of struggle. But the two sides are not equal. While some of these voices still live on in people's understanding of their faith, others died out, and many were actively suppressed as heresy. Overall, women's voices are muted, denied a place in the 'official' history of the Church.

The next step is for women to claim their rights as subject in reading the Bible itself. The obvious starting point is with the women characters. Something is achieved simply by naming them, by drawing them out of the shadows thrown by male lives. The daring and resourcefulness of the judge Deborah and the prostitute/spy Rahab are praised and celebrated. Themes such as barrenness and fruitfulness, that have been associated particularly with women, are re-claimed and followed through in new ways (see *eg* Rebera (ed), 1990). In place of Mary the Virgin, hands clasped and head demurely bowed, we see Mary of the Magnificat, head thrown back and arms outstretched, joyful and visionary, proclaiming her liberation and the liberation of others:

> My soul magnifies the Lord,
> and my spirit rejoices in God my Saviour,
> For he has looked with favour on the lowliness of his servant.
> Surely, from now on all generations will call me blessed;
> For the Mighty One has done great things for me,
> and holy is his name.
> His mercy is for those who fear him
> from generation to generation.
> He has shown strength with his arm;

He has scattered the proud in the thoughts of their hearts.
He has brought down the powerful from their thrones,
And lifted up the lowly;
he has filled the hungry with good things,
and sent the rich away empty ...   ~ Luke 1: 46-53 ~

The whole passage of the annunciation pre-figures the reversals of power which Jesus proclaimed (see Chapter Five). When his child was foretold, Zechariah the man, the priest, refused to believe it, and was struck dumb. But his wife's cousin, a young woman, without even the status of being married, believed and rejoiced in God's will. Even in herself, Mary embodies the contradictions of power. On the one hand she is young and strong, filled with the power of women, the greatest power of all, to nurture new life in her body, to bring new life to birth. On the other hand patriarchal social structures make her vulnerable. She has no man. The archetypal female sinner, her belly swelling with a child who has no name. She is the outsider, standing for all at the margins, all whom social structures of class, gender or race make oppressed; a pledge of faith that it is through such people, the poor, the ones of no account, that God's salvation comes.

Because women's bodies have so often been the targets of male abuse, both physical and verbal, celebration of women's embodiment plays an important part in feminist theology. Bingemer (1994:317) gives a powerful example of this. She draws a parallel between the sharing of Christ's broken body in the Eucharist and poor women in Latin America's daily giving of their bodies in nurturing children, earning income, and political and religious action. Turning on their head all the arguments that identify God and the representatives of God with maleness, she claims:

> It is women who possess in their bodiliness the physical possibility of performing the divine eucharistic action. In the whole process of gestation, childbirth, protection, and nourishing of a new life, the sacrament of the Eucharist, the divine act, happens anew.

Women's re-reading of the Bible is a tremendously creative act. It throws into question not only the received understanding of the message, but also the conventions about *how* the message should be read. The relationship with the text is interactive, restoring women as subject of their own lives, rather than object of others' action. Reversing the hierarchies of gender, class and racial status, the foreign servant girl Hagar is brought centre-stage as the story of Sarah and Abraham's struggle to conceive a son is re-told (see Tamez, 1986 – based on Genesis 16-21). Drawings, stories, poems and dance are used alongside academic methods of textual criticism to tease out 'her-story' from the 'his-story' presented. The poem at the close of this chapter gives an example of this.

While couched in the conservative terms of an appeal to tradition, such re-readings are clearly radical. Not only do they challenge the dominant understanding of the faith, but more fundamentally they claim the tradition as a common resource, refusing to accept its appropriation as the private property of the establishment. This movement is not limited to Christianity. Hindu feminists similarly are re-reading their tradition to recover the veneration of the feminine principle of power, *Shakti*. Muslim feminists are combatting patriarchal understandings of Islam by pointing out how within his social context Muhammed reformulated women's position in society in a positive way. The feminists join the poor at the door of the unjust judge, settled upstairs in bed, beating their fists and shouting and clamouring to be let in (see Luke 18: 1-5).

The importance of reclaiming strong images of women from the tradition is without doubt. But asking 'where are the women?' can only be the first step. Its great drawback is that it reproduces the dominant culture in defining identity primarily by sexual difference. It accepts the prescription that women must look to female role models, and men to male. The next step is to question this. Are the interests of twentieth century women the world over the same as each other, and as those of women in Biblical times? Are the feminine characteristics we praise, of (m)other love, nurturing and enabling those around us, something constant, unchanging, a truth about women, given for all time? There is a real danger that in re-claiming *only* the women in Church tradition, we ascribe to women and men essential characteristics, out of any social context, and box ourselves in to precisely the dualism we aimed to escape.

We pursue this further in the fourth section. First, we back up a little, to consider how development policy has responded to the challenge of counting women in.

Counting Women in

For the development worker to question Raul about their family finances was, in a way, a surprising mistake. As the claim that women are expected to be magicians shows, the common pattern in the Philippines is for women to be the ones to have responsibility for managing the family budget. The worker certainly knew this. But because Raul was defined as 'household head', it was he who seemed the proper person to speak for the family. The idea of the male as household representative overrode the worker's awareness at another level of the kinds of work and responsibilities that men and women have.

This kind of mistake has been very common in development. Even where women had the major role in agriculture – as in many parts of Africa – development programmes assumed that 'the farmer' was male. This meant that extension advice was given to the men, rather than to the women who actually did the work. Attention also tended to concentrate on cash crops grown for sale, which were usually in men's hands, rather than subsistence crops for the family's use, which were often the women's responsibility. This could mean that women had not only been 'left out' of the benefits of development, but were left actually worse off than they had been before. This was what Anne Whitehead (1984) observed in North East Ghana, for example. With 'modern' farming methods, men saw the potential for larger profits from cash crops, and so put a higher priority on their production. This meant there was less land on which the women could grow their crops to feed the family. They also had less time to grow subsistence crops, since the men demanded that the women give more labour helping out in their fields. But the cash that the men received from selling their crops was their own, to do with as they liked. The net result might be, therefore, that the woman was not only having to work harder, but also had a smaller harvest of her own from which to feed herself and the children.

WID/GAD Approaches

Recognising the importance of women's work to economic production and family well-being created in the early 1970s a strong 'Women in Development' (WID) lobby. This label has been challenged more recently, and many prefer the term 'Gender and Development' (GAD). To talk about 'gender' rather than 'women', makes clear that it is society, not biology, that is the basis of the power difference between men and women, and so it is open to challenge. In practice, however, even those who talk about gender focus almost exclusively on women, rather than men. The differences within WID or GAD approaches are at least as significant as any distinctions between them.

Because women are seen as a minority interest, all women's programmes tend to be lumped together within a single category. As with participation (Chapter Five), however, the same label can cover a great range of practices and interests. In this section, we aim to set out some main types of approaches to development for women. The basis of this is the well-known classification of WID approaches made by Caroline Moser (1989). She shows how different WID approaches have mirrored the trends in 'mainstream' development thinking which are outlined in Chapter Three. Figure 6.1 develops slightly Moser's framework, and sets

Programme	Women	Emphasis	Model	Methods
Population Control	dangerous breeders no choice mothers	control population	global limits	top-down women targeted
Welfare	vulnerable groups mothers	family welfare	relief	top-down handout
Equity	backward class disadvantaged by development	equality human rights control	modernisation global limits	top-down women targeted top-down
Anti-Poverty	mothers poorest of poor	fight poverty control	basic needs	top-down women targeted
Efficiency	under-utilised resources resource managers	economic development via market	Structural Adjustment Programme	top-down business
Empowerment	women as powerless need question gender relations	gender as power relations	liberation	bottom-up struggle

it out in the form of a table. This shows for each programme type the dominant images of women it uses, the first being more passive, the second more active; where it places its main emphasis, or identification of 'the problem'; the model of development which it assumes; and the methods it prescribes to achieve a 'solution'.

Figure 6.1   Motives and Interests in Women's Programmes
(See page 132)

Population Control

Population Control is not mentioned by Moser (1989) but has been – and still is – an important motivation underlying many Women in Development programmes. Here the aim is not so much women's development as an end in itself, but as a means to slowing population growth. The chief development concern is the global limits to growth. The methods are top-down targeting of women. This in itself was nothing new. Women had long been the main targets for sterilisation or distribution of contraceptives. What was new was the idea that women have children for lack of alternatives – they are 'no choice mothers'. As in much of development thinking, economics is seen as the basis of all. The theory comes in various forms. One maintains that as women become economically active, the time they spend in child care will come to be seen as having a cost to the household, so they will wish to have fewer children. Another states that women have no incentive to limit their fertility if having children is the main way in which women gain status in society. Also, if women are educated, and so can get more prestigious jobs, they will again feel less need to have so many children. In practice things are much less clear-cut, and the evidence for these connections is more ambiguous.

Welfare

Women first appeared in development programmes under the heading of 'welfare' concerns, and this is still where they are most often to be found. Here again women are often seen mainly as mothers. Mainstream (male-focused) development is directed at economic growth, while women mainly featured in add-on relief programmes. In its more passive form, the welfare approach sees women as a 'vulnerable group', economically dependent on men. Alternatively, the welfare approach sees women as mothers who are responsible for family welfare. In either case, women are viewed as passive recipients of development and firmly anchored to the domestic sphere. Implementation is through top-down methods, with the main emphases put on family physical survival and relieving malnutrition. The aim is not development for women, but the use of women to promote family well-being.

Equity

Equity is what Caroline Moser sees as the original WID approach. It reflected the priorities of the new women professionals within the male-dominated development agencies, and the wider feminist lobby in the donor nations of the North. The approach was again top-down, emphasising particularly legal measures as the way to institute change. These should aim to redress the mounting evidence that development had often resulted in women losing ground to men. In the more passive form, women were seen as a 'backward class' left out of development, which equity demanded should now be 'counted in'. More actively, women were seen to have been incorporated by default into male-biased development strategies and left actually worse off in relative terms than before. Of all the approaches, this is the least common now. It faltered for two reasons. First, even when laws and policies were put in place, it proved very difficult for many women to claim the rights they had on paper. Second, the stress on equality and human rights was seen as too radical, and so quietly dropped.

Anti-poverty

The next WID orientation is 'anti-poverty'. Here the main concern is to fight poverty, with the majority of women in the South identified as 'the poorest of the poor'. This arose as part of the 'basic needs' approach in the 1970s, following the general realisation that growth oriented strategies had not resulted in the 'trickling down' of benefits to the most needy. For poverty to be overcome, it is necessary to increase poor women's productivity through better access to employment and income generating opportunities. In its passive form, this strategy promotes programmes which do not threaten existing patterns of gender relations. Women are seen first and foremost as mothers, and projects are favoured which raise women's productivity in areas conventionally considered women's work. More actively, however, this approach can see the gender division of labour itself as contributing to poverty, and so argue for the need to promote women's rights if poverty is to be overcome.

Efficiency

Operating in the policy context of Structural Adjustment Programmes, the next orientation is efficiency. Women are seen as 'untapped human resources' or 'resource managers' who should be incorporated in development if it is to progress at full capacity. This language shows its instrumental approach. The market is seen as the answer to all development problems. As we have seen in Chapter Three, however, in practice this approach often serves chiefly to shift costs from the paid to non-paid economy, particularly through the use of women's unpaid time. These outcomes can be positively harmful to women.

Empowerment

The final WID approach is empowerment. This is introduced in general terms in Chapter Five. It questions fundamentally the dominant model of development, locating the empowerment of women in the South alongside the goals of national liberation and rejection of neo-colonial, patriarchal capitalism. Casting women in a passive role, it identifies them as a 'powerless group' needing to be empowered. More positively, however, it claims that it is gender relations (seen as power relations) that need to be questioned. In theory at least, this is a bottom-up approach, oriented towards liberation.

Limitations in the Model

Moser's model has provided a useful corrective to the tendency to lump all women's programmes together into the same category. For this reason, it has been widely adopted by development agencies all over the world. This success of course brings its own dangers. In this section, therefore, we note some limitations to the model, which should make us wary of applying it mechanically.

First, even in terms of aid fashions, there has not been a historical progression from welfare to empowerment. The schema is best thought of as an 'ideal type', a model from which actual programmes will differ, rather than a description of how the real world is. Each of these orientations remains (like the four paradigms) as a present option. Second, and allied with this, actual programmes do not in practice fall neatly into one category or another. A women's credit programme, for example, may incorporate some training on (or even provision of) child nutrition (welfare). It may aim to combat poverty of the poorer members (anti-poverty) and to promote greater efficiency of resource use amongst the less poor (efficiency). It may see the process of getting women together in small groups to talk about common problems, as leading to empowerment. These many faces may be because planners have not really thought the programme through. On the other hand, they could reflect the complexity of women's lives, and the fact that the different aspects cannot be kept separate from one another. Third, as seen for participation in Chapter Five, the same programme may be 'marketed' quite differently to different 'consumers'. While these orientations can be *analytically* distinguished, therefore, in practice it is quite common to find welfare, anti-poverty, efficiency and even empowerment aspects all rolled into one.

Fourth, following on from this, it is important to distinguish the character of programmes from their outcomes for women. It is simply not possible to do as Moser does, and deduce from which category a programme fits into, which of women's needs it will meet! A conservative, 'welfare' programme may have unexpectedly radical consequences, and (more commonly) a programme aiming at 'empowerment' may have primarily welfarist results. Believing development outcomes are predictable from an analysis of programme design may be a comforting fiction for planners, but it is very far from the reality. In fact, its indeterminacy may be the key characteristic of the development process.

This is borne out by Albert Hirschmann (1984:16-18) who tells how a project that started out with a sewing class developed into advocacy.

Comas is one of the squatter settlements that sprawl around Lima in Peru. Here, a group of women decided to get together to find ways that they could increase they family income. They started a sewing class. For technical assistance, they turned to a social education and action group. Over time, this partnership developed. At the women's request, a whole curriculum began to be built up with classes in literacy, history, women's sexuality and health, and so on. After two years, some of the classes were taken over and taught by the women themselves. Gradually, the whole of the administration and most of the teaching was in the women's hands. The main obstacle they faced was that some of the husbands resented their wives being out of the house one evening a week. To win them round, the women tried to involve them in some activities, organising community festivals and educational events. In addition, the women have taken part in various demonstrations and petitions to improve public facilities in Comas. From the 'personal' wish to earn more for their families, they have moved into an openly political vision.

Who benefits from a project and how, therefore, is a very complex question. This can only be answered on a case by case basis. The people may not be concerned about the needs identified by planners. Nor is everyone likely to benefit in the same ways, to the same degree, or at the same time. Typically, different people see quite different opportunities in any project, and they may follow these through in ways that the planners never foresaw.

A final problem is that the approaches are clearly ranked in ascending value. The final one, empowerment, gets top marks, while welfare comes out bottom, as fostering dependency and assuming weakness. This can mean that welfare programmes get the thumbs down from planners wishing to be radical on gender. But the pressing needs in one place will not be the same in another. We need to ask whose priorities these are. What space is left for women to assess their own needs, and decide which should be acted on? It is important to be very critical of *outsiders'* desires to identify with the vanguard, and to be sure *whose* needs are really being put first.

Special Programmes for Women

The most common way that development agencies have responded to the challenge to 'count women in' is by creating separate women's programmes, women's desks, women's departments, or women's organisations. These have opened up a vital 'women's space' within organisations and programmes, from which committed people can work to defend and promote women's interests. Having this special provision has been tremendously important in raising consciousness about gender issues – where something is seen as 'everyone's' responsibility it usually means that no-one makes sure it is done.

On the other hand, there is a danger in having special departments or programmes. This is that they allow everyone else off the hook. Gender becomes the business of the women's desk, and life elsewhere continues as usual. Getting people outside the special unit to take on gender issues is often a real battle. A consensus seems to be emerging that both a 'liberated zone' (see Connell, 1985:281) – where like-minded people can support one another and plan common strategies – and key outposts throughout the organisation are needed to push this forward.

Where gender issues have become fashionable amongst aid donors, there is a risk that women's programmes will be established purely as a means to gain funds. Women project holders may be appointed simply as a figurehead for the same reason. While neither of these means that women will in fact gain nothing from the project, they tend to weight women's programmes against success from the outset. These politics are particularly evident at the government level, where Ministries of Women's Affairs have rarely had any effective power. This is partly because resources tend to be organised in sectors (such as energy, agriculture, industry) so that units that cross sectors have very little scope to insist on changes. Compounding this, Ministries of Women's Affairs are typically under-funded and understaffed. Their main purpose may be to establish the progressive credentials of the government, rather than make a real impact.

If the 'liberated zone' cannot expand its frontiers, it may find that gender issues become a new form of 'women's work' with all the old negative associations of that term still attached. Women professionals often find they are type-cast into 'gender people' and that other career paths within the organisation are blocked to them. It is a rare organisation that will face squarely issues of personal politics within its own institution, however progressive its rhetoric when it faces outwards. That gender issues have not, despite all the lip-service paid to their importance, been taken to the heart of development, is shown in reviews of women's projects. These repeatedly find that they are under-funded relative to men's; that they tend to veer off from economic to social issues, often with a welfare orientation; that income-generating activities they sponsor are usually low technology, low productivity, and low profit; and that they operate with stereotypical views of their 'target group's' lives (see for example Buvinic, 1986).

As this brief survey shows, the record of treating gender as a 'women's issue' is not encouraging. This is usually analysed in terms of *technical* failure – inappropriate planning, resourcing, and so on. But to see why these technical failures continually reappear, we need to look at the politics of gender. Development planning does not happen in vacuum. Its context is a battle for limited resources. And the battlefield itself is not neutral, but set up in ways that reflect male dominance.

We pursue this issue further later in the chapter. Here, however, we need to note one final point. Women's programmes are not necessarily the answer to women's problems. The example below shows the importance of understanding the social context as a whole, rather than going in with a pre-defined agenda.

Fifteen years ago the fishing community had been prosperous. The men had gone out to fish and the women had done the marketing of the catch. Now the fishing boats lay idle and in disrepair on the shore. The waters had been overfished by large trawlers, and the shallows where the fishing boats could go were empty. The men sat around, gambling and drinking. The women tried to earn a little income by taking in laundry from the town. They did not like the work, they missed the independence of their fish marketing days, but at least it brought in some money.

A development organisation moved into the area. They could see that there was real distress, something needed to be done. Gender was their top priority for action. What was needed, they said, was a women's project which would give them an alternative source of income from the laundry-work. If they could learn some skill that was conventionally considered 'men's work', so much the better. It would challenge the traditional gender division of labour and lead to the women's empowerment. So the project was begun. A communal farm was established and the women were organised to work in it. The women were glad to have a new source of income, though because the men were not working they kept on with the laundry too. They were very busy, and going to the meetings was an extra demand on their time, but it was a condition of being a member of the project. The men sat on, and the women worked on, and the NGO kept on talking of empowerment.

Gender Interests

At first, the question 'Where are the women?' treats women as a single category. Charts are drawn up showing 'the status of women' through figures on their health and educational levels, the numbers who go out to work and make it into parliament (see *eg* 'The Human Development Report of the UNDP'). Although it may not be stated explicitly, what is meant by 'Where are the women?' is 'Where are the women *in relation to men?*' This is an important question to ask. The problem is, however, that to stop here also reproduces one of the key mechanisms in the structuring of power by gender: the placing of women as 'other', as deviant, with the male as norm.

This is clearly a danger in 'counting women in' to development planning. In Figure 6.1 we saw how each of the WID approaches characterises its 'target group', women, in particular ways. Women are the passive objects that are acted on, and the (neuter?) planners are the active subjects who make decisions and carry them out. Even where the planning is *for women,* rather than to make better *use of* them, this still leaves women as object, rather than enabling them to be subjects in their own right.

The same trend is present in feminist politics. 'Sisterhood is powerful', was an important early feminist slogan. The stress was on a common oppression, a common cause. Like the 'Black is beautiful' movement, the first stage of women asserting their rights as subjects involved appropriating their stigmatised identity, and celebrating rather than denying their essential difference from men. This is how we saw women doing theology in the previous section.

In practice, of course, women are no more all the same than men are. NGOs found that women's groups set up in the early WID years were just as vulnerable to capture by their wealthier members as the cross-class men's groups had been. A new bride in Bangladesh has most to fear not from her husband, but her mother-in-law, who will strictly supervise her work and general behaviour. Relationships between female employers and employees can similarly show at least as much tension as those between men.

To take account of these differences between women, Molyneux (1985) introduces the term 'gender interests' – the interests that women, or men, have because of their gender, rather than other characteristics such as class, age, religion and ethnicity. Molyneux further divides gender interests into 'strategic' and 'practical'. Practical gender interests lie in achieving incremental improvements within the existing structures. In establishing the *shakoy* business Anna was acting in her practical gender interest, since the income she earned enabled her to fulfil her (gender) duties as wife and mother. Women's strategic gender interests lie in structural change, not only to improve their position within the patriarchal system, but actually to overthrow it. Like the poor, women may or may not recognise these interests, and even if they recognise them may not act on them. We have seen this already in Anna's decision not to tell Raul that it is she, not he, who is actually supporting the family. To challenge the myth of the male breadwinner would be a strategic gender interest, but her practical circumstances meant that even when she saw the real situation, she decided it would serve her better to keep quiet.

The practical/strategic terminology has been taken over by Moser (1989) as a tool in gender planning. As noted above, Moser's framework has been enormously influential. There is, however, a danger that it is mechanically applied, reinforcing women as *objects* of planning, rather than *subjects* in the development process. Reflecting on how this can happen helps to indicate an alternative.

When Moser applies Molyneux's framework to gender planning, she shifts the focus from gender interests to 'gender needs'. The major problem is set out by Anna Jonasdottir (1988). She draws the contrast between a theory of needs as opening a perspective from above, while a theory of interests is necessarily a view from below:

> To speak *politically* … only in terms of needs leaves open the question of who is to define what those needs are and who is to act on behalf of them.   ~ ibid: 35 ~

The application of Moser's gender planning framework bears this out. While Moser begins by talking about *planning* needs, these very quickly become the needs of the women themselves. These may then be classified by outsiders, with a minimum of consultation. But as discussed earlier in this chapter, who gets what from a project can only be discovered on a case by case basis; the same patterns of household budgeting may have very different *meanings* in different contexts. The point here is rather similar. Challenging the existing gender division of labour is a strategic gender interest for women. This does not mean, however, that whenever women take on some task previously seen as 'men's work' that women's 'strategic gender needs' are met. What is *seen* to be done depends at least as much on who is doing it, and why, as on the character of the work itself.

A couple of examples will make this clear. The first comes from Bangladesh:

> Maloti, a middle-income Hindu woman, was working hard one day harvesting the family's mustard crop. In the field with her were three other workers. To all appearances, all of them were doing exactly the same work. And yet each of them saw what they were doing quite differently. Maloti was doing her household work, fulfilling her role of wife and mother. A widow neighbour was 'helping out' Maloti with domestic work, getting the usual pay of her meals that day. Their male agricultural worker, who was on a year-round contract with Maloti's family, was doing agricultural labour. He, of course, got the usual male wage rate of food plus cash. And finally there was a researcher, who saw what she was doing in terms of anthropological 'participant observation'.

A change of tasks does not necessarily mean a change in relationships. To understand the significance of what happens we need to look not just at *what* is done, but at the *meaning* that people give it. In Bangladesh, where the outside is identified as male space, women gathering fuel does not *count* as going outside because gathering fuel is part of their family responsibilities. Women may work in the fields, but it does not *count* as work in the fields because they see it simply as an extension of their work at home. As Ursula Sharma (1980) remarks, a woman may even take a job outside the home as a way of fulfilling, not challenging, her role as wife and mother.

The second example comes from the Philippines:

> Ploughing in this area is considered a man's job. One man, however, decided that he would do the lighter work, while his two daughters would do the ploughing. He sent his son away to school, to get an

education and so better his position in life. Neither of the daughters was allowed to go to school. They were kept at home to support the rest of the family by their labour.

A reversal of the usual gender division of labour certainly took place. But could it be said that this met the women's strategic gender needs? On the contrary, the *relations* in which the work was done meant that their ploughing simply intensified the daughters' subordination. To understand gender, like other power relations, analysis must be *contextual,* and take seriously how the people involved see what is happening and whose interests it serves.

A further point follows on from this. Seeing 'gender needs' as things 'out there' that women 'have', can mean they are classified as 'practical' or 'strategic' in a very static way. In Molyneux's discussion of gender interests, however, there is no opposition between the practical and strategic. Rather, it is the *politicisation* of practical interests that transforms them into strategic interests. Practical interests are where a programme must start if it is to secure women's support. It is the *way* that practical interests are pursued that secures their strategic, transformative potential. This recognises that the process of development planning is political, rather than being primarily technical. This is emphasised strongly by Kate Young (1988). Good intentions are not enough. What is needed is to make gender a 'pressing political problem' for planners, so that effective action is in fact taken. Alliances between women – and men – are thus essential. Recognising the diversity of interests, these should look to build up a visible constituency on the grounds of 'affirmities of position rather than identity of position' (ibid: 12). Strategies should not focus narrowly on the planning process, but mount a multi-pronged assault to engender a widespread climate for change and guard against backlash. Women's rights cannot be pursued in isolation. They are intimately linked with the broadening of effective democracy in general.

To assert unity, and to construct it in spite of difference, is vital to the process of empowerment. But there comes a stage when people need to go beyond this. In the course of struggle, real differences of interest arise. There are tensions between individual and collective goals. There are different emphases, different priorities, different levels of commitment. When such differences emerge, they are often deeply threatening. The movement falters. Where there used to be just one voice, differences spell division. But the emergence of difference is in fact a sign of growth. So long as people are defined only by their oppression, then they may appear all the same. When they come to have names and faces, to be subjects commanding their own identity, then the diversity that was always there can emerge.

Recovering Relationship

Molyneux's introduction of the idea of gender interests is a great advance on the tendency to see women – and their interests – as all the same. We need, however, to press the analysis of gender a bit further than she does. Take the example of Sarah and Hagar (Genesis 16-21). As written in Genesis, the relationship between these two women is contradictory. The story is well known. Abraham and Sarah cannot have children, so Sarah suggests that Abraham should have a child by her maidservant Hagar. When Hagar conceives she 'looks with contempt' on Sarah, and Sarah – with Abraham's permission – punishes her so she runs away. God tells Hagar to return to her mistress and submit to her. Things, it seems, settle down between the two women. Then 14 years later, Sarah finally gives birth herself. Hagar's son suddenly becomes a threat. Sarah goes to Abraham again and tells him, 'Cast out this slave woman with her son'. Abraham checks it with God and then does as Sarah says.

In Molyneux's framework, the analysis of this would be clear. United by gender, the two women have contradictory interests by class (and race): Sarah is mistress and Hagar the (foreign) maid. At times their both being women is paramount. Presumably Sarah would not have recommended just anyone as surrogate mother to Abraham. Hagar must have been something of a favourite with her. At the same time, of course, the class difference never goes away. Hagar's sexuality and fertility were at her mistress' disposal: we never hear what she felt about having to sleep with her aged master. But when the crisis points come, class interests win out over gender. By looking at her with contempt, Hagar threatens Sarah's superior status. When Sarah herself bore a son, she wanted all Abraham's inheritance to go to him alone.

The problem with this analysis is that the contradiction between Sarah and Hagar was rooted at least as much in their gender identities, as in their class. What was at issue between them? Childbearing, the essential womanly act. The class difference was obviously significant, but it was Sarah's identity *as a woman* that required she bear a son, and it was Hagar's proving herself *as a woman* that gave her grounds to mock her mistress. There are two ways then that Molyneux's framework needs to be adapted. First, interests of class, race, or gender can be distinguished analytically, but in practice they always shape each other. White working-class men and black working-class women may make a common wage claim, but the form their protest takes will differ. Second, gender identities do not only establish divisions between men and women. They also construct contradictory interests between women and women – and between men and men.

This means that the 'add women and stir' approach in either theology or development will never be adequate to the challenge that gender presents. To take gender seriously means a much more fundamental review of the whole social structure. It means seeing gender, like power, as fluid and variable, something that belongs in relationship, not dividing the world simply into two opposing categories. The importance of gender does not end with the subordination of women to men. It is also deeply implicated in the subordination of men to men, and of women to women.

In this section we begin to explore what this might mean. It is potentially such a huge subject that we cannot cover it in depth. We therefore choose two points as focus. First, we assert the importance of analysing male identities as a gender issue, alongside female. And second, we consider what this would mean for a core theological perspective in the liberational paradigm, the poverty of being.

Men and Gender Interests

While churches and development agencies persist in seeing gender as a 'women's issue', women are managing men's gender interests on a daily basis. This is why Anna, even when she saw that she contributed more to the household than Raul did, chose not to confront him. She knew that his idea of himself, as a man, depended on him being the main provider. What men do and how they feel is affected at a very basic level by what it is to 'be a man' in that society. This is in fact so sensitive that, like most other women in relationships with men, Anna decided to work around it, rather than take it on directly.

Taking account of men's gender interests is important for a number of reasons. First it helps to understand how the view of how the world is or should be *even in women's programmes* assumes male gender identities as norm. This can have serious negative consequences for women. Income-generating projects provide the most obvious example of this. Women's subordination in the household, the argument goes, comes from their economic dependence on men. Since men are the norm, and women the deviation, the problem for women becomes (in very crude terms) that they are not men. Women therefore need to become like men, through generating income by employment or small businesses. All the change needs to come from women. Because men's gender identities are not at issue, domestic labour remains women's responsibility. Women are thus left to do all that they were already doing, but with the additional burden of providing income, which was seen before as a male role. It is a short step from here to women's 'double day'. Men may even come to keep more of their income for their own use, and contribute less to the support of the family, as they see their wives taking over more of the providing role.

On the face of it, it often seems that the women are already doing more than their fair share. It is the men who need to face up to their responsibilities, not the women who need to take on more.

Second, leaving men's gender interests out of the account seriously underestimates the forces against change. We saw earlier how failures of women's programmes are put down to technical problems. More often than not it is women staff or project participants who are blamed (see eg Buvinic, 1986). This is like blaming black people for the racism they suffer. Clearly there are some complementary interests between men and women, particularly at the practical level. But there are also real contradictions. Not wanting to seem 'soft', as well as simple self-interest, makes men resist their wives' attempts to get them to share in domestic work. Historically, working men in the UK have tended to defend their rights to better pay and privileges against those of women. And yet better working conditions for wives would help the household as a whole. In Chapter Five we saw how empowerment, even if it takes the form of increased power *to*, at very least threatens others' established power over. Women do not struggle for their rights in a vacuum. It is time that men's active resistance was recognised and worked on, rather than women being given the sole responsibility for change.

Third, as we have already noted, patriarchy prescribes not only the dominance of men over women, but also of some men over other men. To see gender as *only* about relations between men and women is therefore to abstract one dimension from a much wider structure. In polygynous systems, senior men demonstrate wealth and status *vis a vis* other men by the number of their wives and children. In Arab and Latin cultures, women's chastity is seen as the badge of the family honour. At one end of the social scale the ability to support the family, at the other end having on one's arm a leisured wife dripping with gold, establishes a man's status amongst men. A practical outcome of this is that men at the bottom of the male hierarchy may compensate by asserting themselves against their women. More generally, if gender is seen as part of the overall structure of social subordination, then ideas about tackling class first and gender 'after the revolution' clearly need to be revised. Class dominance is predicated on and interwoven with subordination by gender. Struggle against the one cannot be undertaken apart from struggle against the other.

Following on from this, the character of women as 'natural symbol' means that shifts on gender may not be primarily 'about' women, but a way of one male faction moving against another. The moves spearheaded by President Zia Ul Huq in the late 1970s and 1980s towards the establishment of an Islamic state in Pakistan provide an example of this. These left women structurally much worse off. Under the banner of a campaign for 'public morality', women's freedom of movement was curtailed. Under the Law of Evidence, 1984, women's evidence in court was made to count for only one half that of men's. The Hudood Ordinance, 1979, made sex outside marriage a crime against the state. Charges of rape could be substantiated only by the evidence of four male eye-witnesses. Women who alleged rape could find themselves in the dock on a charge of adultery instead (Mamtaz and Shaheed, 1987). These moves, which might be seen as serving men's gender interests, were strongly protested by women's groups. But alongside the women were also many men, who rightly perceived these moves as the attempt by one political faction to gain legitimacy through appropriating Islam, and so consolidate its power.

Fourth then, recognising the cultural construction of men's gender identities may indicate unexpected allies. Masculinity is not given, it needs to be defended or achieved. For many men, like many women, the gender roles they are called on to play simply do not fit. It is an immense pressure on some boys and men to 'act like a man', to deny weakness and display strength. Criticisms of men often take the form of implying they are not masculine enough – they are 'effeminate', or 'wet'; they fuss like 'old women'; they are 'tied to her apron strings'. They may feel oppressed by the need to be competitive and ambitious, not to talk about their emotions, to demonstrate heterosexual conquest, to spend much time away from home while their children are growing up. Even men who can 'succeed' in the masculinity stakes may wish to have women as equal partners, and see the existing culture of gender as limiting the development of full human potential. This opens up the possibility that some men may actually choose strategically to fight against the dominant model of gender relations, and be ready to build alliances with feminists for change.

Fifth, and finally, looking at how gender identities are constructed and maintained shows up that gender is about values. Masculinity and femininity are not 'about' men and women in any straightforward way. They are cultural values, not descriptions of what men or women are actually like. As a value, masculinity is available to women as well as men. It was, for example, during Margaret Thatcher's time as Prime Minister in the UK that the term 'wets' was coined for those members of the Conservative Party who did not agree with her hard line. Getting even further away from people, cultures often use gender to describe other qualities. In European societies, as we have seen, male tends to be identified with (higher) culture, female with (lower) nature. Figure 6.2 shows some other common examples:

Figure 6.2   Masculine and Feminine as Values

<u>Masculine</u>	<u>Feminine</u>
hierarchy	community
individualism	relationship
competition	sharing
opposition	commonness
orthodoxy	diversity
domination	adaptation
aggression	gentleness
strength	vulnerability

Many such pairs of oppositions exist, though what is seen as 'masculine' or 'feminine' varies by context within the same society as well as cross-culturally. Clearly, there is no essential relationship between these values and male and female persons. Each person will show a combination of characteristics, and express different values on different occasions. It may be, however, that what are seen as 'masculine' qualities in any society are *more* available to *more* men than they are to women, and that for so-called 'feminine' traits the opposite applies.

Gender is a 'women's issue', but it is not *just* a women's issue. Nor is it the only women's issue, for class, ethnicity, age and disability issues affect women just as they affect men *in gendered ways*. Focusing on gender only in relation to women reinforces women's being sidelined from 'mainstream' affairs. It also lets masculinity too easily off the hook. We need to take masculinity apart, to de-construct it, to identify its weaknesses and contradictions, not to reinforce male dominance by identifying male gender identities as natural and impregnable.

Poverty of being revisited

Christianity is the religion of incarnation. God is not abstract and unknown, but appears in human form. The fact that what Christians believe to be the fullest revelation of God was made in the male person of Jesus of Nazareth has been used down the ages as an excuse for male privilege. The exclusion of women, or their inclusion on male terms, is intimately tied up with their embodiment. Menstruation and childbirth are seen as unclean; women as physically weaker and dependent; women's bodies as the objects for male desire or violence.

Women's move to reclaim their bodies as natural symbols *for their own use* is mentioned earlier. The aim of this is to generate for all images that resonate with womanliness, rather than to trap women within the confines of specifically female bodies. The themes of barrenness and fruitfulness, for example, are recognised by some as biological realities. The extent to which this is identified with women is itself changing, as male fertility drops and more is known about the reproductive process. Taking barrenness as generative theme also provides an opportunity for people to reflect on how the system makes them barren, or the ways in which they themselves refuse to bear fruit (Rebera (ed), 1990). Similarly, motherhood is celebrated in its own right but it is also politicised, in groups like the Mothers of the Disappeared in Argentina, or the Peace movement.

In doing theology and development, the embodiment of women and men has to be taken seriously. This encompasses both physical embodiment, and the social embodiment of the meanings their bodies carry at any particular place and time. Recognising that men have gender interests too, that they are not simply the norm from which women are the deviation, suggests that we need to look hard at the embodiment that our theology has taken, expecting that its face will not be neutral, but turned more than half-way towards men. Here, we consider what this might mean for just one doctrine, the poverty of being. Has this been understood in a male-biased way? And if so, how does it need to be revised to be of use to women? In reflecting on this we follow the lead given by Daphne Hampson in her book *Theology and Feminism*.

Hampson's point of entry in this discussion is the theology of sin of Reinhold Niebuhr, one of the foremost 'social' theologians of the twentieth century. What we have called poverty of being – the sense of one's limitedness, or as Hampson puts it, 'a basic dis-ease' (p 122) Niebuhr terms 'Angst'. This he sees as presenting a choice. Either it leads people to trust in God, to become the *anawim*. Or it leads people into sin. Sin takes two forms, pride and sensuality. For Niebuhr then, it is the will to self, to use others for one's own purposes, that is the core of sin.

Feminists criticise this analysis on two counts. First, they question whether it fits women's experience: is too much self women's main problem? Second, they dispute its individualism, where women see themselves as essentially in relationship. Reflecting on the figure of Clara (p 79) should help us here. Her problem was not an over-developed sense of self, but the opposite. In seeking to meet others' needs, she had lost a sense of who she was. Her problem was not in giving, but in being able to receive. She felt she deserved nothing, was nothing, had no value at all.

To tell someone like Clara that pride and self-love are sin, would simply compound her problems. For her, salvation would lie in the healing, rather than the breaking, of self (Hampson, 1990:127). Women like Janet (p 62) are torn apart with self-blame as they struggle to succeed in a system set up for men and experience themselves 'failing' to balance the dual demands of motherhood and career. Christianity's stress on service, on self-giving, on the self as bad and sinful, may thus be totally inappropriate for women already struggling in a system which identifies their bodies as impure and their minds inferior. The experience of poverty of being may be quite different for men and women. In doing theology, they need to begin from where they are. The irony is again that what begins by emphasising gender difference, ends up by transcending it. Once we recognise that the dominant understanding of the poverty of being does not fit for women, we can see that similar problems may apply to men. Men can also be destructive of self and others because they have too weak a sense of self, rather than too strong. The feminist vision presents a key challenge to Christianity to move beyond the sense of self and other in contradiction, and to develop new models of complementary mutual growth.

Rosemary Radford Ruether (1981:54) makes a beginning towards this, as she says that the Christian ideal of servanthood should not be confused with servitude. Its essence is the free gift of liberated persons. This is surely the meaning of the pledge that the first shall be last and the last first. For those in positions of power, their challenge is to deny themselves and seek to enable others. But for the marginalised, the oppressed, the challenge is to gain that freedom that transforms servitude to service.

In celebrating their own embodiment, women are re-claiming the creation pledge that they are 'made in the image of God'. Clearly, this has implications for how they view themselves, but it also requires searching for new and different images of God. Many of these stress the importance of being in relationship. Elizabeth Dominguez, quoted by Kyung (1994:253), for example, states that we realise the image of God not as individuals but together in community. Although Biblical images of God are overwhelmingly male and hierarchical, as father, king and judge, in the mysterious doctrine of the trinity, relationship is seen as being at the heart of God. Communion in community is similarly a recurring theme. God forged the Covenant with the entire people of Israel and the whole of creation. The disciples were a community centred on their common search for communion with Christ. The community of the early Church was celebrated in the communion of holding all things in common. Even the contemporary Church strives, in its better moments, to realise community.

Although male terms predominate, female imagery of God's care are also used interchangeably. Psalm 131 gives an example of this:

O Lord, my heart is not lifted up,
my eyes are not raised too high;
I do not occupy myself with things too great
and too marvellous for me.
But I have calmed and quieted my soul,
Like a child quieted at its mother's breast;
Like a child that is quieted is my soul.

Passages like this can be reclaimed to show that we should relate to God as mother, as well as father. This is valuable on two counts. First, it celebrates femaleness by making clear that this is as much a part of God's person as maleness is. Second, it is important in freeing God from the male body we have trapped God in. It is a challenge to our anthropomorphism, our tendency to make God in our own image. 'Making an issue' of God's gender is a step towards recognising that we need to go beyond gender if we are to understand the fullness of what being human means.

Jesus similarly seems to have felt no contradiction in using female imagery in speaking of himself. Looking down on the city as he entered it for the last time, he said:

O Jerusalem, Jerusalem, killing the prophets and stoning those who are sent to you! How often would I have gathered your children together as a hen gathers her brood under her wings, and you would not!

~ Matthew 23: 37 ~

In Jesus' ministry also, he rejected the conventional masculine model of an imperialist messiah, who would overthrow the existing order by force and establish a new empire with himself at its head. This style of power was a temptation from which he precisely turned away, preaching the paradox of strength in weakness. The last would be first, one must lose one's life in order to gain it, the seed would have to be buried in the soil in order to grow and bear fruit. As we saw in Chapter Five, the image Jesus chose for himself was that of a servant. Not someone subordinated by outside forces, but one who in his freedom chose to serve others.

Jesus' care for the women he encountered has to be seen in the context of his overall ministry. As Rosemary Radford Ruether (1981:55) points out, the significance of this is not that the women embodied some mystical 'feminine essence', but that they were *socially* subordinated, and so in need of liberation. They were oppressed not only as women, but often additionally as women whose foreignness, widowhood or sexual behaviour put them right at the margins. He meets these outcast women where they are, as persons deserving of care, just as he meets and responds to people with mental illness or physical disabilities, and those who are hungry, or poor.

There are seeds of transformation of gender power within the Christian tradition. But it would be false to claim that these represent anything like its major character. There is a difference between re-reading tradition to recover elements that have been lost in the dominant interpretation, and virtually re-writing the historical record to make it say what we would like to hear. The Biblical texts reflect the patriarchal societies in which they were formed. There is much within them, and in subsequent traditions of interpretation, that is anything but liberating to the human spirit. One of the ways in which the female body differs from the male is in its capacity to change its shape over time (Kyung, 1994:256). Claiming God's body as female may therefore point us also to the need to go beyond. We may not only need to re-read the old stories, but tell new ones, find new myths in which to discover our liberation.

Conclusion

Gender is a justice issue. Its starting point is the subordination of women to men, the oldest form of social inequality. Recognising how intimately this is tied up with other power structures should make clear to those committed to liberation how vital it is to work on gender issues, not as a concession to the women, but as a central part of the agenda for change. No call for liberation is complete without taking this into account. The twin feminist slogans – 'the personal is political' and 'sisterhood is powerful' – strike to the heart of the liberational world-view. The personal is political for women who, gathering together in small groups, discovered that what they had seen as individual problems were shared by others. But the personal is political also in pointing up the part that each of us plays in challenging or reproducing gender power. How we treat our lovers, wives or husbands; how we bring up our children; how we behave towards our colleagues; even the language we use … all of these strike a small blow for freedom or help to maintain the way things are. But the stress on sisterhood means the battle need not be fought alone. If the problems are shared, are collective, then so also are the solutions. Solidarity is the way to fight them. This must be established between men and women, as well as amongst men and women as they struggle to establish new gender identities for themselves. What divides us is less important than what unites us. There is a world to win.

Bathsheba

Based on 2 Samuel 11:2-12:25

Didn't Bathsheba have any feelings then?
Was it only, as always portrayed, the men who made the decisions?
Big King David, with his many wives and riches,
And poor man Uriah, with his one treasure, her,
His one lamb to David's many flocks?

Could it be that instead, she loved David?
Loved Uriah too, but felt impelled to leave
That being his treasure was not enough,
That she needed, rather, to find her treasure for herself?

Was she not a lamb at all,
But a full grown ewe.
With the strength to love and be loved equally.
Attracted to the ram, David
For what he saw in her
And she in him.
For the greater possibilities that were suddenly opened up
A life where the scale of opportunities was suddenly transformed,
Where she could dare, tremblingly, to live for herself?

Bathsheba, I hope you were happy.
That you didn't just exchange that poor man's hut for a jewel encrusted
    prison.
I know that when Uriah died you wept,
For the love you had shared, and the part of you that died with him.

But I hope the son you bore brought you joy.
That you found in him the fuller wonder of what you knew yourself
    to be.
That it was your brokenness, your strength,
That founded him in wisdom.
That he learned to know others from what he knew of you.

CHAPTER SEVEN

Environment

Introduction

Environmentalists have become the new prophets of the apocalypse for the late twentieth century. Judgement will come not from a heavenly throne, but from the earth itself, as the abused and exploited planet finally turns on its oppressors. The pursuit of endless economic growth is exposed like the alchemy of earlier times – there is no magic formula that will turn all to gold. The cries of prophets down the ages echo in our present: 'Mend your ways while there is yet time.' Fitting our generation, the old appeal takes a modern form, marshalling the apparatus of science and technology against itself. Graphs, statistics and calculations demonstrate the horrific scale of destruction done already, and the prospects of future disaster. Their message is clear: we cannot go on as we are, the earth simply cannot sustain exploitation at the present rate. Sean McDonagh (1990:87) portrays this well in an imaginative compression of time:

> To grasp the impact of human activity, particularly since the beginning of the Industrial Revolution, it might help to put the Earth's story in a timescale which we can comprehend. If the total history of the universe were somehow compressed into a single year, human beings would appear on Earth at 11 pm on the 365th day. The Industrial Revolution, which is having such a deleterious impact on the biosphere, would take place during the last half second of the year.

The imagery of time running out conveys the urgency of the need for change.

Like people down the ages, when we look at our environment we find reflected in it the social world. There is meaning for us in the felled forests or the polluted waters, just as some cultures see trees and rivers as the dwelling places of spirits, guardians of the natural order. The degradation of the environment is the more frightening, because in it we see an image of ourselves.

As we see our impact on the world we also re-evaluate our place in the world. The search for better ways to relate to our environment is inseparable from the search for a better society. In this sense, environmental destruction is not only a threat to our way of life, but also a challenge to find new ways of living. Encountering material 'limits to growth' calls into question both the dominant strategies for development and the values and assumptions on which they are built. They demand an urgent re-assessment of where we are and where we are going. It is this challenge that is the subject of this chapter.

The chapter begins with some stories which explain the framework within which we search for a new approach. We then go on to explore three major ways in which environmental concerns have been incorporated in development. We go on to a fuller reflection on the implications of our framework for our understanding of development. We close the chapter by exploring how we belong to our world and one another, and how we can find new ways of living that relationship.

Explaining the Option

When the people first settled in the hillside village of Kinapat, the Philippines, one hectare brought them sixty to eighty sacks of maize. By the mid-1980s they were very lucky if they got ten or fifteen sacks. The fruit trees in the village could be counted on one's fingers. Half of the men had already left to work more fertile lands elsewhere.

Three farmers volunteered to form a research team. They undertook training and then interviewed everyone, collated and analysed the data. The results of the survey were transposed into charts, graphs and pictures to tell the story of the village. These were all presented in a village assembly. The first farmer had come to the area in 1960, just after the loggers had cut down the forest. He could not believe how fertile it was. He wrote and told his relatives and friends, even offering to pay the boat fare for them to come and join him. The yield was so abundant that they had to advertise by radio for people to help with the harvest. When the survey was conducted a generation later, Kinapat had a small chapel and primary school. But yields were so low that the farms could no longer support the families. As the men went to work outside, only the women and children were left in the village during the week. Three families had even left the village completely.

When the findings of the survey were presented to the village meeting, people could see how migration was related to the productivity of the farms. But why had productivity gone down? Agricultural officers and advertisements told them that low production was due to out-dated farming methods. They should use high yielding varieties (HYVs), chemical fertilisers and pesticides if they wanted to get a good harvest. But in the 1980s they used the same planting techniques, seed varieties and natural fertilisers as in the 1960s. For the first time they came to a common conviction: the propaganda for 'modern' methods was false. It was not their agricultural practices that were at fault. The crucial factor was the fertility of the soil!

Some farmers admitted that they knew about the Sloping Agricultural Land Technology (SALT) which can prevent soil erosion and rehabilitate farms. The problem was not technical: they could easily implement it. Their objection was on other grounds. As one farmer said: 'Why should we stop further soil erosion when we have no guarantee that we can hold on to our farms? The infertility of the soil may not drive us away, but the rich and powerful can.'

One of the community organisers summed up the discussion by challenging the group to take a risk.

> If you do not implement SALT, sooner or later the land will drive you away. You have a saying, *'Kung mogimaw na ang mga bato, mahanaw ang mga tao'* ('When the stones start to appear, farmers will disappear'). Someone rich and powerful may evict you one by one from your land. But if all work together as a team in the implementation of SALT, anyone who wants your land will not be up against one of you. He will have to face you as a group. Will he dare to go against an organised group? Besides, the local government will have greater reason to push for the release of the area as 'Alienable and Disposable' and you can then apply for titles to your farms.

All the 21 families decided to form the Kinapat SALT Farmers' Association. Within a year of contouring the land, the process had started for them to gain titles. Three years later, land that had produced nothing was growing rice again. One hectare's yield of maize had grown to forty sacks. Families that had always been in want were now able to live off the produce of their land.

Doing the survey forced the villagers of Kinapat to re-examine their understanding of development. Up until then, they had accepted the dominant model. The land on which they settled had been waste land. It was forest, wilderness, inhabited only by primitive tribespeople, little better than animals themselves. It was a land without value, without history – dark, dangerous, disordered. Development began when the loggers moved in. In cutting down the trees they created value out of what had been worthless: timber for export and ground cleared for houses and farms. What the loggers had begun, the settlers completed. In working the land, in building houses and planting crops, they developed the area. What had been savage, useless, was tamed, trained, made valuable and productive.

In settling the forest areas, the Kinapat villagers acted as pioneers extending the frontiers of development. But, ironically, they were also the victims of this same model of development, further down the line. The Philippines' national commitment to export-led growth (see Chapter Three) means that the best land is given over to huge agri-business plantations. This is the reason that the Kinapat villagers, like many other poor people, were pushed out of the fertile lowlands and forced to grow their food on marginal hillside farms. Some clear the land for cultivation themselves, others follow in the trail of loggers who cut down the rainforest for a quick profit. Once the area is settled, there is no way for the forests to grow back. When soil fertility falls, like the men in Kinapat, settlers start the cycle of destruction again by moving on to new sites. Ironically, the loss of the rainforest makes farming even more precarious. Rainfall has dropped drastically. Delayed rains mean that planting cannot take place at the right time, and crops become more vulnerable to pests, drought or flash floods. In the Philippines, deforestation, plantation agriculture and upland ploughing are causing the loss of top-soil equivalent to a metre depth over 100,000 hectares every year. And the effects of this do not end with the land.

The soil washed away from the hillside is carried down to the sea. There it silts up the coral reefs which are the breeding ground of fish, slashing fish stocks within three kilometres of the shore. The situation has been made worse by the destruction of the fishing grounds by dumping industrial waste into the sea, trawl fishing by high technology boats, and dynamite fishing. In the experience of Julian and Teresa we have seen how these new methods of fishing have destroyed fishing communities' livelihoods. They have also shattered the balance between human beings and their natural surroundings. Whereas the local people caught fish with a hook and line, one by one, the large trawlers trail huge heavy nets. Not only do these trap fish indiscriminately, but they also destroy their habitat, in the shape of the sea-beds and corals.

From the perspective of the environment, the pursuit of development means a spiralling cycle of destruction. Poverty plays a part in this, but on the land, as on the sea, the maximum damage is done in the race for profit of the rich. In the Philippines, the prime agricultural lands are in the hands of rich landlords or multi-national corporations producing cash crops for export, like pineapples, bananas and sugar. These make their own contribution to the degradation of the soil. Growing a single crop over up to 30,000 hectares, these agri-businesses use the soil only to *anchor* the plants. For nutrients they rely heavily on oil-based fertilisers and on other chemical inputs to control weeds and pests. But constant use of chemicals also kills organisms which are beneficial to the soil and naturally control pests. They leach phosphorus, potassium, iron and manganese from the soil. Though chemical inputs increase production, they also destroy the long-term fertility of the land.

When the yields in Kinapat began to decline, the response of the development 'experts' was to prescribe more of the same. Cultivating crops the 'natural' way was not enough: more and more radical intervention was called for. By purchasing HYVs and applying chemicals, the settlers could take control of the growth process itself. Not only their land, but they themselves would be developed, as they left behind their traditional farming methods for the new, 'modern' techniques. Their own value, like that of their crops, would rise. They were already worth more than the backward hill-tribes who had lived there before. With the new technology, they would take a step nearer towards the smart townspeople who so despised them at present.

The villagers of Kinapat accepted this diagnosis. The only problem was that they did not have the money to follow the experts' advice. The HYVs and chemicals were simply too expensive. It was only when they undertook the survey themselves that they began to see that the answer to their problems lay elsewhere.

The participatory research enabled the villagers to see their situation with new eyes. The key change was that instead of seeing one part of the picture – falling yields – in isolation, they began to look at the connections between all the different parts, so that they could see their position as a whole. This showed up that their problems were not only economic. Their family lives were suffering as the men spent most of their time away from home. Their political situation as squatters without titles to the land kept them from terracing their farms to halt erosion. This meant that family by family they were very vulnerable, it was in acting together as a community that the answer to both their poverty and their degraded environment was to be found.

In forming Kinapat SALT Farmers' Association, the villagers were not opting out of development. They were re-defining what development might mean. They began where they were, not with a ready-made solution, but by analysing their particular situation in all its complexity. This was itself a political action, re-claiming from 'the experts' their rights and ability to diagnose their own problems and forge their own solutions. It also made them recognise that they had to act politically in a more direct sense, applying for titles to their land and building a strong community to withstand collectively any attempts to dispossess them. Development therefore became a political and collective issue, not simply an economic and individual one. In addition, they questioned the idea of development as progressive transformation of their environment by new and more invasive technologies. Instead, they chose to adapt to and work within the natural limits by caring for the land, holding as valuable the complex system of relationships within which they came to see themselves as belonging.

Overall, what comes out of the Kinapat story is a message of hope. What seemed like the end became instead a new beginning. In working towards harmony with nature, the villagers also built community with one another. Like human beings, the natural environment is remarkably resilient. The search for alternatives is not an empty option. With some give and take on the human side, environmental systems can re-establish equilibrium to accommodate changed circumstances. Shifting from relationships of exploitation to nurture holds the promise of new life.

Widening the Picture

The model of development advocated by the extension agents in Kinapat was adopted by the farmers of Asha's village. In the 1970s and 1980s, mechanised irrigation was introduced to the area. This was part of a push by the Government to make Bangladesh self-sufficient in food-grains. As in other countries, all the emphasis was on a few crops: in this case wheat and rice. In some ways this was a great success story. From a single harvest a year, rice in Asha's village can now be grown virtually all year round. Land that was left fallow is now under cultivation, with even poorer families having some access to land through sharecropping arrangements. Some irrigation is also used to grow wheat, mustard, potatoes and vegetables in the cold season. With increased yields from HYVs, there is no doubt that the prosperity of the area as a whole has increased. There is, however, a down-side.

Pressure of population and the desire to maximise profits mean that forest areas have been cleared to provide more agricultural land. With more land under cultivation for more of the year, it is increasingly difficult to find grazing for animals. Numbers of dairy cattle in particular have fallen sharply. Since keeping goats and cattle is one of the few ways that women alone can earn some income, this is a very serious loss. It also means less proteins and vitamins in the diet as milk becomes scarce. In addition, cattle dung is used along with wood and bamboo as domestic fuel. The loss of these resources has increased the time that poorer women spend gathering fuel and pushes them towards more and more marginal sources such as leaves and bark, which cuts down further the number of trees. Other common resources have also declined. The canal, which used to be a good source of fish, now dries up early in the season, as water is drawn out of it for irrigation. This threatens fishing families' livelihoods and lowers the general quality of the diet. Fruit and vegetables that used to grow with little or no tending, now give much lower yields. Hand-pumps which provided clean drinking water now run dry as the water table falls under the demand for irrigation.

Such changes affect everyone to some degree, but they do not do so equally. Poorer households are far more dependent on marginal, common resources to eke out a living. The worst affected are those without adult males, since they cannot balance out their losses with the benefit of more agricultural work being available. Like natural disasters, therefore, environmental changes hit hardest those who are already worse off. The major benefits of irrigation have gone to those who were already wealthy, and to men. The 'big people' of the village have bought more land, diversified into new businesses, and built new larger houses. Male toys, headed by flash motorbikes and followed for the less well off by bicycles, cassette players or rings and watches, are other visible signs of the new prosperity. But the gains have had their cost: reduced diversity in vegetation and diet for those without means to buy; heavier work-loads for poorer women; and lost access to resources for some of the most vulnerable, who already had very limited options.

Seeing the knock-on effects of new methods of food production points up how intricately environment and society are bound up together. They form a single system, in which the parts are related in complex ways. Human beings and different aspects of the natural world belong fundamentally in relation to each other. What people do affects the plants, animals, land, air and water in which they live, and this in turn acts back on them. Because the system is made up of living things, it is dynamic, not static. As one aspect changes, all the others will shift to some degree, so that the system as a whole will readjust, or 'find its level'. The drive for development means that more is changing, and more radically, than would otherwise be the case. This poses considerable challenges to the capacities of both human beings and the natural world to readjust. The story of Asha's village, like those from the Philippines, points out very clearly that in the scramble for change the costs and benefits are not equally shared.

What the long term effects of this intensive cultivation will be, no-one yet knows. There are some signs that crop yields are on the decline, and the rains seem less predictable than they were. It is not clear what are the reasons for this. Some believe that recent disastrous flooding in Bangladesh is the result of de-forestation 'upstream' in Nepal; others blame low water-tables on the extraction of ground-water for irrigation; or on major dams in the river system in India, which divert water which used to come to Bangladesh. Evidence for these positions is hotly contested. What they do suggest, however, is that 'the system' needs to be considered very broadly. What happens in one context may have implications for locations far away.

Development again plays a part in this, as it serves to draw different systems more tightly together. In Asha's village, for example, people used to store and germinate their own seeds, keeping aside some of one year's harvest to sow the next year. This cannot be done with the HYVs, so people have to buy new seeds each year. More cash is needed for the chemical fertilisers, pesticides and irrigation, without which the crop will not grow. People still produce for their subsistence needs, but they have also to produce for sale. Roads have been improved to allow trucks in to collect rice. Travel to and from the town becomes more frequent. More shops are open daily in the bazaar, where there used to be little on sale outside the weekly market. As more options become available, tastes change and develop. In consumption as well as production, there is much greater dependence on the market. What was, for better or worse, a comparatively self-reliant community, is now tightly enmeshed in state structures and the international market system.

The impact of development is now felt right up to the global level. The destruction of the rainforest and carbon dioxide emissions are trapping solar heat within the earth's atmosphere. The 'greenhouse' effect could melt the polar ice-caps and raise the level of the sea. The potential consequences for low lying lands like Bangladesh are frightening to imagine. Holes in the ozone layer have been caused by the release of nitrous oxide from nitrogen fertilisers, emissions from supersonic aircrafts and chlorofluorocarbons (CFC gases) which are mainly used as propellant substances for aerosol sprays and as refrigerants. The ozone region protects human beings from skin cancer caused by the sun's rays. The reproductive processes of micro-organisms like plankton could also be seriously impaired or destroyed with the depletion of the ozone region. Since the photosynthesis of plankton is vital for maintaining the earth's atmosphere, this could result in the ozone layer being destroyed even more quickly.

Alarm about the environmental costs of 'normal' development is compounded and heightened by periodic disasters. These again point to the inter-dependence of all of our worlds. In the mid 1980s, the Bhopal explosion and the Chernobyl accident became world news headlines. A decade after the nuclear disaster in Ukraine, sheep farmers in Scotland and North West England are still unable to produce meat safe for human consumption. Other incidents have had a more local impact. The Love Canal Tragedy caused the abandonment of residential areas in New York because toxic chemical waste from a dump-site filtered into ground water causing birth defects, liver and kidney damage, respiratory ailments and various forms of cancer. A subsequent investigation in 1979 revealed that there were 50,000 such toxic dumpsites in the United States and less than 7 % had proper disposal facilities. Such 'accidents' cast doubt on both the safety and sustainability of the current technological culture. They also make one thing very clear. No one any more can say 'it's not in my backyard'. The current model of development is *everybody's* business. If we look to our environment as an image of society, we have good reason to worry. But one thing stands out above all others. Rich and poor, black and white, male and female, old and young, human and animal, vegetable and mineral: we belong to one another as perhaps never before.

New Environmentalisms

The push for development has presented, as we have seen, major challenges to society-environment systems the world over. The example of Kinapat shows that this process is not all one-way. When the assault on the natural world becomes too great, it may also counter-attack. In this case it literally withdrew the ground on which the model of development was based. At the global level also, the environment has now weighed in with heavy protests against rapacious human exploitation. Whereas all the dynamism once seemed on the human side, the situation is now reversed. Like it or not, human society is faced with a fundamental challenge to its development policies and practice. In this section we discuss three different ways in which that challenge has been taken up.

These responses represent three distinct trends in contemporary environmentalism. Nonetheless, as with the four paradigms, in practice they are often mixed up together. A particular group or institution will not necessarily fall neatly into one of these categories, but may use any or all of the approaches at different times.

We begin with the response of mainstream development policy, as represented by institutions like the World Bank. Following Timothy O' Riordan (1976) we call this approach 'techno-centric environmentalism'. The keystone of this is environmental management. The aim is to rehabilitate the current model of development. Greater economic growth and better environmental protection are not contradictory, but complementary goals. As in classic modernisation theory, the way forward lies in policy and institutional change, and the better application of science and technology. New Right and liberal faith in progress and the benefits of economic growth are re-affirmed.

The next trend that we discuss is green consumerism. The vision of this is a new form of development based on social and environmental justice. The quality of a product depends not only on its finished form, but also on the circumstances in which it is produced and marketed. The aim is to shift tastes away from commodities that are made or traded in wasteful or exploitative ways and to substitute more humane, 'greener' alternatives. At its most radical, this is a practical attempt to move towards the liberational paradigm of development.

The final approach is what O'Riordan characterises as 'eco-centric'. This contains an absolute rejection of development and all its works. It fuses elements of the conservative and liberational paradigms, seeing the natural world as a harmonious order into which human beings have intruded. People should therefore seek to adapt to the natural system, rather than attempt, as in the techno-centric approach, to re-fashion it to meet human needs. In discussing this approach we concentrate on one influential strand within it – ecofeminism.

Despite their differences from one another, all of these approaches are vulnerable to decline into 'green packaging'. This is the term we give to their co-option, as existing products, policies or philosophies are simply re-packaged with a 'green' label, leaving the substance unchanged. As we have already seen, co-option is always a danger when a new and challenging critique becomes accepted as part of the dominant development agenda. We note green packaging as it arises as we discuss each of these approaches in turn.

Techno-centric Environmentalism

In 1992, the World Bank devoted its major annual publication, the *World Development Report*, to the issue of Development and the Environment. This argues strongly against the view that the dominant model of development is bad for the environment. The interests of human development and the natural world match one another, they are not in competition. If the environment is degraded, development will be undermined. Health problems will offset gains to quality of life through rising incomes; decline of natural resources will sabotage future productivity. Similarly, the greatest threat to the environment is poverty and underdevelopment. Poor countries do not have the resources to invest in environmental protection; poor people are hit hardest by environmental degradation. Sound environmental policies should therefore bring particular benefits to the poor. There is no need to re-think the overall strategy. On the contrary, according to the World Bank (1992:iii):

continued, and even accelerated, economic and human development is sustainable and can be consistent with *improving* environmental conditions ... the positive (win-win) links between efficient income growth and the environment need to be aggressively exploited.

The macho language of development triumphalism needs no emphasis.

Productivity is still the main concern. Environmental protection may at times involve trade-offs with growth in income. But with appropriate policies the economic costs are likely to be small, and in any case result in economic pay-offs in the longer term. Natural resources should not be conserved for their own sake, development will inevitably involve some destruction. What matters is that the environment should be counted in by policy-makers as a significant form of 'capital', alongside 'human capital' of skills and education, or 'physical capital' of manufactured products. The environment could then be included in the established process of assessing projected costs of development programmes against the expected benefits. The main concern is to ensure that total productivity is increased. Some additional weight is given to environmental 'capital', as the Bank recognises that its 'costs' may be uncertain, intangible, irreversible, and very long term. But the overall message is clear. The natural world is something to be used instrumentally in the pursuit of human progress. It is one form of capital among others, the technical characteristics of which simply need to be taken more carefully into account than they have been up till now.

This translation of the natural world into its cash value indicates how little the Bank has really changed. The tone of the whole report is masterful and authoritative. It expresses tremendous self-confidence, both in its own economic policies and in humanity's capacity more generally to re-fashion the world in development's image. This assurance comes in part from the World Bank's immense institutional and financial power. But it also draws on the cultural power of science, which in Western society has replaced religion as the source of ultimate authority. Charts, tables and statistics clearly assert an objective, rigorous approach. Elements such as air or soil quality are abstracted from their setting, breaking the connections between different parts of environmental systems. Each factor is then transferred to the new context of the laboratory, where it can be analysed separately with scientific precision. The 'wild' is transformed into raw data for the human production of graphs or bar-charts. On the face of it, the purpose of these is to present information on the state of the planet. But there is a further underlying message. In Hebrew thought, it was through naming the plants and animals in the Garden of Eden that Adam gained dominion over them. The World Bank employs more sophisticated methods, but the basic idea is the same. Simple naming gives way to complex measurement and calculation. The use of scientific techniques, along with the text itself, conveys the message again and again that humankind is in control.

At a global level it is clear that the World Bank must be right in equating efficient use of resources with environmental sustainability. At the level at which decisions are actually made, however, there are often clear trade-offs between efficiency and renewal of environmental resources. For the Kinapat villagers it was consistent with economic efficiency to run down soil fertility while there were other lands to move to. It may make economic sense for local people to kill wildlife for food or sale, while conservationists wish to protect national parks to preserve wild species, and the government to encourage tourism. As in Asha's village, high-yielding varieties of rice have led to higher rates of production in much of Asia. They have, however, proved much more vulnerable to crop hazard than the lower yield indigenous varieties. Researchers are now trying to gather together the remaining original strains of rice in order to foster agriculture that will be sustainable in the longer term. But few of them survive. One of the aspects of the 'efficiency' of the new varieties was in largely wiping out the old.

There are contradictions between local and national, and between different national interests. Gordon Conway and Edward Barbier (1990:72) cite the example of Indonesia in the mid 1980s, when it gained an increase in its quota for cassava imports to the EEC. The need to raise revenue to service the national debt led the Indonesian government to raise cassava prices to encourage production. The resulting increase in cassava helped the national balance of payments, but was achieved at the cost of falls in production of other crops which had been grown in a more sustainable ecological balance.

What of the Bank's understanding of the links between poverty, development, and the environment? The report does admit that the pursuit of economic growth has resulted in some environmental damage. It also states that combatting poverty is a vital part of better environmental stewardship. What it fails to recognise, however, is that the hazardous living conditions of many poor people are the direct result of development, not of being 'left out'. Nancy Scheper-Hughes (1992) shows how mistaken this is in her study of a Brazilian shanty town. The economy of the area is dominated by sugar, grown in huge monocrop plantations. She writes how the word *bagaceira* originally meant the sheds which stored the debris fibre left after cane was crushed. In everyday speech the word has now come to mean junk, garbage, riff-raff, or a marginalised or 'low-life' person, such as a prostitute or drug addict. In this way, as she points out, local people link the development of plantation agriculture directly with the production of human and social 'waste'.

Techno-centric environmentalism responds to the environmental challenge by making it a *policy* problem. With appropriate policies, institutions to police them, and technologies to put them into effect, 'win-win' links between economic growth and environmental safeguards can be achieved. As we saw in Chapter Three, the Bank believes that the interests of rich and poor are also complementary. Poorer countries should learn from the success and failures of the rich. New technologies mean that the environmental mistakes of the past can now be avoided without inhibiting growth. Richer countries need to solve the environmental problems that result from their affluence: damage to air quality and the ozone layer, global warming, acid rain, and hazardous wastes. They also need to make available funds and skills to countries of the South, to enable them to adopt policies from which the whole world will benefit. In short, the new prescription simply echoes classic modernisation approaches: development will come through the transfer of technology, capital, and skills from the more to the less-developed world.

What of the 'major shifts' in policies and institutions that the Bank says are required to make the most of potential 'win-win' links? The report's opening chapter sets these out. Removal of subsidies; population programmes; privatisation of property rights; curbs on 'heavily polluting state companies'; agricultural extension and research; local participation to promote efficiency; and open trade and investment – the policies recommended simply re-confirm the New Right economic paradigm to which the World Bank was already committed. Some concession to the limitations of the market is made as the report states that strong public institutions will be necessary to enforce environmental protection. It softens even this, however, as it insists that 'policies need to work with the grain of the market rather than against it' (p 3). It is business as usual, with the same model of development as before. The 1990s World Bank has taken environmental responsibility in its stride.

It is possible to see this whole report as an elaborate form of 'green packaging'. Even if this is not the Bank's intention, it may be the outcome, because of the way that projects are implemented. Take the recommendation that environmental interests be figured into cost/benefit analyses, for example. The typical way that this happens is that an environmentalist is included in a development project team. This person's responsibility is to ensure that the environment is considered alongside economic, political, technical and social concerns. The problem is that, like gender issues, environmental perspectives cannot simply be tacked on as an additional technical specialism. To be effective, they need to be built into the framework of the project as a whole. As we saw above, the major characteristic of environmental perspectives is looking at the system as a unit. But the World Bank, like other official development agencies, is still committed to the classic model of scientific expertise.

When an official agency is considering launching a project, it sends out a team to assess its viability. Following the scientific paradigm, the team is invariably made up of 'experts' who each know a great deal about one aspect of the system, and nothing about the others. After just a few weeks, or even days, they are expected to come up with a framework which suggests the timetabling and budgeting for inputs over the life-time of the project, usually three or five years. In this framework, a generalist attempting to look at the whole system is at a great disadvan-tage. The soil scientists, plant biologists, engineers and so on, come with clear criteria for analysing problems, and robust ready-made solutions to apply. By contrast, insisting on considering the local context, looking into the connections between things rather than particular aspects in isolation, can seem woolly and unconvincing. Personal politics within the project team may compound this if the environmentalist is younger and (even worse!) female, while the 'real scientists' are older males. The limited time allowed may also make it impossible for her/him to do an effective job. Including an environmentalist team member may thus bolster the legitimacy of the project, while the overall framework ensures that s/he does not have sufficient power to make a significant difference.

Putting faith in technical solutions and top-level policies masks the fact that the use of resources is highly political. Apparently 'objective' instruments such as cost/benefit analyses have long been manipulated to produce the desired results. A further example of green packaging in techno-centric environmentalism is given by David Pepper (1984) in his analysis of the nuclear industry's propaganda in the UK. In 1980-81 the Conservative Government in the UK reduced grants for research into renewable sources of energy to £11 million. In the same year it gave £170 million to nuclear research. While phrased in scientific terms, the clear sub-text of the Government's strategy was to break the back-bone of the trades union movement, the miners. Since then the nuclear indus-try has launched an impressive public relations offensive. The public have been invited to take guided tours around nuclear plants, to reassure them of their human face. The nuclear industry has sponsored high-powered conferences on the environment, in which eminent people, well-fed and watered, surprisingly conclude that nuclear energy is the most environ-mentally friendly form.

Figures on the destruction of forests by existing fuel use are employed to back up this assertion. The fact that we still have no safe method for disposing of nuclear waste is underplayed. Repeated assurances are made that safety systems are so tight that a nuclear accident simply could not happen – despite recurrent instances that show they do. The nuclear industry has been re-packaged, and the key legitimating element is the green label. At the same time, anti-bomb activists, who in the 1950s campaigned under the banner 'atoms for peace', have joined forces with the anti-nuclear environmentalists. They now believe that nuclear energy and nuclear bombs are inextricably linked.

The World Bank's advocacy of 'win-win' policies masks the fact that green issues have come to the fore because of environmental degradation leading to resource scarcity. Sometimes scarcity brings out people's sense of community, but often it leads to competition and conflict. This was very evident in the early days of the current upsurge of environmental awareness. Alarmist predictions forecast that 'exploding' populations in the South would make claims far beyond the earth's 'carrying capacity'. In the 1960s some even argued that it was irresponsible for the North to provide aid to the South: there simply would not be enough to go around and everyone would end up worse off (O'Riordan, 1976:27ff). The image was used of the earth as a life-boat in which there were only a limited number of places. If those in the boat gave up their seats, they would be replaced by others with less social conscience, so the good of the whole would suffer. The self-interest of such arguments made in the North does not need to be underlined.

Like development, environmental protection is often presented as being in the general interest. In practice, however, this often means acting in one sectoral interest at the expense of others. Cecile Jackson (1993) points out, for example, that colonial conservation measures depended on the exclusion of non-white people and particularly women. The problem of soil erosion perceived by Southern African colonial states was met by forced labour to build contour ridges. Forest policy in Zimbabwe in the 1930s identified Africans as to blame for deforestation. Tree-cutting for mining continued, but legislation was enforced against local people cutting live trees for wood. Judy Adoko (1993) sees similar trends in contemporary Uganda. She points out how poor women are blamed for environmental degradation, when they rarely cut trees for fuel wood anyway, but collect dead wood that is lying on the ground. Since much greater damage is done by large-scale commercial interests, she argues, it is businessmen and wealthier groups who should be targeted for environmentalist action.

Similar trends are evident at an international level also. Many countries of the South are infuriated by new Northern claims that they should 'clean up their act'. Debt and unequal terms of trade underlie present practices of environmental destruction. The North achieved 'development' with little concern for the environment. Are environmental policies simply the latest measure by which countries of the North aim to keep those of the South in their place? The World Bank may advocate it, but is the North really willing to transfer resources to the South to enable it to implement more environmentally-friendly forms of development? Or does talk of 'sustainable development' really mean the sustaining of existing inequalities?

Green Consumerism

Green consumerism is a potentially radical challenge to the dominant economic culture. It is a practical way that individuals and organisations can begin to live out their commitment to solidarity with the poor, and social and environmental justice. Its immediate concern is with the circumstances of production: that workers should receive proper pay and work in reasonable conditions; that animals should be humanely treated; that re-cyclable materials should be used where possible and that natural resources should not be run down. It also brings attention to the unfair terms of trade between producers in the South and consumers in the north. Ironically echoing the World Bank's preferred strategy, this movement aims to work 'with the grain of the market', rather than against it. Instead of putting faith in policymakers from on high, however, this approach appeals directly to ordinary people. It acts on the insight that 'power comes from below' (see Chapter Five) by aiming to build a barrage of pressure on big business through millions of tiny consumer choices. By changing tastes, a market is created for ethically produced and fairly traded goods. It therefore comes to make economic sense for mainstream companies to supply and retail outlets to stock these products. Green consumerism thus aims to co-opt the mechanisms of the 'free market', to beat the system at its own game.

In line with the logic of the green movement as a whole, this approach draws attention to the connections within production-consumption systems that are generally hidden. Since coffee was one of the first products to be targeted for action, we take this as an example. We follow the method of the 'life story of maize' introduced in Chapter Four. A jar of coffee on a supermarket shelf appears as a free-standing individual unit. There is no hint of the long journey that it has travelled or the many hands through which it has passed in order to get there. But even a jar of coffee has a history. Most coffee is processed and packaged by huge multinational companies. Some buy direct from the producers, others from international traders. The price paid to producers is regulated by the international market in coffee beans. This is again dominated by the multinationals. In line with Singer and Prebisch's thesis of the decline in terms of trade of primary products (see Chapter Three), this price has fallen considerably over time. Countries of the south thus find themselves as Mr or Ms *Pila,* how much?, when they come to sell their produce. In order to sustain income, more land has to be planted with coffee, leaving less for the production of food crops. As we saw in the case of Kinapat, this pushes small farmers onto marginal lands to produce food for their own consumption. In the north, meanwhile, consumer prices remain high. They are set by the multinationals, who allow themselves large profits for processing and packaging the final product.

Alternative Trading Organisations have stepped in to by-pass the multinationals' stranglehold. They buy coffee direct from small-scale producers, usually organised into co-operatives. The price they pay is a proportion of the consumer price, rather than the low and unstable rate for coffee beans given by the international market. By cutting the middle-traders' profits, they are able to pay better prices to the producers, while not demanding more from the consumers. At the same time, their packaging serves as development education. They provide a brief description of the original producers and the terms on which the coffee has been traded. In this way they make visible what the mainstream manufacturers cast into shadow: the system which connects the person who places the coffee in their supermarket trolley, and the people who were involved in growing it in the first place.

Most Alternative Trading Organisations place the emphasis on social justice rather than the environment, while seeking to avoid practices that are clearly harmful. Another strand of green consumerism takes the opposite approach, paying little attention to the terms of production or trade, but laying heavy stress on the environmental outcomes. The range of products marketed under a green label is huge. Washing powder advertisements promise not only better cleaning power but also less waste. Plastic bags and writing paper are claimed to be re-cyclable. Spray cans proclaim they are 'ozone friendly'. In this form, green consumerism is highly vulnerable to co-option into green packaging. Sometimes this happens literally, as products are re-packaged in 'minimum waste' containers, or with a green label over unchanged contents. Environmental concern has become a new marketing ploy. Instead of challenging the culture of consumption, this makes for good business. In some cases, a lower price offers an additional incentive to 'purchase green'. 'Ecologic' washing machines offer cut bills by lower use of water and electricity. Evidence on the damage of lead pollution to children's brains has led to unleaded petrol being sold more cheaply than leaded. More often, however, 'green' has become a mark of quality, which justifies sale at higher prices. In diversifying the products on offer, it serves to differentiate the market, giving a new axis for the addition of 'manufacturing value added'.

The social content of this is very clear in the case of bottled water. Rather than pressures being applied to ensure the quality of piped water for all in the UK, 'pure' bottled water is marketed for the relatively wealthy. The tendency for 'green' consumption to become a social marker is found throughout the movement for 'organic' products. It is striking how much more common wholefood stores are in middle class than working class areas. Green products have become one further way in which consumption tastes and habits set apart the poor and non-poor. It is not the *volume* of consumption that should be cut, but the *quality* of consumption that should be monitored. It does not matter how much is consumed as long as the product is 'green'.

Another strand in green consumerism draws attention to connections in 'the system' in a rather different way. The emphasis here is on the integrity of individuals, and it involves a central concern for body purity. This rejects the dualism between mind and body which has dominated Western thought, having much more in common with Hindu and Buddhist understandings of the self. Control over the 'pollution' of wider society is exercised by a vegetarian diet, avoiding additives or vegetables grown with artificial fertilisers, or using 'pure and simple' lotions that are kinder to the skin. For some people the motivation for this is explicitly religious. Alternatively, it ironically confirms a tendency in secular Western culture, towards the body as a cult in itself. One's 'body image' becomes a key part of one's self image. Correct body form has to be cultivated by rituals of dieting and exercise, or even surgery. The body itself is commercialised, a consumer item to be 'produced' through financial investment. For some, this has chronic personal outcomes as they suffer the new illness of anorexia or bulimia, in which the body size itself becomes a pathological focus. While it seems to reject the dominant culture of mind-body dualism, therefore, there is a danger that the concern with 'holistic' consumption slips into reconfirming the values of *homo consumens*. The cult of the body seems an ironically fitting spiritual expression for a culture of extreme individualism.

In summary, the radical sting of the green consumerism challenge can be removed in a number of ways. The most blatant is by 'greening' the external package while leaving the content unchanged. But even when the products are truly 'green', the inducement to consume in quantity, as long as it is the right quality, denies the limits to the earth's resources. Green consumerism may provide an important first step towards challenging the dominant culture of consumption. The danger is that it lulls people into a false sense of security that they are 'doing something', while the reality, as in techno-centric environmentalism, is 'business as usual'.

Ecofeminism (Eco-centric Environmentalism)

Eco-centric environmentalism takes the values of techno-centricism and turns them on their head. It is like the negative of a photograph, in which the dark parts are highlighted, and the bright thrown into shadow. The dominant model of development can never be generalised to all. It is a profane, high-cost, Western patriarchal model, which has built into it exploitation of the 'other': women, non-Western peoples, and the natural world. The roots of this are in colonialism, when Europeans 'discovered' the Americas, Africa and Asia, and claimed them for their own use. What was there already counted for nothing: people, plants, minerals and land were seen simply as raw material for plunder, extraction or annexation.

History began with the white man. Development took up where colonialism left off. It also proceeds by violence, by dispossession. It also is fuelled by desire (see Mies and Shiva, 1993).

For ecofeminism, value lies in what development discounts. All creatures and eco-systems have 'biotic rights' which should be respected. Inverting the 'normal' hierarchy of development and mainstream Western thought, what is 'nearer to nature' in human society – 'savage' peoples and women – is seen as superior to the cultured, the civilised, and the male. The natural stands for the good, the true, the integral, the spiritual. As in the conservative paradigm, therefore, the natural is viewed as a moral order. People are the children of Mother Earth, not her masters. We therefore need to seek the good life within the limits of what she has provided for us, fostering a relationship of mutual respect and nurture, not plunder and exploitation.

This implies not only a revolution in development, but also in the model of science on which it is built. As scientific knowledge involves dissecting, reducing, separating out, it is unable to comprehend the integrity of natural systems, which lies not in the separate elements, but in the linkages between them. It is these 'spaces in-between' that maintain ecological stability and productivity in situations of scarcity. It is also in these connections between sectors that much of indigenous people's and women's work and knowledge exists. Only by substituting a more holistic approach, which re-claims these areas from the periphery to the centre, will genuinely sustainable livelihoods be achievable for all.

The radicalism of ecofeminism's critique of development links it to the liberational paradigm. While techno-centric environmentalism bolsters the existing social and political structures, ecofeminism calls for major change. Its critique of development as violence, dispossession and desire also links with awareness of the poverty of being (see Chapter Four). The violence of development is seen in its devastation of the natural world; in its spawning of militarism and sophisticated weaponry; and its destruction of subsistence in the pursuit of 'surplus' at any cost. Dispossession is experienced by the poor in being torn from their cultural roots and often their own land; losing their self-reliance, for example in seed germination; and having the value of their subsistence labour discounted. It is experienced by nature through genetic erosion and the profanation of its sacredness, as development introduces a purely instrumental relationship between humanity and the environment. Ultimately, even the wealthy are dispossessed, the development 'experts' or transnational companies, as they lose their home in claiming the whole world as their property.

Finally, ecofeminists analyse development as desire. As Mies and Shiva (1993:145) put it:

> Before yearning there was destruction, before romanticising there was violence.

The desire they identify is not only for endless growth and consumption. It is also for 'the world we have lost' which is destroyed as soon as it is found. This is seen in the cultural or individual yearning for 'unspoilt nature', the 'noble savage', the wild, childhood, authenticity, home, community, the sense of belonging, and security.

We have seen many of these features of development as we have reviewed what it has meant for the poor and non-poor. By using the language of emotion, ecofeminism snatches development from the neutral, 'objective', sanitised world of policy-speak. It also makes clear that development does not involve the creation of something out of nothing, but the displacement by something else of what was already there. As the waters of a massive dam thunder down, and people above admire it as a feat of human ingenuity and enjoy the electricity and irrigation it supplies, ecofeminism speaks for the 'others'. The perhaps thousands of people who lost their homes as the land was flooded, the creatures that lost their habitat, the soils and plants now drowned beneath the pounding waters. In this sense it gives a voice to those 'below', to those whom development 'disappears' and silences. And it is a voice ringing with the fullness of life, with the passion of love and pain, hunger and feasting, with the wonder of the sacred and the brutality of its denial.

Ecofeminism gives a much-needed corrective to the blinkered materialism of most development analyses. But there are some problems in the way it is set out. The first is the tendency to generalise – and idealise – about indigenous peoples and women (especially 'third world women'). This damages the long struggle to establish that women differ from one another just as much as men do (see Chapter Six). It also means they cannot take into account that how people treat the environment does reflect their cosmologies, but these are also related to such things as poverty, land rights, work-loads, and so on. Not recognising this opens up the danger of co-option, so that women actually become more exploited, as their 'natural' affinity with the earth makes them 'naturally' suited to doing (unpaid) environmental work (Jackson, 1993). This approach also has the potential to be politically very reactionary. Contraception, for example, is seen as invasive to the integrity of women's bodies, which is cold comfort for women wishing to limit the number of children they have.

This political ambiguity is common to all eco-centric approaches. Typically, they take a strongly populist tone, with bio-ethical, romantic and utopian values. Simple, adaptive technology is preferred to complex. Small-scale organisation, in which local people can have greater say, is preferred over large-scale centralised control. Participation is favoured over hierarchy, and 'feminine' approaches of co-operation and adjustment over 'masculine' ones of competition and technical control. An ideology of biotic rights could, however, be used by an authoritarian dictator such as Pol Pot in Cambodia, to try to exterminate all evidence of modernity – and the people who opposed him. As the scarcity of natural resources comes to be felt ever more acutely, the use of eco-centric arguments *against* people 'below' unfortunately becomes a more likely possibility.

The final shortcoming of ecofeminism is an ironic one: that in its praise of diversity and hostility to dualism, it actually fails to present variability and is highly dualistic. Stereotyped images of harmonious rural environments which 'disenchanted' modern society has lost give no sense of tension or discord. Individual interests do not necessarily coincide with the social, nor older women's with younger women's, nor the lion's with the gazelle's. To see society-environment as a 'system' should not mean a denial of conflict. Systems may reflect an uneasy and shifting balance between opposing interests, as well as 'natural' complementarity.

In contrast, the picture that ecofeminism paints of development is too bleak. As we saw in the case of Kinapat, society-environment systems do adapt to new challenges, there is room for hope. In Asha's village one of the knock-on effects of irrigation was that new, power-driven rice mills were introduced. Although the immediate effect of these was that some of the poorest women lost their main opportunities for paid work, they did find alternatives in time. Meanwhile, the heavy burden of husking rice by traditional methods was removed for women in the vast majority of households. The cost of husking rice was met by male cash instead of female labour. The key issue is not *whether* new methods should be developed – they are bound to be. Rather, we should ask *what kind* of technologies should be used, who has *control* over them, what are the *relations* in which they are introduced, and who gets what benefits.

Living a New Relationship

> My book is the nature of created things. In it when I choose I can read the words of God.
>
> ~ Sorrell, 1988:16 ~

These are the words of Antony, a hermit who died around AD 350. They hold the conviction that there is a wider context for the relationship of human beings to their environment: the world of nature speaks of God.

In this section we explore how this has been understood in the Judaeo-Christian tradition. As in other areas, the tradition is plural and at times contradictory. The overarching context, of course, is the view of nature as creation, and of the glory of God as creator. But within this, we distinguish three further images, which recur and even intersect at different times. The first sees nature as disorder, lower, something to be conquered and subdued. In the second, nature appears as a garden, a place of beauty, play, and bounty to meet human needs. Finally, nature figures as wilderness, a place of retreat, of struggle, and of the search for wisdom.

Conquering Nature

In his address to the American Association for the Advancement of Science in 1966, Lynn White (1967:1203) drew on the first of these themes:

> … we shall continue to have a worsening ecological crisis until we reject the Christian axiom that nature has no reason for existence but to serve man …. Both our present science and our present technology are so tinctured with orthodox Christian arrogance toward nature that no solution to our ecological crisis can be expected from them alone. Since the root of our troubles are so largely religious, the remedy must essentially be religious, whether we call it that or not.

Distrust of nature, the body, and sensuality, is strongly rooted in the Christian tradition, as in many religions. The doctrine of original sin expresses this most clearly, as human nature is seen as fallen, in need of redemption. As noted in Chapter Six, this fed on and into the antagonism towards women, who were seen as nearer to nature and so lower, dangerous and in need of control. In the Middle Ages, monasteries were rather like early development projects, setting out to subdue nature and so restore the hierarchical order of human dominion established by God in Eden. Even the language of the early scientists betrays this idea of man's (*sic*) dominance. Francis Bacon (1561-1620) for example, wrote how Nature had to be 'hounded in her wanderings', 'bound into service', and made a slave. The role of the scientist was to 'torture nature's secrets from her'. The fact that nature is seen as female is not, of course, a coincidence.

What religion began, science therefore took over. This is not surprising, because initially there was little difference between the two. In the Middle Ages, the main goal of science was to understand the meaning and significance of the natural world, in the context of questions about God, morality and the human soul. Physicians, for example, understood the human body as made up of 'humours', which mixed together the material, emotional and spiritual. It was only in the sixteenth and seventeenth centuries that scientists in Europe began to break away from the control of the Church and to assert their right to learn through a process of doubt and experimentation, not faith and tradition. The Church began to move from the centre to the sidelines of society as other professions and institutions came to the fore. The dominance of the conservative paradigm was broken, as the liberal took its place (Chapter Three). The material was divorced from the spiritual, and the human body understood as something physical, which could be treated like a complex, animated machine. Ideas of hierarchy and order gave way to those of equality, reason and progress. The myth of creation was replaced by the theory of evolution. History told not of the Fall, but the ascent of humankind, *through the progressive transformation of nature*.

The story of the growing supremacy of science ends with an ironic twist. *What happened was not the victory of science over religion, but wider social changes in which both religion and science were transformed, and subordinated*. The magical aspects in religion made it vulnerable to being displaced by the superior technical control of science. In the same way, the myth of objectivity and value neutrality have laid science wide open to co-option by the dominant culture of industrial society. The core of the scientific approach is its critical attitude, its progress through doubt. But science has become the new magic, to which people look to solve all their problems. It has become the new authority, which people use to legitimate their views. The 'problems' science has 'solved' are not random. Heart transplants are possible, the provision of clean drinking water for all is not. Thousands of children die daily in the South, while couples in the North follow expensive and biologically intrusive fertility treatments. The driving impetus to split the atom was to manufacture the first nuclear bomb. The great majority of scientific research is either under-taken or sponsored by commercial firms or governments with commer-cial or military aims. Development has been fuelled not by the thirst for knowledge, but for resources and power. It is economics, not natural science, that has replaced religion as the arbiter of life and death.

Seeing the dominance of economic rationality offers a corrective to Lynn White's view that a religious 'remedy' will be the full answer. It is a part of the answer, but it must be grounded in a praxis of social and political transformation. This follows the example of many poor commu-nities the world over, who have mounted protests in defence of their environment. A few of the best known are often quoted: the opposi-tion to the massive Narmada dam in Western India, which sent shock waves through the World Bank; the Chipko movement in North India, of hugging trees to prevent more logging. But these cases are just the tip of the iceberg. Even in the UK, it is remarkable what a cross-section of people are prepared to join environmental protests, for example against new motorways. In concern for the natural environment, people time and again assert the centrality of spiritual concerns against the instrumental-ism of the economic system. They are motivated to organise, to demand rights of participation in decision-making, to assert the values of quality against quantity, mutuality against individualism. Through their argu-ments for the environment, people assert their values for themselves. The recurrence of environmentalist movements shows an underlying momentum of resistance to the poverty of the dominant culture of conquest and subjection.

Like the formation of the Kinapat SALT Farmers' Association, these are deeply political actions, in which people assert their own rights against the experts', and forge community as they struggle together. And, like the people of Kinapat, they may go on to tackle wider issues. Although some of them had once been workers of the logging company, many of the Kinapat villagers supported the campaign to cancel the logging concessions which destroyed the forest to pay for the country's debt. They had long felt uneasy at the violence of the forest's destruction, but had never felt the confidence to voice this, much less to act on it. One of the farmers in the picket line put it into words:

When I go to the forest and hear the rustling of the leaves, the rumblings of the streams and the singing of the birds, I hear God's voice. If logging is allowed to continue, the day will come when I will no longer hear the sound of the leaves or streams or the birds. When that day comes, I will cease also to hear God's voice.

A woman who was six-months pregnant was also with the group. She explained why she was there:

I believe that God created us as the trustees of creation. For years I have been an irresponsible trustee by being blind and dumb about what was being done to the forest. I want to show my repentance.

Nature as God's Bounty

In seeing things this way, the Kinapat villagers were reaching back to the remains of a world-view that saw the earth as something living. The trees, plants, rivers, stones, everything around were the dwelling place of spirits. Like many other Christians in the South, the people of the local tribes believe these spirits exist alongside the Christian God whom they worship. Mainstream Christianity has tended to dismiss this as 'syncretism', 'pantheism', or 'nature worship'. Some liberation theologians similarly write it off as conservative, superstitious, 'folk religion'. But in some sections of the Church at least, the search for liberation has led to repentance for this arrogance, and a new readiness to learn from the understandings of peoples previously dismissed as 'primitive'. This is in line with the changing sense of God's body as female, which we suggested in Chapter Six. One Manobo woman explained how they prayed:

Forgive us, *Magbabaya,* for cutting down this our brother tree. From its trunk we can get lumber to build houses to protect our families from the sun and the rain. From its branches we can get firewood to cook our meals. Forgive us, *Magbabaya,* for killing this our sister hen. From its meat we can get nourishment and energy to do our work.

She explained what she was doing in this way:

We pray to *Magbabaya* (Creator) because we do not own things. The *Magbabaya* does. We humans are the most beloved creatures and the other things are given for our use. But we need permission to use them because they are not ours.

This perspective echoes the second motif in Biblical understandings of the natural world: the image of the garden. The classic statement of this is found in Genesis 1: 27-28:

> So God created humankind in his image, in the image of God he created them; male and female he created them. God blessed them, and God said to them, 'Be fruitful and multiply, and fill the earth and subdue it; and have dominion over the fish of the sea and over the birds of the air and over every living thing that moves upon the earth'.

The character of this dominion is given in the next chapter: 'The Lord God took the man and put him in the garden of Eden to till and to keep it.' The Jerusalem Bible translates the second purpose as 'to take care of it' (Genesis 2: 15). The cosmology that this reflects is hierarchical, in line with the conservative paradigm. This makes it open to the co-option for exploitation which Lynn White points out. But to emphasise human dominion alone means leaving out a key part of the picture. As we saw in Chapter Five, human power is always provisional: ultimate authority rests with God alone. Psalm 8 makes this clear:

> O Lord, our Sovereign,
>> how majestic is your name in all the earth!
>
> You have set your glory above the heavens.
>> Out of the mouths of babes and infants
> you have founded a bulwark because of your foes,
>> to silence the enemy and the avenger.
>
> When I look at your heavens, the work of your fingers,
>> the moon and the stars that you have established;
> what are human beings that you are mindful of them,
>> mortals that you care of them?
>
> Yet you have made them a little lower than God,
>> and crowned them with glory and honour.
>
> You have given them dominion over the works of your hands;
>> you have put all things under their feet,
> all sheep and oxen,
>> and also the beasts of the field,
>
> the birds of the air, and the fish of the sea,
>> whatever passes along the paths of the seas.

O Lord, our Sovereign,
how majestic is your name in all the earth!

Perhaps this is what Antony meant when he said 'my book is the nature of created things'. Through the ordinary, the extraordinary is revealed; through the profane, the brilliance of the sacred. To experience this is to make one's own what Matthew Fox (1983) calls 'original blessing', in a celebration of life and joy. To feel a sense of awe and wonder at the magnificence of creation and the generosity of God's provision. Like the Manobo tribe, the Psalmist sees human beings as the most beloved of the Creator. But the context is not one of domination, but of worship, spreading out the arms and throwing back the head to revel in God's glory. It is an embrace also of the poverty of our own being, in the context of the wonder, the giftness, the richness of Being.

The love of God is revealed not simply in creation as a one-off action, but in the continual renewal and sustaining of all that is made. This insight was revealed in a vision to the fourteenth century mystic, Mother Julian of Norwich. She recounts it:

[Christ] showed a little thing, the quantity of a hazelnut, lying in the palm of my hand, as me seemed, and it was as round as a ball. I looked thereon with the eye of my understanding and thought, 'What may this be?' And it was answered generally thus, 'It is all that is made'. I marvelled how it might last, for me thought it might suddenly have fallen to nought for littleness. And I was answered in my understanding, 'It lasteth and ever shall, for God loveth it, and so hath all thing being by the love of God'.

~ Quoted in Tugwell, 1984:194 ~

The scope of this assurance is also affirmed in the story of the flood in which Noah and the creatures in his ark were saved. After the flood, God promised never again to send waters to cover the face of the earth. The covenant was not only with Noah and Noah's descendants, nor even only living creatures:

I have set my bow in the clouds, and it shall be a sign of the covenant between me and *the earth*.

~ Genesis 9:13, emphasis added ~

Ignatius of Loyola would perhaps be expected more on the 'original sin' than 'original blessing' side of the balance, but in his 'Contemplation for Achieving Love', he also encourages people to see God living in all creatures:

in matter, giving it existence,
in plants, giving them life,
in animals, giving them consciousness,
in people, giving them intelligence.

He then proceeds ...

> Think of God energising, as though He were actually at work, in every created reality, in the sky, in matter, plants and fruits, herds and the like: it is He who creates them and keeps them in being, He who confers life or consciousness, and so on.   ~ Ignatius (1963:80) ~

Twentieth century theologians have pushed considerably further the idea of the one-ness of all things. Teilhard de Chardin (1971:101) has this to say:

> It is essential to note that in this emergent state the idea of the Whole is still extremely vague in my mind and to all appearance ill-defined. It is simply that, above the complete linked body or ensemble of beings and phenomena, I can glimpse, or sense, a global reality whose condition is that of being more necessary, more consistent, richer and more certain in its ways, than any of the particular things it embraces. For me, in other words, there are no longer any 'things' in the world; there are only 'elements'.

Teilhard, like many more contemporary theologians, was deeply impressed by recent developments in natural science. Observations at the sub-atomic level now suggest that the absolute division between observer and observed, the touchstone of scientific objectivity, may not be sustainable. The path of sub-atomic phenomena after a collision can only be charted by a holistic perspective in which both are seen, with the observing instrument, as part of a single system. The established language, categories, concepts, the whole way of thinking, is inadequate to under-stand and explain these subatomic phenomena. They cannot be pictured as 'things', very small bits of matter. Instead they are the interconnections between 'things' – which in turn are interconnections with others. The reductionist perspective seems to have reached its limits.

Similar tendencies are also evident in health care. The machine model of the body is being questioned, as people reject narrowly technical treat-ment for holistic remedies which recognise persons as integrated, body mind and spirit. At the global level too, some scientists are now advocating new understandings of the earth which are organic and holistic. James Lovelock, for example, talks of the global system as 'Gaia', an ancient goddess, to suggest not that it *is* a 'being', but that its flexibility and ability to regulate itself makes it seem like one in many ways. As at the sub-atomic level, a full description means not *abstracting* and isolating an element from its context, but recognising its relationship to other things as constitutive of what it is. There are no static structures in nature. What we have is stability in dynamic balance. Some physicists, though still a minority, even suggest that consciousness may be an essential aspect of the universe. The scientific division between spirit and matter seems finally to be cracking from within.

In the Christian tradition it is Francis of Assisi (*d* 1226) who is popularly seen as the 'nature saint', so it seems fitting that we should close this section with him. Rejecting the wealth and ethos of the monasteries, Francis sought special 'places' for contemplation, with a minimum of establishment, where he was able to live out his delight in creatures simply for their own sake. For Francis, contemplation of creation was not just a starting point from which to move to abstract ideas. Instead Francis chose to be among them, and was filled with warmth, love, respect, and family feeling towards all creatures. They responded to him in turn, reflecting the mutual dependence and willing service that God had ordained. This relationship was not one of equality, but of courtly respect. Reflecting the culture of his time, Francis believed a code of honour, as well as love and a sense of family, united people with their fellow creatures. But again, there is this recurring sense of one-ness. For it was through the senses and emotions of his intimacy with nature that Francis experienced mystical union with the divine.

Wilderness

The wilderness is not always something to be tamed; it may also be something to which we need to surrender. There is a long established tradition of people leaving human society, to go out into the desert to seek God there. The children of Israel had to journey through the wilderness before they could reach the Promised Land, and it was there that they came to know and depend on their God. For Jesus also, it was in the wilderness, alone and hungry, that the calling of his baptism was tested and confirmed. This withdrawal marked a turning point in his life. It was only when he came back from the wilderness that his ministry began. The Desert Fathers, like Antony, whose words opened this section, were highly significant figures in the development of Christianity in North Africa and West Asia. In our own times, this witness is still carried by hermits like Carlo Caretto. If for most of us at secondhand, the desert still plays an important part in contemporary spirituality.

This pattern is common across many times and cultures. Amongst tribal peoples, for example, initiation ceremonies often involve a time away in the bush, a time outside society, before young people can return to take their new place as adults. The wilderness is a place to be feared, but also a place of wisdom. It is a place which strips away what has been, and yet restores one to a new self.

Amongst liberation theologians, this tendency can be mistrusted, as it usually takes the form of an individual withdrawal. In Chapter Four, however, we show the need to hold in tension the personal and political in the search for liberation. There may be a time for each of us that we need to withdraw into whatever the desert or forest is for us. It is frightening, because it involves surrender. Like being with the poor, it means losing control. The outcomes are never certain. The importance of the wilderness, the waste land, to our religious inheritance should caution us against the wholesale destruction of it that we are seeing. It may be that it is only in being willing to relearn the wisdom of the desert that the secrets of the poverty of our being will ever be revealed.

Conclusion

Viewing development through an environmental lens points us powerfully to our connectedness. As individuals and in community, life is shown as an integrated whole, with profound connections between physical, emotional, psychological and spiritual well-being. This reaffirms our option to do theology and development, as we see the importance of drawing together economic, political and spiritual perspectives in seeking better ways of relating to the natural world. The stories of Kinapat and Asha's village show that parts can only be understood in relation to the whole. This makes us question models of science and knowledge that divide and abstract, rather than seeking to comprehend the whole picture. We also see that the 'objectivity' these models claim has been co-opted for their use in sustaining and intensifying relations of inequality and domination. We need to move beyond understanding development as growing freedom *from* the realm of necessity, to seeing development as seeking a good life *within* the realm of necessity, which is both environmentally sustainable and genuinely open to all.

This means that 'the environment' cannot be treated as something separate from us, that can be dealt with by special policies with no implications for the rest of life. Any action is like a stone thrown into a pool which sends out ripples in ever-expanding circles. The shape that these take is given by the habitat of the pool, the rocks, branches, water-lilies or creatures that lie within it. In the same way, politics and economics shape the impact that human action has on its environment, and mean in turn those ripples hit different sets of people in different ways. In guitar-playing, there is something called the 'minimum movement principle', which governs the action of the left hand which holds the notes. Perhaps adopting a 'minimum movement principle' in relation to the environment would be a useful corrective to our present practices. Finally, the beauty, diversity and adaptability of the natural world should arouse our wonder. It inspires hope for a new future, in which we learn to see our environment not simply as what we inhabit, but as a part of what we are.

CHAPTER EIGHT

Violence and Nonviolence

Introduction

'Development is the new name for peace,' Pope Paul concluded his encyclical of 1966, *Populorum Progressio*. But the twentieth century, the century of development, has seen unprecedented levels of militarisation and organised violence. 'Progress' through science and technology has supplied weapons of greater precision and destructive power than ever before. The rise of nation-states has been matched by the multiplication of national machineries for war. The given aims are not 'aggression', but 'national security' or 'national defence'. As noted in Chapter Three, these are used to terrorise the states' own citizens, at least as often as to combat an external threat. The build up of nuclear arsenals during the Cold War was similarly justified as deterrence against possible attack. Peace, it was claimed, would be maintained only by a stable 'balance of terror'. But the drive to accumulate nuclear weapons took on its own dynamic. Sydney Carter satirises this in his song 'I wanna have a little bomb like you':

Now everybody says the same:
'I wanna have a little bomb like you.'
I am not the one to blame,
I wanna have a little bomb like you.
Who will be the first to say:
'I'll throw the bloody thing away'?
I don't wanna be the first, do you? no,
I don't wanna be the first, do you?

The 'nuclear peace' was peace in name only. The superpowers fought out their 'cold war' over the bodies of countries in the South. Violent struggles for 'liberation' were supported and opposed by the super-powers and their allies, supplying the warring factions with training, funds and arms. In cases like Mozambique and Nicaragua, foreign-backed wars continued even after 'liberation'; crippling the nascent state and its people. In the course of armed conflict, millions of people have been killed, raped, maimed, or displaced. The effects of war on development have been disastrous. Production has collapsed. Combined with the destruction of roads and bridges which provided distribution networks, this has led to widespread famine. The environment has been plundered to fund military manoeuvres, or destroyed by mines and bombs. In Vietnam, it was even the direct target, as the United States used 'Agent Orange' to defoliate trees and so destroy the guerillas' hiding places.

Of course there have also been some winners. It has been a good century for the arms trade. The spectre of increased unemployment is raised against any call to cut spending on armaments. More locally, wars always generate additional opportunities for profiteering. The war against Iraq in 1990 was followed almost immediately by a rush of foreign companies seeking to win contracts to 're-build' Kuwait.

In the midst of the violence, there have also been calls for an alternative path. Advocates of nonviolence have had to pay a heavy price for their stand. They have been denounced as naive, harassed as subversive, imprisoned as unpatriotic cowards, and killed. But the vision of a nonviolent strategy lives on. It draws together other values that we have explored in the previous chapters: people's participation, gender justice, and environmental sensitivity. Within Christian tradition it speaks, perhaps most sharply, of the way of the Cross.

In this chapter we set out our option for nonviolence. This is based in experience, rather than being an *a priori* stand. At this point Sarah has to stand aside, because she has not been faced with a situation that demands that she choose for or against violence. It is therefore Romy's experience that dominates this chapter. We begin, however, by reflecting on the 'everyday violence' that makes up the experience of poor and marginalised people the world over. It is a profound error to separate out the violence of those who seek change from the violence of the structures against which they are protesting. They are part of the same system, and have to be understood as fruit of the same bitter tree.

The choice between violence and nonviolence as a strategy for change hangs on the understanding of political power. In the next section, therefore, we discuss this, drawing on the discussion of the nature of power in Chapter Five. This leads us on to explore violence and nonviolence as different kinds of culture. As we analyse the logic of different forms of struggle, we show why we believe the option for nonviolence is more consistent with the longing for liberation. The chapter ends by showing how the option for nonviolence constitutes a profound challenge to our way of being in the world, and affirms and deepens the core values we have identified in doing theology and development. Although we recognise the importance of interpersonal violence as an issue within development, our discussion here is limited to the use of violence as a political strategy.

The Violence of Oppression

Before we consider violence or nonviolence as an *option,* we need to recognise that violence is the given, the norm, in many people's lives. This is the insight of 920 Latin American priests who submitted a document to the 1968 bishops' conference in Medellin, Colombia. They argued that it was wrong to condemn as violence only the actions of the revolutionary forces. 'For centuries,' they claimed, 'Latin America has been a region of violence' (Torres, 1971:442). There was violence in the poverty of the people, denied education, decent housing, and even sufficient food. There was violence in the political system, which allowed the poor no voice. The Church too was implicated, by continually siding with the ruling classes. There was violence in national and international economic structures which spawned debt and militarism. This perspective is echoed even in the relatively tranquil terrain of rural Bangladesh, as Betsy Hartmann and James Boyce (1983) write: 'a quiet violence is stalking the villages.' While it only sometimes flares up into direct attack by fists or weapons, this violence of hunger and injustice is a fact of everyday life.

Condemnation of a shallow 'peace' that is only a mask for injustice, goes back to Biblical times. Here, for example, is the Prophet Jeremiah:

'For from the least to the greatest of them,
everyone is greedy for unjust gain;
and from prophet to priest,
everyone deals falsely.
They have treated the wound of my people carelessly,
saying, "Peace, peace",
when there is no peace.
They acted shamefully, they committed abomination;
yet they were not ashamed,
they did not know how to blush.
Therefore they shall fall among those who fall;
at the time that I punish them,
they shall be overthrown,' says the Lord.   ~ Jeremiah 6: 13-15 ~

We do not have to look hard to find people crying 'peace, peace' when there is no peace, hastily covering over the wounds of injustice that afflict others in their society. Up to the eve of the first all-race South African election in April 1994, there were still white people in the so-called liberal English-speaking community who condemned the African National Congress (ANC) because they had accepted armed struggle. They were quite unable to see the violence inherent in a system where black people were relegated to small, infertile areas; where money spent on education for a white child was many times that spent on a black child; where blacks provided almost all manual labour, while whites almost all the managerial; where residential areas, restaurants, parks, even public toilets, were segregated according to colour; where black people had no vote. Perhaps even more surprisingly, they saw themselves as non-violent. Their heavy investment in electronic security systems, training in fire-arms and guns in the pantry were like their army, simply a form of defence, a legitimate force against the 'outsiders' who threatened them.

For many people outside the system, and the blacks within it, the apartheid state provides a particularly clear example of the 'structural' violence built into the fabric of society, and the armed force needed to sustain it. In Chapter Five we saw that power is not always expressed in visible conflict. Similarly, structural violence goes far beyond the open use of force. But there are often links between the two. These show, for example, in the murder of Latin American street children, which is tacitly accepted as a form of 'pest control' during movements for urban 'beautification'. They show in the troops' firing on students who dared to protest in China's Tianenman square. They show in the Indonesian government's massacre of the people of East Timor.

Violence, like death, is not the great leveller, but the great discriminator. In the United States it is young black men who are by far the most likely to be victims of violent crime, and murder is their most common cause of death. Brazilian shanty-town dwellers experience as normal levels of state, and particularly police, terrorism that would create outrage if used against 'respectable' citizens (Scheper-Hughes, 1992:220). In India too, 'marginal' populations of Adivasi ('tribal') people and urban slum dwellers are used to routine police violence, and suffer periodic massacres. The same pattern can be seen in the UK. It is poor housing estates that have the highest levels of violent crime, and also the highest levels of police surveillance. New-age travellers, gypsies and squatters are open to physical abuse by police and citizen alike, with very little hope of redress.

We saw in Chapter Two how the experiences of poverty and powerlessness are very closely linked. This is expressed in a particularly sharp way in the violence of many poor people's everyday lives. The power of the industrialised nations, the state, the patrons, and the bosses is founded in the structures and culture of society, but also embodied in their control over the machinery of violence. It is not therefore surprising that for some who want to smash that power, taking up arms themselves can seem the only effective way.

For Sarah, it was while she was in Gaza, teaching English in a refugee camp one summer, that she first began to understand how this might be. This is her story.

Sarah:

I had come to Gaza with a group of other British students. Many of us, like me, had known little more about the Palestinians than their identification as terrorists in the British media. The warm and generous people we met were very different from those scarf-masked, gun-carrying stereotypes. The Palestinians were eager for us to hear their history. Our whole stay was like an intensive course in political education. But one incident brought the situation home to me, more than all the talk and argument.

One weekend, one of my 'students', Awad, decided to take me to visit Beer Sheba, in the state of Israel. A friend of his owned a taxi, and agreed to take us along with one or two others. The taxis are huge Mercedes, and normally they wait until they are full with seven passengers before they set off.

On the way back from Beer Sheba, I asked for the car to stop. I wanted to take a photo of the desert. Out of nowhere, it seemed, an Israeli army jeep was suddenly alongside us. What was I doing? This was a restricted area! No photographs allowed! Awad began to speak up for me. The soldiers rounded on him.

'*Meen inte?*' – who are you?

Who are you? Who are you to speak? Who do you think you are?

Because it was a taxi, the soldiers would assume we just happened to be travelling together. To show that we knew each other would only make things worse. It would mean more questions, more suspicion. It could endanger the driver, Awad himself, even perhaps the English project. Awad stepped back.

The rest of the drive home was very quiet. The soldiers' words were ringing in our ears. *Meen inte?* No one. No man, able to protect the woman he was travelling with. No citizen, with rights or a state to call his own. A refugee, living in a camp on occupied territory, ringed by military observation posts. Not even the camp could be called their own, as houses were repeatedly bulldozed to make a 'security road' wide enough for the Israeli tanks. In the nearby city, municipal buildings were crowned not by their own, but by the Israeli flag. The person I knew as strong, confident, capable and full of fun was humiliated, made nothing. Nobody.

For the first time I began to feel how you might reach for a gun.

The denial of humanity lies at the roots of violence. For some people, there is nothing left but the struggle for what they have not, to assert their claims of who they are.

An Option for Nonviolence

The choice between violence or nonviolence does not come to everyone. It is the 'time of trial' from which we may all pray to be delivered. But when it does come, it confronts the whole person. Abstract arguments are forgotten, as people are torn between what they see happening and the ideals which they have held. Neutrality is not an option. Either way, one's life may be on the line. This is how the moment came for Romy.

Romy:

When I first arrived in the parish, I was not fully committed to non-violence. I refused to have formal links with the New People's Army, but I knew my political awareness seminars provided fertile recruiting grounds for them. 'I am prepared to plough and to sow the seeds. Let others do the nurturing and the harvesting,' was the way that I explained it.

One day, Al came to see me. He was a regular military officer, who had command of the local platoon of Special Police. These were young men who were given arms and a crash course in military train-ing to assist in combatting the guerillas. Unlike his fellow soldiers Al was never drunk or abusive, so he was well-liked and trusted by his men. He explained to me how they had told him that their monthly allowance was always late, and less than they had been promised. Al had found out why: some of the regular officers had been taking a cut. Nothing happened when Al raised the issue at headquarters, so the Special Police decided to stage a protest. Al joined them. They were immediately declared 'absent without leave' and ordered to return their firearms. The group refused. Regular soldiers were sent out to arrest them. It was said there was a shoot to kill order.

As Al was talking I saw marksmen behind the trees. He sheltered behind me as we made our way into the rectory. Al and his group stayed in the rectory that night. In the early hours they left to try and find a safer place. Before he went, Al gave me his .35 mm pistol.

I hid the gun in the sacristy, behind the container for consecrated bread and the chalices. Each morning, as I prepared for the Eucharist, I looked at the bread, the chalices, and the gun, as I wondered what was happening to Al and his men. Days, weeks and months passed. I got more and more disturbed. If Al were killed, would I one day open the sacristy and take out the gun instead of the chalice?

One day one of the servers at the Eucharist asked if he could talk to me. He told me that I had changed. Was something wrong? I had become so impatient and easily got angry. Members of the Parish Council and some parishioners also came to me saying the same thing. I seemed to have become a different person. As the months passed, the gun and the violence it represented had eaten up something inside me. I decided to return the pistol to Al.

Instead of me owning the gun, it had possessed me. As I feared the military would kill Al, I was taken over by the urge for revenge. I started to hate those officers. It did not matter any more that if I killed them it would leave their wives and children widows and orphans. But eventually owning the gun made me reject the power and the culture it represented. I could not reconcile it with the message of love I was preaching. There was a contradiction between the justice I sought and the urge to take justice into my own hands. I could no longer block out the fact that most of the families of the officers were members of the church community under my care. I had no right to discount or disconnect them from it. The death of the officers would not bring anyone freedom. It would only lead to more suffering and pain. A number of farmers had told me, 'If you join the armed struggle, we will come with you'.

The debate between violence and nonviolence is highly charged. So much is at stake. People on both sides passionately believe in the right-eousness of their cause. The temptation is to see everything is right on one's own side. The others are not only tactically, but also morally wrong. Their hearts are not with the people, as ours are.

The ethical issues perhaps appear clearest to those who are least involved. It is easy for armchair revolutionaries to assert their radicalism by advocating armed struggle. It is equally easy for those who have known nothing but safety and comfort to insist that violence can never be justified. Until faced with the situation ourselves, none of us can know for sure what option we would take.

There are people of good-will, people of conscience, people utterly committed to peace and justice, on both sides. There are also people whose motivation is less pure. In this chapter our aim, therefore, is not to establish the morality of one side against the other. It is rather to consider concrete experiences and trace where the logic of violence leads to. We believe that this shows fundamental contradictions between the praxis of violence and the ideals of justice and peace it is supposed to bring about.

Before going on, one initial point needs to be made. So far, neither violence nor nonviolence has succeeded in establishing the dream of a new society they promise. To take a stand for *either* violence *or* non-violence is to make an act of faith. There is room for rational discussion, but this can only go so far. Beyond this, one can only 'read the signs of the times'. Recognising these limitations in their own stance may help to make both sides more tolerant of the other.

Political Power

At one level, the option for violence or nonviolence may be a matter of temperament. There is a sense in which the choice is beyond rational discussion. But it also reflects different understandings of political power. Before looking in more detail at the cultures of violence and nonviolence, therefore, we back up a little to consider the nature of political power.

Our starting point in thinking about power is set out in Chapter Five. We draw on this in this section, along with the framework set out by Gene Sharp (1973) in his book, *The Politics of Nonviolent Action: Power and Struggle.*

Power from Above

A new mayor visited villagers, asking them what the government could do to help them. Everywhere he went, the people's reply seemed like a memorised formula:

> Mr Mayor, we are only peasants. You know what is best for us. We do not know what to say. We depend on your goodness, kindness and mercy.

He had really to press the villagers to get any concrete suggestions. Their initial and spontaneous response was that it was up to him to decide. *He* was the one with the power. Power came from above. By becoming mayor, he had assumed power. They were simply dependent on his support.

The Philippines equivalent to 'power corrupts' is more picturesque:

> Look at the fly. It has forgotten that it is a fly because it is perched on a water-buffalo. It now behaves like a water-buffalo.

This is how people describe their peers who act as the 'bully boys' of those in power. They throw their weight about to prove their power over those who were their equals. Power comes from above and a few favoured ones below get a share in the power. They keep this share by demonstrating unquestioning loyalty to those at the top.

This power from above is seen as concentrated, self-perpetuating, and durable. As the common saying goes, 'All power corrupts and absolute power corrupts absolutely'. The power holder clings on to power at all costs. During the time of Marcos a favourite joke among the people ran like this:

> Jesus Christ held an audience with the top leaders of several countries. John F Kennedy came forward and Jesus Christ stood up to greet him. Brezhnev approached and the Lord Jesus also stood up. Several other Presidents and Prime Ministers took their turn and Christ got up from his throne to greet each one. Finally, President Marcos stepped forward, but Jesus shook his hands sitting down. St Peter, who watched the proceedings, bent down and whispered, 'Master, why didn't you stand up?' Christ answered, 'You can't risk the throne with this man. He will never abandon it if once he gets hold of it!'

In Marcos' inauguration as President, an anthem from Handel's Messiah was sung as the background music: 'And he shall reign for ever and ever.'

According to this view of political power, there are three ways to check the ruler's abuse of power. The first is his/her voluntary self-restraint. The institutional Church has a role to play in this. Its mission is to befriend the ruler and provide him/her with spiritual direction. Through guided reflection, the ruler is asked to meditate on Christ's exercise of his kingship and encouraged to follow the examples of ideal Christian sovereigns. This should help the ruler learn to use but not abuse his/her power. A succession of senior priests thus acted as President Marcos' confessor. In his case, the strategy did not work.

The second method is through constitutional checks and balances. The threat of elections or impeachment modifies abuse of power, or the power itself is limited through the separation of executive, legislative and judiciary powers. Faced with an absolute ruler who re-writes the constitution to suit him/herself and uses the army to enforce his/her power, this method also fails.

The last resort is violence. Opposition groups within the state machinery launch a *coup d'etat,* or those outside begin a guerilla war. If power comes from the top, then the top must be attacked. If it is concentrated and self-perpetuating, then it can only be overcome by a superior use of force. This is the zero-sum view of power taken to an extreme. If the ruler and his/her henchpersons 'have' all the power, then the only way of gaining power is to destroy them, and to 'seize' the power for oneself. But power, as we have seen, also comes from below. What are the implications of this for political strategies?

Power from Below

During election campaigns in the Philippines, the candidates for political office deliver set-piece speeches:

> Sovereign people, I am here to implore your support. My fate is on the tip of the pen which you hold in the power of your hands. If you write my name on the ballot, you can make me your humble servant. Driven by the desire to serve you, I am asking you to vote for me.

The view that power comes from below sees the government as dependent on the people's goodwill, decisions and support. Power is not something 'out there', an object that people can get hold of. It is a property of the relationship between the government and its citizens. The power of those at the top is dependent on the response of those below. Like the teacher needing her students' attention and co-operation, so people in positions of political power require their citizens' compliance. Many institutions sustain the political structure, illustrating all of the three dimensions of power (see Chapter Five). People's choices are far from altogether free. But still, their consent is *necessary*. Power is not self-perpetuating. It does not 'belong' to the government in isolation, but depends on the co-operation or collusion of different sectors of society. Without this sustaining compliance from below, political power cannot continue. And that compliance may or *may not* be given. In this view, political power can therefore be broken simply by the withdrawal of support.

The dependence of supposedly 'absolute' rulers is visible in a number of ways. Military abuses continue unchecked because dictators rely on the support of the military establishment. Top-ranking officers are showered with privileges and special favours to ensure their loyalty. The strong military the dictator needs to rule may too easily turn into his/her chief threat. Patronage keeps the business sector, the Church and the bureaucracy sweet as they see the dictator promotes their interests or fear the people's uprising that might be the alternative. The obedience of the people is never complete. James Scott (1985), in his study of the 'weapons of the weak', points out the persistence of peasants' resistance to their rulers. This appears in foot-dragging, petty pilfering, evasion, arson, sabotage, and ridiculing their rulers behind their backs. But these actions are usually hidden, sporadic and unorganised. It is relatively rare that their rumbling dissatisfaction erupts into organised rebellion. As long as the majority of the population renders at least formal compliance, the established order stands firm.

There are many ways in which people's dissatisfaction can be contained. One is to allow sufficient benefits to 'trickle down' that a significant number of people feel they have some stake in the system. This is particularly effective if different sectors of society are made to compete against one another for limited resources, rather than unite against the government. Holding constant negotiations for piecemeal reforms is another strategy often successful in dividing the opposition. Absence of a credible opposition may encourage people to privatise their interests. They withdraw from collective activity into protecting themselves and their families, trying to ensure that they, at least, will not be the ones to go under. Citizens may also simply be worn down into hopelessness or apathy by their government's war of attrition against them.

In authoritarian or totalitarian states, people also give consent because they are afraid. Civilian informers are found in every sector of society, even among church personnel. People fear that their neighbours could be informers making reports to Party authorities. Advancement comes through toeing the Party line. In Chile in the 1970s and 1980s, thousands of people judged subversive were summarily executed by Government-backed death squads. The sanctions enforcing 'consent' may be very high. But those sanctions themselves depend on the co-operation of at least some of the people. The ruler has only two hands, two feet, two eyes, two ears, one mouth – s/he cannot maintain coercive rule on his/her own.

Political power, then, is dependent on the people's willing or unwilling consent. If this is withdrawn, the leader's power dissolves. If power belongs to the relationship between ruler and ruled, then non-co-operation is the way to undermine it. Gene Sharp (1973:63) describes how this can happen:

> People do not always do what they are told to do, and sometimes they do things which have been forbidden them. Subjects may disobey laws they reject. Workers may halt work, which may paralyse the economy. The bureaucracy may refuse to carry out instructions.

Soldiers and police may become lax in inflicting repression, they may even mutiny. When all these events happen simultaneously, the man who has been 'ruler' becomes just another man. Political power disintegrates when the people withdraw their obedience and support.

The view of power from above logically leads to the conclusion that when self-restraint and constitutional provisions fail to curb the abuse of power, violent force is the only effective strategy for radical change. But the understanding of power from below shows that the powerful persons on top of the pinnacle of command are dependent on the obedience and co-operation of a multitude of institutions and individuals. By cutting off the sources of power from below, the powerful may be rendered powerless.

The Culture of Violence

The Latin American priests who pointed out the violence in society's structures did not leave it at that. They went on to say that to condemn oppressed people for using force to liberate themselves, would be to 'commit a new injustice upon the people' (Torres, 1971:445). There was no neutral path: 'not opposing the violence of the oppressors is equivalent to provoking indirectly the legitimate violence of the oppressed' (p 446). They therefore called on the bishops to take an unequivocal stand in condemning the structural violence of the existing system and in encouraging all Christians to work for liberation. Their aim was not to idealise violence,

> … but to give a new dimension to the principle, repeatedly recognised, of the right of every unjustly oppressed community to react, even violently, against an unjust oppressor.
>
> ~ ibid: 447 ~

For the Philippines, Father Pedro Salgado (1991:49) spells out this view further:

> Church people who take up arms profess they do so by the imperative of their faith. They follow to its ultimate consequence Christ's command of love for neighbour, offering their lives to remove through armed struggle the political and economic structures that oppress them.

Since Spanish times, Salgado says, the Church hierarchy has used violence against the interests of the common people. The use of violence by Church people is therefore nothing new. The difference is in the results. While the violence of the hierarchy has been self-perpetuating:

> The armed violence of the small section of the Church, used as it is to stop injustice, ends all violence. For when justice is achieved, there is at last peace.   ~ ibid: 50 ~

The culture of violence expressed in these writings is dualistic. There are only two options, to support the violence of the existing structures, or to oppose it, by armed revolution. There is no third way. To seek mediation, or compromise, amounts to appeasement. There are three main implications of this: the logic of violence; the dualism of means and ends; and the absolute distinction between 'us' and 'them'. These are discussed in turn in the following sections.

The Logic of Violence

Lauro was a quiet and softly-spoken 16 year-old. One day he invited a friend to go fishing. On their way back, a military patrol stopped them and asked for their residence certificates. They explained that they had none, they were students at the local school. But the soldiers were not satisfied. They were suspicious of Lauro's friend because he came from another village. As Lauro tried to defend him, one of the soldiers hit Lauro in the ribs with the butt of his rifle. Lauro bent over in pain, and the soldier struck him again in the back, knocking him to the ground.

Months passed. Lauro said very little about the incident. But soon after graduating from high school, he disappeared. One night, some months later, Lauro returned. He was carrying an AK-47. He was full of revolutionary language. In his own quiet way, he talked about US-Marcos dictatorship, fascism, capitalism, imperialism .... Political education by the underground had taught him to link the poverty of his community, displaced when their land was allotted as a sugar plantation, with the military harassment. He sounded convinced of the cause. But his reason for joining the underground he admitted later to a friend. He wanted to take revenge on the soldiers.

Lauro died when he was 21. He had become a local hero. To his credit were a number of successful ambushes and a daring daylight raid on a military headquarters. It is not clear whether his commitment to the armed struggle stayed to the end. His mother said that Lauro had talked about laying down his arms and asked whether, if he did, he would be granted an amnesty. She even hoped to find a way to smuggle him out to another island. But Lauro never came down from the hills. He was killed by a land mine as he led another raid. He was afraid to surrender because he thought that the government forces would never forgive him for what he had done.

That the violence of oppressed people has its roots in the violence of the oppression they suffer is quite easy to see. In Lauro's area, military raids were part of everyday life. In extreme cases women were raped by the soldiers. But it was commonplace for men to be hit with rifle butts or kicked, for eggs and chickens to be snatched from their nests, for dogs, pigs or goats to be used as a target for 'shooting practice'. The given reason for these raids was to trace the underground forces. Some of the young men had already left for the hills, other 'barefoot' soldiers were farmers by day and armed rebels by night. But the raids also had a second purpose. They were to intimidate the villagers into withdrawing support to the guerillas.

Such raids did not make Rommel, a Regional Commander of the New People's Army, sad. They made him angry, very angry. But a part of him was also glad. The more the people suffered, the more ready they would be to take up arms. For Rommel, Lauro died a hero – he died with his boots on. His death would hasten the revolution. For every one fallen Lauro, ten others would rise up and take his place. And the statistics bear this out. in 1968 there were less than a hundred armed members of the New People's Army. When Marcos was deposed in 1986, the government said that the NPA had become an armed force 20,000 strong. But the military had also grown. The government forces of 60,000 in 1972 had expanded to 300,000 in 1986.

What then are we to make of Salgado's assertion that 'armed violence … used … to stop injustice, ends all violence'? This indicates the first dualism that we noted above, as it assumes a complete reversal in the logic of violence, depending on who is responsible. On the one hand, violence is seen to breed violence, as the violence of unjust structures brings out the violence of the revolutionary forces. On the other hand, however, the *just* violence of the revolutionary forces is believed to bring peace. The two sides are seen as absolutely different from one another. But does this hope reflect reality?

If the underground forces had stayed away from his village, Lauro might still be alive. In villages where there was no active armed group, there were also no military outposts. Lauro and his classmate would not have been stopped and beaten up. The villagers were the target not only of the violence of the military, but also of the underground. Some genuinely supported the guerillas' cause, but others supplied their needs simply out of fear. A band of hungry young men with guns is not easily turned away. People judged to violate 'revolutionary discipline' could be punished severely, even killed. Anyone believed to be an informer would almost certainly be executed. The local label for an informer was *demonyo,* demon.

John Pilger's grim report from Cambodia similarly suggests the picture is not as clear-cut as Salgado presents it (BBC, 25.4.93). A doctor remarked that Cambodia was being demined 'one leg at a time'. The mines laid by the Khmer Rouge, under instruction from British officers, were still killing civilians, regardless of the fact that peace talks were at last underway. As the land retains the marks of violence, so also do the people.

In practice, it has proved very difficult to de-mobilise combatants of armed struggle. Despite all the special provisions that were made for them, United States soldiers who had served in Vietnam found it very difficult to return to civilian life. They had been changed by the brutality they had gone through. Similarly, the wounds of people who have seen friends and family butchered do not simply heal with the formal ceasing of hostilities. Resentments can smoulder on to be re-ignited in a later struggle. Declaration of amnesties for laying down of arms never lead to the full recovery of all weapons. Many remain in the community, all too ready to hand if tempers fray or new divisions arise. The Lebanon provides just one of many examples of countries now split into feuding factions each with their rival militia.

The Dualism of Means and Ends

Violence is rarely seen as a good thing in itself. It is usually seen as an undesirable but necessary means to a justified end. The dualism here is the dualism of means and ends. The end envisaged by liberation struggles is the establishment of a new society. Its characteristics are often rather vague. The impulse to revolution comes from dissatisfaction with what is, rather than a clear vision of what will be. They seek justice, against present injustice. National sovereignty, against present subordination to outsiders. Meaningful participation for the people, against domination by an elite. Truth and transparency, against the lies and deceit of corrupt governments. And finally, they seek peace, against the present violence.

In this dualism between means and ends, the culture of violence is founded in a very basic contradiction. This is located in its view of political power. As noted above, the strategy of armed struggle sees political power as coming from above. The structure of armed forces reflects this: they too are organised in a top-down way. Yet the society that is envisaged is one in which the people themselves will be empowered, where, that is, political power will come from below. This section explores the implications of this contradiction.

One day, a MuCARD group member came to see Romy. 'Who,' she asked, 'really is Ricardo? Is he one of you?' The question took Romy by surprise. Ricardo was one of MuCARD's longest serving staff. Andrea went on to explain:

'Ricardo sent my husband a note. He made three requests: send three or four members of the village to a seminar, bring some food provisions and cash donations for the movement. But what troubles me is what he said at the end of the letter. Burn this after reading it. And don't tell Romy about this.'

Armed struggle is a military operation. Guerilla forces, just like any other army, must have secrets. Their success depends on the element of surprise. Opposing forces send spies to try to discover each other's secrets. The fewer people who know, the safer it is. Absolute obedience is required. Soldiers are trained to obey first, and question later. Their judgement is not required. Their duty is to do as they are told. The danger of this became clear in the awful chorus of German soldiers charged with 'crimes against humanity' after World War II. Almost all made a single defence of what they had done: they were only obeying orders. Military planning is not done democratically. There is an inner core within a core group which controls the organisation and its operations. Plans are made by an elite few, and passed down to the many.

This tendency can spill over into non-military operations also. The Party must not be questioned, it is always right. When the Communist Party of the Philippines decided to boycott the Marcos-Aquino election, it was in complete disregard of the sentiments of majority of the people who wanted to participate. Even in a democratic system, ordinary members may vote for people of whom they know nothing, because that is the instruction passed down the Party line. Dissenters are challenged: 'Are you pro-Party, or pro-people?'

The dualism of ends and means also shows itself in the politics of language. A video of a massacre put all the blame squarely on the government side. The speaker hammered the message home. But a member of the audience who had actually been present, objected. He did not condone the military's action, but pointed out that some of the marchers had seemed deliberately to provoke the soldiers to use their guns. After the meeting the speaker went to the objector and said, 'I am involved in propaganda. If I paint the picture 51 % against 49 %, I will never convince others to join my cause. I have to portray the truth 80 % against 20 % in my favour'.

As is often pointed out, one group's terrorists are another's freedom-fighters. 'Truth is the first casualty in war' is a common saying. Propaganda takes over from observational reporting. What was in shades of grey is presented as though it were black and white. To boost morale, victories are blown up larger, news of defeats suppressed. Atrocities by the other side are exaggerated, those of one's own side go unreported. Taken a step further, one side may even deliberately provoke the other into abusive behaviour, in order to gain more support for itself. The end justifies the means. The propaganda of the establishment has to be countered. If people are to risk their lives, they must be convinced of the cause. In the process, 'the enemy' becomes less than human. Perhaps even more alarmingly, as Rommel's response to the raids and Lauro's death indicates, 'the people' become less important than 'the cause'.

What are the implications of this for the kind of society that is formed if the struggle succeeds? Can the active, participatory democracy that revolutionaries envisage be brought about by a strategy that depends on blind obedience for its success? We know how political parties in so-called democratic societies also 'economise' on truth. This shows the difficulty of achieving participation that genuinely represents people's interests, even in societies with a long history of 'democracy'. Will it help people participate maturely in the political process, if they are taught in the struggle to obey without question? Will the new elite learn to listen to their people when they have spent many years not consulting, but simply telling people what to do, and massaging the 'truth' to fit their interests? Will openness and accountability to the people replace the instrumental use of propaganda? Will army commanders who have known near absolute authority be able to let hold of power to allow others, better qualified to establish a civilian government, to take their place?

Us against Them

The world portrayed in the culture of violence is a world of black and white; good against evil; righteousness against injustice; us against them. The humanity of the other side gets lost. They become either sub-human – brutes, barbarians – or super-human – demons or monsters. Only the uniform is seen, not the person inside it. There is no common ground.

As the following stories show, in practice this distinction between 'us' (good) and 'them' (evil) is much less clear

> Edna was a card-carrying member of the Communist Party of the Philippines. Her work with an NGO had brought her into direct contact with the sufferings of the poor. She was fully committed to

revolutionary armed struggle, seeing no other way to combat the structural violence of the state. But her brother was quite different. He was often drunk and violent at home, and sometimes screamed threats to inform on NPA sympathisers. The NPA decided he should be killed. As member of the Communist Party's regional committee, Edna heard about the decision. She negotiated that her brother be given three months grace to reform.

Four weeks later, Edna was informed that her brother was dead. He had been shot 38 times with his hands tied behind his back. Holding her brother's body, Edna cried out: 'Why did they kill him like this? The three months are not over. They are no better than the government soldiers.'

★ ★ ★

Ben got a lucky break to work for three years in the Middle East. The family saved all his earnings and when he returned they were able to make a down payment for a passenger jeep. When it was paid off, they got a second loan to buy another. While Ben drove one jeep, a neighbour's son drove the other. As far as possible, they did all the maintenance themselves. Some months later, they decided to buy a third jeep. Another neighbour's son had learned how to drive.

Ben and his wife seemed to be doing well. But when they had got the three jeeps, they attracted the attention of the local underground forces. The guerillas began to demand free transport at any time of the day or night. They also called regularly to extort protection money. The family's income began to get tight. Ben went to the patrol and explained that he could no longer pay his monthly 'contribution'. He thought the guerillas would understand. But one day they received a warning that their son would be kidnapped if they did not keep up the payments. There seemed to be no option. Ben and his wife closed down the business they had struggled to set up. They took their family and left the town. They have never been back.

The dualism of drawing an absolute division between the two sides distorts as it caricatures each of the opposing camps. The example of Al shows that the forces of the state may be divided amongst themselves. The summary 'justice' meted out on Edna's brother does not seem to square with the revolutionaries' claims to stand against the brutality and human rights violations of the State. Financing their operations through protection rackets sits uneasily with the underground group's opposition to exploitation. The dualism of means and ends can lead the revolutionary forces also to perpetrate injustice, in the name of the greater good.

This dualism applies initially towards the opposition. But it may also arise in relation to those who have the same goals, but disagree on the means. The hostility between factions committed to different revolutionary alternatives is often very bitter. Those who take a different view are condemned as 'deviationists', 'reformists', 'revisionists'. They are seen as traitors to the vision of ideological purity. Nonviolent activists in particular, may be seen as dangerous anti-revolutionary elements. Their right to make a different option is disputed. Those committed to violence may therefore take steps to sabotage the nonviolent strategy. There are many ways this can be done. A simple one is for a group committed to armed struggle to join a nonviolent demonstration. They then agitate to get the crowd to throw stones or abuse at the police or military. The armed forces of the state respond with violence. The people scatter, with the bankruptcy of the state confirmed, the hopelessness of nonviolent protest demonstrated, and a few more martyrs made to strengthen resolve for the cause.

Whatever one's position regarding the ethical justification of armed struggle, it is very important to question whether or not the strategy will effectively bring about the desired changes. The need for secrecy, for concentration of decision making in the hands of an elite few, the use of propaganda, the assassination of the 'enemies of the people', the conscious and willing use of force to destroy lives and property – these are not simply strategies and tactics that revolutionaries can pick up and throw away as the situation demands. The dualism of 'us' and 'them' leads into brutality, where 'the people' become a means to be exploited like any other. The use of rape as a war crime shows how the so-called 'legitimate' violence of military combat is deeply inscribed in a negative culture of masculinity, which is expressed in the instrumental disregard for women's integrity. The culture of violence is not easily discarded, once it has become established. Like all cultures, it tends to reproduce itself. The people who have shaped it find that it is shaping them in turn.

The Culture of Nonviolence

The culture of nonviolence begins with the belief that political power comes from below. It rejects dualism, holding that justice cannot be achieved through injustice. Rather than the ends justifying the means, the means should pre-figure the ends. The new society should be forged through the struggle itself, not postponed until after the battle is won. As people claim the power that is theirs, they use it to re-build society from below. The strategy thus begins from the small and immediate, and only slowly spreads outwards. It begins with the people, believing that the first and most important move is for people to change themselves.

Nonviolent mobilisation may start with initial acts of non-co-operation which are very ordinary, not radical at all. This was so in the case which launched the civil rights movement in the United States, of which Martin Luther King became the national leader. On 1 December 1955, Rosa Parks, a seamstress in her forties, was coming home after a long day. At that time in Alabama, buses were segregated. Whites sat at the front, and blacks at the back. She sat down in a seat for black people. At the next stop more whites got on. She was ordered to give up her seat to a white man. If she did, she would have to stand the rest of the way home. As Coretta Scott King (1973:126) puts it:

Rosa Parks was not in a revolutionary frame of mind. She had not planned to do what she did. Her cup had run over. As she said later, 'I was just plain tired, and my feet hurt'. So she sat there, refusing to get up.

Rosa Parks was arrested. Her bail was paid by someone already involved in civil rights activities. Coretta Scott King goes on:

Suddenly [the activist] also had had enough; suddenly, it seemed, almost every Negro in Montgomery had had enough. It was spontaneous combustion. Phones began ringing all over the Negro section of the city. The Women's Political Council suggested a one-day boycott of the buses.   ~ ibid ~

The bus boycott in Montgomery, Alabama, went on for over a year. At the end of that time, the Supreme Court ruled that buses in Alabama should be desegregated. Black people stayed faithful to the boycott, even though for some it meant a daily walk of twelve miles to and from their work. During that time Martin Luther King was arrested, and he and many others were threatened with violence. Some people were beaten up, others shot, churches and homes were bombed. But the Freedom movement remained committed to nonviolence. As Coretta Scott King (p 163) puts it:

Black people had found in nonviolent, direct action a militant method that avoided violence but achieved dramatic confrontation, which electrified and educated the whole nation.

Political non-co-operation may begin with the 'everyday acts of resistance' described by James Scott. But to be effective it must build on and politicise these. Bus boycotts had been tried before, and they had failed. Rosa Parks could easily have become just one more black person punished for an isolated act of defiance. The Freedom Movement was born because there was the will and the organisation to turn her individual act into a collective action. The time was clearly right for the Montgomery boycott. It was also, without doubt, strengthened by the vision and charisma of Martin Luther King. But he could have done nothing without the people's *organised, active* support. It was their courage, their discipline, their commitment, their self-sacrifice, that carried the movement through. There is nothing passive about nonviolence. It cannot succeed without effective organisation and strategy. But most crucially it cannot, unlike other kinds of power, persist unless it has people's wholehearted support.

This is the strength of nonviolence, but it is also its weakness. The people are rarely wholehearted. The kind of activism that nonviolence requires is difficult to sustain. It may be achieved in times of crisis, but it can quickly fall away if the situation eases. As new structures become established, the old patterns of passivity are likely to re-emerge. The following example from the Philippines makes this clear.

Non-violence can bring down, but can it build up?

'What the armed struggle failed to do in 14 years, active nonviolence accomplished in fourteen days.' There is some truth and some falsity in this statement. It is accurate in stating that the New People's Army was unable to oust President Marcos with its 50 mm machine guns, grenade launchers, AK-47s, M-16 armalites and other weapons of war. But it is a gross exaggeration to claim that the nonviolent struggle took only 14 days.

The 'revolution' of Epifanio delos Santos Avenue (EDSA) did not happen in a vacuum. Mass demonstrations had been happening for years. NGOs had been waging the 'parliament of the streets' even before the declaration of Martial Law. The funeral in 1983 of Ninoy Aquino became a mass rally which millions joined. He was returning to the Philippines from self-exile in the United States. He was tipped to be a sure winner against Marcos, if an election were held. But as Ninoy Aquino stepped down from the plane under full military escort, he was murdered. If such a prominent person enjoying the friendship of the US government was not safe from the brutality of the regime, then who was? The massive cover-up which followed stripped the government of any vestige of legitimacy. Opposition against Marcos erupted in all sectors of the population. When Marcos finally yielded to pressures to hold an election, Ninoy's wife, Cory Aquino, agreed to become a unity candidate for the opposition. Her initial unwillingness was overcome by a petition of a million signatures asking her to stand. These had been collected within only a few weeks. Despite the Communist Party's boycott, the people went out to vote.

The results showed Marcos had won, but Cory Aquino accused him of massive ballot rigging. Her call to boycott the national papers published by the cronies of Marcos, sent their sales cascading downwards within a few days. General strikes and non-payment of taxes were planned. As Cory campaigned around the country for massive civil disobedience, a *coup* against Marcos was discovered. When the 'rebel' soldiers were surrounded by Marcos' forces at Camp Crame, the citizens responded by defending the camp with their bodies. The tanks turned back. The pilots refused to drop their bombs. The soldiers became the allies of the people. The differences among the opposition groups were shelved as they confronted a common enemy. They all knew the one thing they did not want: Marcos. The simultaneous withdrawal of support by multitudes of individuals, groups and institutions reduced the most powerful ruler of the Philippines into an ordinary man in three days.

But soon after the disappearance of the 'common enemy', the 'rainbow' coalition started to crack. Cory's election promises of radical changes in the ownership of land and repudiation of foreign debt were broken. In the re-organisation of the new administration, she had to repay the different groups which supported her challenge against Marcos. The rich and powerful few proved to be more influential than the many poor. Most of the key government posts were given to the members of the elite. The landlords, industrialists and bankers had the money and organisation to lobby for their interests, while the vast majority of the people neither had the funds nor the cohesion to exert a strong influence on the policies of the 'revolutionary' government.

A year later national elections were held to mark the end of the 'revolutionary' government and the restoration of democracy. The President lost her power to rule the country by decree. Legislative power was given back to the House of Congress and Senate. But traditional politicians once more dominated the 'ownership' of elective posts. Radical changes through legislation became impossible. Ironically, it was the power of the ballot that put the members of the elite into power. 'People power' overthrew a dictator, but it could not build a new society.

But did 'people power' really fail in its second challenge? It did not. The failure was more fundamental. It did not exist! As already noted, the population may be divided horizontally according to income. But vertical alignments cut across this. There is no automatic solidarity amongst either the non-poor or the poor. Poverty does not automatically generate a class identity. People's awareness of their power was sufficient for them to rally in the crisis. But when the crisis passed, they lapsed back into consenting to the old patterns of relationship. The poor were split. They voted in different ways according to ethnic origin, religious affiliation and/or patron-client relationships. Or they sold their votes for a favour or a price to get at least some benefit from the elections. The solidarity of non-poor with poor in opposition to Marcos similarly quickly fizzled out once Marcos was removed. It had no solid base. It was simply an instrumental alliance. In the elections, the wealthy simply bought their way back into power. 'People power' to rebuild a country had not failed. It had not been tried.

The same is true at the international level. With the world economy so interdependent, the power of nonviolent action, such as political isola-tion or economic sanctions, is potentially very great. But governments do not seem willing or able to act together to bring significant pressure to bear on aggressors. In the UK, arms continued to be sold to Iraq despite warnings to the government from high level military advisors. The atrocities in Bosnia Herzegovina were allowed to continue without protest, until the military option seemed the only one possible. President Bush and his military commanders could pose as heroes in the 'swift and surgical' bombing of Iraq. But they left behind them, as always, the rubble of ordinary people's lives, who had never sought a place in the conflict.

Nonviolence and Vulnerability

The time and effort involved in building solidarity to achieve change is one aspect of the difficulty of sustaining the nonviolent option. Another is more immediate. The irony of nonviolence is that in rejecting the dualism of the violence of state and revolutionary movements, it becomes a target for both. Before EDSA, in the battle against Marcos under Martial Law, the choice for active nonviolence became more and more difficult to make. So much blood had been shed and brutality inflicted that anger and hatred filled the air. In such an atmosphere any talk about nonviolent action seemed futile. The self-discipline, education and organisation necessary to make nonviolent action effective were almost impossible to achieve in such a situation. To the regime, community organisers were subversives, and could be the target of summary execution. For those committed to armed struggle, nonviolent activists seemed 'dangerous liberals' and anti-revolutionary. Their small projects promised to fill the bellies of the people and so to blunt their hunger for revolution. Their nonviolent stance might lessen the people's readiness to take up arms. They must be silenced. It did not seem possible to transform the social structures of society through nonviolent action, nor to prevent a bloody civil war from happening. From a pragmatic person's point of view, the efforts were doomed to failure. It felt like hanging on to a sinking ship hoping that somehow it would stay afloat.

Holding a gun can give a person a sense of power. People have to listen or take the risk of being shot. By comparison, taking a stand for nonviolence means to accept powerlessness. It is to make an appeal, which may be rejected, as well as accepted. Making the option for non-violence does not mean that violence will not be used against you.

Beyond Dualism

The culture of nonviolence strives towards unity, rather than dualism. This is seen most powerfully in the life of Mahatma Gandhi, who first popularised nonviolence as a strategy for political opposition. For Gandhi, this was the inevitable outcome of his religious search for Truth. The personal was inescapably political. Religion could not be divorced from politics. Nonviolence, *ahimsa,* is a long established principle within Hindu thought. It is based on the idea of the unity of all life, so that one should treat all creatures with compassion and generosity. Where violence sees dualism and opposition, nonviolence sees oneness and interdependence. Many things flow from this. Gandhi was a strict vegetarian, believing that to kill animals for food was a form of violence. Beyond this, he sought to purify himself by restraining the passions for food, sex, and material comfort. He aimed always for a life of greater simplicity and self-reliance. This was itself revolutionary within the Hindu context, as caste rules of purity and pollution required that the 'lower' castes did the dirty work of the 'higher'.

From very early in his career, Gandhi used his professional skills as a lawyer to represent the interests of the poorest members of the Indian community. This began in South Africa, with the indentured labourers who were virtually slaves, and continued with numerous oppressed groups when he returned to India. He also encouraged the people themselves to take nonviolent action to oppose injustice. The term given to this movement was *Satyagraha,* truth-strength. It involved political education, so that the people should see officials not as their masters, but as the servants of the people, who paid their salaries through taxes. At a national level, justice required self-rule (*swaraj*) to free Indians from their subordinate status within the British empire. *Satyagraha* methods included strikes, boycotts, prayer, fasting and civil disobedience.

Some of these tactics are clearly oppositional, but this is belied by the spirit in which they were undertaken. For Gandhi, civility was a vital element of *satyagraha,* though it was also the most difficult for people to develop. Civility meant not just verbal politeness, 'but an inborn gentleness and desire to do the opponent good' (Gandhi, 1983:364). The oneness of all life did not stop with the opposition. On the contrary, Gandhi strove to have good personal relations even with those whom he opposed politically. Personal hostility would violate the ethic of *ahimsa.* Where possible, conciliation should be sought. Compromise was a consequence of the pursuit of Truth, which for Gandhi was synonymous with Love. It was the fulfilment, not a breach of principle.

For Martin Luther King, the framework for nonviolence was the Christian rather than the Hindu tradition. As he drew great inspiration from Gandhi, however, there are many points in common. For Martin Luther King also, nonviolence began at the personal level. It was only later that he saw it as a strategy for action at the community and ultimately international level. Like violence, nonviolence could also arouse hatred (King, 1977:152). But for those who practised it, nonviolence brought them new self-respect and made them newly aware of their resources of strength and courage. Also, in stirring the conscience of the oppressor, it made reconciliation become a reality.

The strength of nonviolence is in its power to generate support in society more widely. As we have seen above, the tendency of violence is towards exclusivity. Even those who share the same goals may be identified as enemies if they disagree on the means. Nonviolence, on the other hand, is inclusive. Instead of hardening the opposition, it may soften their hearts. If Ninoy Aquino had sought to fight Marcos with the gun, his death would not have aroused such tremendous sympathy. Soldiers approached as people, offered food and drink rather than stones and curses, are more likely to consider the arguments of the opposition. The women in the Greenham Common Peace Camp recognised this as they sang: 'Nuclear bombs kill policemen too!' This is the insight of the old fable of the wind and the sun.

> The wind and the sun had a competition: who could get the man to take off his cloak? The wind blew and blew, cold and strong, but the man only pulled his cloak around him more tightly. Seeing the wind wear himself out with puffing, the sun asked if he could take a turn. Softly and warmly, the sun shone on the man. His hunched shoulders eased, his tensed body relaxed. After a little while, he undid his cloak and laid it on one side, to enjoy the warmth of the sun more fully.

Like Gandhi, Martin Luther King saw the foundation of nonviolence as love. The Freedom movement called for justice for white as well as black people. Loving one's enemies meant realising that the evil they did never expressed all that they were. There was some evil in the best and some good in the worst people (*ibid*: 49). Hatred just begets more hatred. The aim of love is to transform the enemy into a friend, in order that both might be enabled more fully to become the children of God. Through experience, rather than theory, Martin Luther King came to see unearned sufferings as redemptive. They could be transformed into a creative force for good. It was in struggling for justice that he experienced more powerfully the reality of a personal God by his side.

Mahatma Gandhi and Martin Luther King are inspirational figures in the movement for nonviolence. But they are also testimonies to its futility. Both suffered a violent death. Gandhi's death meant that his ideals played only a small part in the new India that he had helped to bring independence. The Gandhian tradition continues, but it has never been dominant in the formation of national policy. Martin Luther King, the day before he died, said he had no more fear. God had led him to the mountain-top, and he had seen the promised land. He foresaw that he would not enter it with his people. Black people in the United States are still waiting for the day when that land will be theirs.

The Way of the Cross

The plurality of religious tradition means that both violence and nonviolence can be justified by appeal to the Bible. For the writers of many psalms, the Lord's reward to the righteous would include the physical destruction of their enemies. The land promised to the Children of Israel was already inhabited, the Israelites took it by force. They did this not only in the name of God, but actually saw the violence as itself the work of God:

> Know therefore this day that he who goes over before you as a devouring fire is the Lord your God; he will destroy them and subdue them before you; so you shall drive them out, and make them perish quickly, as the Lord has promised you. ~ Deuteronomy 9: 3 ~

A common Christian response to this is that Jesus radically revised earlier Jewish teaching. Where the law had taught 'an eye for an eye and a tooth for a tooth', he proposed a new ethic: 'If anyone strikes you on the right cheek, turn to him the other also; and if any one would sue you and take your coat, let him have your cloak as well' (Matthew 5: 39-40). A few Christian 'Peace Churches', such as the Quakers and Mennonites, have taken this seriously and given a consistent witness for non-violence despite the persecution it has brought them. It has to be recognised, however, that Christian tradition has largely failed to live out this orientation. The term 'holy war' is now predominantly identified with the Islamic *jihad*. But it is just as much a part of the Christian heritage (see O'Brien, 1993). The crusaders wore the cross as their battledress. In ordinary life, times of danger, suffering, uncertainty and closeness to death make people turn to prayer. Generation after generation of Christians have taken up arms in the conviction that 'God is on our side'. Neither violence nor nonviolence is the monopoly of any particular religion. Hindu, Muslim, Buddhist, Jewish and Christian faiths, all have been used in incitement to take up arms. But all also contain an alternative vision, a vision of oneness and harmony, of a new humanity, restored to one another through their union with the divine.

In the cleansing of the temple, Jesus showed his capacity for righteous anger and destructive action. In John's gospel Jesus is described as using a whip to drive out the animal traders, and pouring out the coins of the money-changers and overturning their tables. There is no doubt about Jesus' capacity to feel with great passion. In Mark's gospel, this episode figures as a turning point, when the religious authorities began to seek ways to destroy Jesus.

It is in the passion of Christ, his *undergoing* of suffering and humiliation, that the option for nonviolence is made most clear in Christianity. In human terms, Christ failed in his mission. He could not convince the leaders and the people of Israel that the liberation he wanted to bring about was something other than the fulfilment of an earthly Davidic kingdom. He knew of the promised Messiah. But he did not choose to join or lead the armed struggle that the Zealots were planning to liberate Israel from the Romans. Instead he submitted himself as an ordinary person needing repentance, going to be baptised by John. After the feeding of the five thousand, Jesus withdrew from the crowds planning to make him king (John 6:15). Liberation was not a question of the seizure of economic and political power. For the Reign of God to be established, people needed to be freed from their enslavement to the 'mammon' of wealth, status and the abuse of power. The kingdom which he saw was a kingdom of reversals, where the last would be first, love would replace force, and leadership would be shown in service.

The vulnerability of Christ's witness is starkly clear in the figure of the cross. Stripped and beaten, Jesus was reduced to his essential humanness, pinned to a piece of wood, denied even the courtesy of privacy in death. He hung there as an image of human weakness, and of the power of the state to determine life and death. Just a little earlier, Jesus had spoken as a prophet, that whoever followed him was his mother and brothers. On the cross he speaks simply as an earthly son, commending his mother Mary to his friend's care. Jesus had asked to be delivered, perhaps had even hoped that at the last moment God would intervene. But at the same time he had freely surrendered himself to God's will. He was silent, refusing even to defend himself. Amidst the hopelessness and brutality, he believed himself in the hands of God.

Throughout his ministry, Christ showed a capacity to transcend the dualistic categories that were current in his society. This is perhaps clearest in one of his most famous sayings: 'Love your enemies and pray for those who persecute you.' In his words and actions, that love was incarnate. Even as he was arrested in the Garden of Gethsemane, Jesus rebuked his followers for trying to resist with violence, and healed his assailant whose ear had been cut off. Faced with the woman caught in adultery, Jesus rejected the conventional condemnations, challenging anyone who was without sin to cast the first stone. He rejected also opposition along ethnic lines, mixing with people from Samaria, and healing the centurion's servant. The power of nonviolence to transform the opposition is also indicated. It is no coincidence that it was a Roman soldier, standing at the foot of the cross, who proclaimed: 'Truly, this man was God's Son!' (Matthew 27: 54).

It is in John's gospel that the potential for mystical union is most clearly explored. The vine and its branches are used as an image of Christ and his followers, along with the promise of unity brought by love. It is in the passage immediately following this that Jesus makes his statement of the ultimate test of love: 'No one has greater love than this, to lay down one's life for one's friends' (John 15: 13).

If the cross is the most powerful image of the vulnerability of non-violence, it is also the promise of an alternative world. The hope of Christianity is that the cross was not the end, but the means for resurrection. Somehow, after his death, Jesus' presence re-entered and invigorated his broken and frightened disciples. His resurrection was experienced in their healing. Just like Jesus in his earthly life, the risen Christ met each of them at their point of need. To Thomas he offered his wounds, that he might believe. To Peter he asked three times, 'Do you love me?' In answering three times that he did, Peter was able to reclaim the reality of his commitment to Christ, and put behind him his three-fold denial.

The resurrection is mystery, it is something we cannot fully understand. In small ways we see it is true: that seeds have to be buried if they are to bear fruit; that crises and disasters in human lives can lead to a new life. Jesus of Nazareth was one of many prophets of his day, one of many people crucified in first century Palestine. And yet his death has made the world a different place. In succeeding generations, the witness of Christ has been an inspiration for many to work towards the kingdom of his vision. Where one died, many have found new life. This is the power and the hope of nonviolence: to soften, to renew, to make the unbelievable happen.

Conclusion

The challenge to live the paradox of the Cross still remains today.

To love and defend justice but become the victims of injustice;
To love and defend freedom but end up in prison;
To love and defend life but be deprived of it;
To love and defend nonviolence but become the victims of violence;
To love and build a better world but be separated from it too soon;
To accept defeat and failure because they are the greatest triumph and witness that our true happiness is not tied up with earthly possessions.

For nonviolent activists, the vision of justice, truth, freedom and peace are worth dying for, but not worth killing for. The culture of violence will not transcend violence, but only generate more killing and brutality. If the present oppressors are defeated, they will try to regain what they have lost through the same means. In spite of its rhetoric, armed struggle in practice seems to uphold the same values as the present oppressive social structures. The likely prospect of armed revolution is that the oppressed of today will be the oppressors of tomorrow. A genuine alternative needs to reach beyond this dualism. The tendency to draw up oppositional categories needs to be resisted. To see the world this way is to settle for half-truths, like the propaganda of war. The culture of nonviolence steps aside from the categories of 'us' and 'them'. It seeks the common humanity in both sides. It believes that only as we recognise and call God out in one another, can we restore in society the fractured image of the divine.

Epilogue

Coming to write an epilogue is hard. There is a wish to have the book go, to be finished with it, to move on. But there is also a sense in which it has become an old friend. We have fought with it, fought over it, been frustrated and excited by it. In one way it can never be finished. It has been a part of our lives the past three years.

We stated in the Preface that the book did not represent a point of arrival. As we draw it to a close, we feel this all the more strongly. There are parts that we wish we could take back and write over again. There are others in which we know we have still only glimpsed what we would like to say. The stories reflect the people we have known and the ways we have come. Much of the analysis challenges us to move beyond where we now are.

This tension between past, present and future is an integral part of doing theology and development. Chief Openg of the Bukidnons, an indigenous group of the Philippines, expressed it in this way:

> We are like the fresh waters of the Pulangi river which come from the mountains and flow down to meet the salty waters of the sea. Life moves on. We need to sift our traditions carefully, to gather what has served us well in the past and will serve us well in the future. Some of what has been precious to us we will also have to let go. A still water is a dead water. Change is a condition of life. We need also to sift through the ways of living of others outside our own traditions. We cannot go back to the way we were.

Unlike the Presidential Assistance for National Minorities, the Bukidnons did not romanticise their traditions. They did not want their community to become a living museum, a show piece to attract the tourists. They welcomed the flow of life that carried them forward. They did not wish to lose their identity, and knew that elements of their tradition would always form a part of who they were. But even what they took along with them would be open to change. The colour of the sand and stones they sifted out would look different in the new waters to which they travelled. Their culture would grow and develop as they entered into dialogue with others.

Through writing this book we have experienced something of this process of sifting out and moving on. The four paradigms that we have presented are not just parts of a historical sequence, but remain as present options. Within each of them, and between them, there is also a dynamic. Theory may always be challenged by practice, and experience re-shaped by new ideas. Doing theology may enrich our understanding of development, and doing development encourage us to quarry deeper our theology.

The overall theme that has emerged through writing this book is the search for wholeness. This means overcoming the dualisms and dichotomies between rich and poor, material and spiritual, North and South, private and public, individual and collective, personal and structural, religion and politics, men and women, humans and other creatures and text and context. The way to achieve this is not by denying the tensions and conflicts that exist, but to struggle towards reconciliation.

Pursuit of wholeness through reconciliation can never be a gift from one to another. It is a process in which everyone must participate. In our relationships with one another as poor and non-poor in all the many dimensions of poverty, the necessary changes are both personal and structural. Both poor and non-poor need to denounce exploitation, confront in themselves their complicity in oppression and begin to live alternative values and attitudes in their own behaviour. The establishment of new structures and relationships founded in justice is a joint venture, not only between the poor and non-poor in solidarity, but also of humans in sympathy with the rest of creation.

To achieve trust and unity across real difference is an ongoing struggle. Nor do the boundaries that mark people off from one another form an automatic basis for solidarity amongst those on each side. Within and among persons, as well as in politics, there is need for a 'permanent revolution' so that old patterns of distance and domination do not creep up upon us once more. Perhaps the key challenge for us in doing theology and development is to move beyond a sense of self and other in opposition, and to discover that in relationship we are each genuinely more than we are alone.

Although the way may seem difficult, we travel in the assurance that the reign of justice is God's promise. This vision gives us a guide not just to where we are going but also to the means we should choose to take us there. The ultimate context of our pursuit of wholeness together is our belonging to one another in the family of God. We close the book, therefore, with a vision to inspire us, of the new realm of justice set out by the prophet Isaiah:

For I am about to create new heavens
     and a new earth;
the former things shall not be remembered
     or come to mind.
But be glad and rejoice forever
     in what I am creating;
for I am about to create Jerusalem as a joy,
     and its people as a delight.
I will rejoice in Jerusalem,
     and delight in my people;
no more shall the sound of
     weeping be heard in it,
     or the cry of distress.
No more shall there be in it
     an infant that lives but a few days,
     or an old person who does not
          live out a lifetime;
for one who dies at a hundred years
     will be considered a youth,
     and one who falls short of a hundred
          will be considered accursed.
They shall build houses and inhabit them;
     they shall plant vineyards and eat their fruit.
They shall not build and another inhabit;
     they shall not plant and another eat;
     for like the days of a tree shall the
          days of my people be,
     and my chosen shall long enjoy
          the work of their hands.
They shall not labour in vain,
     or bear children for calamity;
     for they shall be offspring blessed
          by the Lord –
     and their descendants as well.
Before they call I will answer,
     while they are yet speaking I will hear.
The wolf and the lamb shall feed together,
     the lion shall eat straw like the ox;
     but the serpent – its food shall be dust!
They shall not hurt or destroy
     on all my holy mountain, says the Lord.

~ Isaiah 65: 17-25 ~

	Conservative	Liberal	New Right	Liberational
Why Poor?	'God did not create us equal'	'left out' of development	'because we're lazy, we're ignorant'	'because the rich are rich'
Core Values	social as moral order, stability, consensus, adjustment, tradition, conformity	progress, rationality, liberty, problems as *technical* puzzles, toleration, division public/private, objectivity	individual moral responsibility, freedom of choice, competition, law and order	poor central, starting 'from below; social justice, transformation, community
Who Poor?	weak, needy, disadvantaged	backward, primitive, left out, ignorant	the undeserving, irresponsible scroungers	the oppressed, marginalised, *anawim*
Action	traditional rights and obligations	campaigning for reform	individual acts of charity	critical reflection, conscious-ness raising, community organisation, active resistance to oppression
Political/ Economic Model	moral economy	secular state, mixed economy, welfare capitalism via market	authoritarian state, free market economy	people-power, populist socialism
Policy	mechanisms to ensure minimum for all	state welfare, education/ training, legal equality, structural mechanisms/ institutions	minimise state provision to discourage dependence, legal structures to enable 'wealth-creators'	federation of people's organisations, dismantling structures that sustain oppression
Church Role	part of hierarchical social order	separate from state (secular/ pluralist), spirituality private matter but source of values to inform institutions, reconciliation	separate from state but support role in social control (individual morality)	make option for the poor, be church of the poor, oppose establishment and renounce domestication role, internal reform vs hierarchy

Texts	Hebrew prophets (Isaiah 1: 11-17) righteousness as community issue	historical documents need de-coding for present reality, de-mythologise	'render to Caesar ...' parable of the talents, prosperity Gospel, 'sanctity of the individual'	'God's Word for us' in inter-action text and context; stress Exodus, promised land, justice prophecies, Kingdom of God, 'structural sin', Way of the Cross
Faith	traditional/conservative; pietistic	questioning, distancing, academic, distrust emotion	conservative, pietistic	personal – what does this mean for us? and political – social action
Fit Experience	how many poor people feel – indicates powerlessness, not absence of human causes of poverty, moral economy *may* operate – but not reliable safety net	'modernisation' itself leads to poverty, political equality does not ensure social, let alone economic, its equality ideal exclusive – assuming exploitation elsewhere (women, nature, third world), does 'objectivity' leave vacuum for New Right?	'wealth-creators' ignores structural framework and workers' contribution, 'undeserving' label denies individuals, underestimates structural obstacles/ advantages, esoteric inter-pretation of Gospel message	poverty has human causes – within and outside us, danger romanticising materially poor, may not be *anawim*, need material changes to sustain changed consciousness; dangers: backlash, identity politics, lose personal in the structural, same values just reversed roles

APPENDIX A

The Four Paradigms

APPENDIX B
Bibliography

Adoko, J (1993): 'Environment and Women in Uganda: The Way I See It', in *Focus on Gender: Perspectives on Women and Development*, 1 (1) (Oxfam).

Allen, T and Thomas, A (eds) (1992): *Poverty and Development in the 1990s* (Oxford: Oxford University Press).

Bailey, F G (1971): 'Peasant Perceptions of "The Bad Life"', in T Shanin (ed): *Peasants and Peasant Societies* (London: Penguin).

Banuri, T (1990): *Dominating Knowledge: Development, Culture and Resistance* (Oxford: Clarendon Press).

Beck, T (1994): *The Experience of Poverty: Fighting for Respect and Resources in Village India* (London: Intermediate Technology Publications).

Bell, D (1980): 'The Return of the Sacred?', in *The Winding Passage: Sociological Journeys 1960-1980* (Cambridge, Massachusetts: ABT Books).

Berger, J (1989): *Once in Europa* (London: Granta).

Berger, J (1992): *Lilac and Flag* (London: Granta).

Bingemer, M C (1994): 'Women in the Future of the Theology of Liberation', in U King (ed): *Feminist Theology from the Third World: A Reader* (London: SPCK).

Brooke, J (1991): *Science and Religion: Some Historical Perspectives* (Cambridge: Cambridge University Press).

Brueggeman, W (1978): *The Prophetic Imagination* (Philadephia: Fortress Press).

Burdick, J (1992): 'Rethinking the Study of Social Movements: The Case of Christian Base Communities in Urban Brazil', in A Escobar and S Alvarez (ed): T*he Making of Social Movements in Latin America* (Boulder/ Oxford: Westview Press).

Buvinic, M (1986): 'Projects for Women in the Third World. Explaining their Misbehaviour', in *World Development*, 14(5).

Capra, F (1982): *The Turning Point* (Suffolk: Richard Clay Ltd).

Cardoso, F (1982): 'Dependency and Development in Latin America' in Alavi, H and Sharlin, T (eds): *Introduction to the Sociology of 'Developing Societies'* (London: Macmillan).

Chambers, R (1983): *Rural Development* (Harlow, Essex: Longman Scientific & Technical).

Connell, R W (1987): *Gender and Power* (Oxford: Polity Press).

Conway, G and Barbier, E (1990): *After the Green Revolution: Sustainable Agriculture for Development* (London: Earthscan).

Cornea, G; Jolly, R; Stewart, F (ed) (1987): *Adjustment with a Human Face: Protecting the Vulnerable and Promoting Growth*, a study by UNICEF (Oxford: Oxford University Press).

Douglas, M (1970): *Natural Symbols: Explorations in Cosmology* (London: Barrie and Rockliff: The Crescent Press)

Duchrow, U (1995): *Alternatives to Global Capitalism* (Utrecht: International Books).

Ekin, P (1992): *A New World Order* (London: Routledge).

Elliot, C (1985): *Praying the Kingdom* (Darton, Longman & Todd).

Elliot, C (1987): *Comfortable Compassion?* (London: Hodder & Stoughton).

Elson, D (1988): 'Dominance and Dependency in the World Economy' in Crow, B (et al) (eds): *Survival and Change in the Third World* (Oxford: Polity Press).

Elson, D (ed) (1991): *Male Bias in the Development Process* (Manchester: Manchester University Press).

Ferguson, J (1994): *The Anti-Politics Machine: 'Development', Depoliticisation and Bureaucratic Power in Lesotho* (Minneapolis: University of Minnesota Press).

Forrester, D and Skene, D (1988): *Just Sharing* (Epworth).

Fox, M (1983): *Original Blessing* (Santa Fe, New Mexico: Bear and Company).

Friedmann, J (1992): *Empowerment: the Politics of Alternative Development* (Oxford: Blackwell).

Gandhi, M K (1983): *An Autobiography* (Ahmedabad: Navajivan Publishing House).

Gaventa, J (1980): *Power and Powerlessness: Quiescence and Rebellion in an Appalachian Valley* (Oxford: Oxford University Press).

George, S (1992): *Debt Boomerang* (London: Pluto Press).

Gorringe, T (1994): *Capital and the Kingdom* (Maryknoll New York: Orbis Books).

Goulet, D (1989) in Baum, G and Ellsberg, R (eds): *The Logic of Solidarity* (London: Macmillan), pp 127-142.

Griffiths, B (1984): *The Creation of Wealth* (London: Hodder Christian Paperbacks).

Guhathakurta, M (1991): *The Politics of British Aid* (Dhaka: Centre for Social Studies).

Gutierrez, G (1974): *A Theology of Liberation* (London: SCM Press Ltd).

HMSO (1992): *Social Trend 22* (London: Crown Copyright).

Hampson, D (1990): *Theology and Feminism* (Oxford: Blackwell).

Hartmann, B and Boyce, J (1883): *A Quiet Violence* (London: Zed Books).

Hirschmann, A (1984): *Getting Ahead Collectively* (Oxford: Pergamon Press).

Holland, J and Henriot, P (1983): *Social Analysis: Linking Faith and Justice* (Maryknoll: Orbis).

Humphrey, C (1983): *Karl Marx Collective: Economy Society and Religion in a Siberian Collective Farm* (Cambridge: Cambridge University Press).

Humphrey, J (1985): 'Gender Pay and Skill Manual Workers in Brazilian Industry', in Afshar, H (ed): *Women, Work and Ideology in the Third World* (London: Tavistock Publications Ltd).

Hutton, W (1995): *The State We're In* (London: Jonathan Cape).

Ignatius of Loyola (1963): *Spiritual Exercises* (London: Burns and Oates), Corbishley SJ (trans).

Jackson, C (1993): 'Environmentalisms and Gender Interests in the Third World', in *Development and Change* 24 (4).

Jacobs, M (1996): *The Politics of the Real World* (London: Earthscan).

Jahangir, B K (1986): *The Problematics of Nationalism* (Dhaka: Centre for Social Studies.

Jonasdottir, A (1988): 'On the Concept of Interest, Women's Interests and the Limitations of Interest Theory', in Staudt, K and Jonasdottir, A (ed): *The Political Interests of Gender* (London: Sage Publications).

Kandiyoti, D (1988): 'Bargaining with Patriarchy' in *Gender and Society* (2).

Kaplan, A (1996): *The Development Practitioners' Handbook* (London: Pluto Press).

Kay, C (1989): *Latin American Theories of Development and Underdevelopment* (London: Routledge).

King, C S (1973): *My Life with Martin Luther King Jr* (London: Hodder and Stoughton).

King, M L (1977): *Strength to Love* (Glasgow: Fount Paperbacks).

King, U (ed) (1994): *Feminist Theology from the Third World: A Reader* (London: SPCK).

Kruijer, G (1987): *Development Through Liberation: Third World Problems and Solutions* (Basingstoke: Macmillan).

Kyung, C H (1994): 'To be Human is to be Created in God's Image', in King (ed): *Feminist Theology from the Third World* (London: SPCK).

Leech, K (1992): *The Eye of the Storm* (London: Darton, Longman & Todd).

Lehmann, D (1990): *Democracy and Development in Latin America* (Cambridge: Polity Press).

Levine, D and Scott, M (1989): *Power and Popular Protest: Latin American Social Movements* (Berkeley: University of California Press).

Lukes, S (1970): *Power: A Radical View* (London: Macmillan).

McDonagh, S (1986): *To Care for the Earth* (London: Geoffrey Chapman).

McDonagh, S (1990): *The Greening of the Church* (London: Geoffrey Chapman).

Mamtaz, M and Shaheed, F (1987): *Women in Pakistan: One Step Forward Two Steps Back* (London: Zed).

Marshall, R (1991): 'Power in the Name of Jesus', in *Review of African Political Economy* 52.

Menike, T (1993): 'People's empowerment from the people's perspective', in *Development in Practice* 3(3).

Mies, M and Shiva, V (1993): *Ecofeminism* (London: Zed Books).

Mills, C W (1964): *The Power Elite* (Oxford: Oxford University Press).

Molyneux, M (1985): 'Mobilisation Without Emancipation? Women's Interests, the State, and Revolution in Nicaragua', in *Feminist Studies* 11(2).

Montefiore, H (1990): *Christianity and Politics* (London: Macmillan).

Moser, C (1989): 'Gender Planning in the Third World: Meeting Practical and Strategic Needs', in *World Development* 17(11).

Nolan, A (1989): *To Nourish Our Faith* (London: CAFOD).

O'Brien, N (1993): *Island of Tears, Island of Hope* (Maryknoll, New York: Orbis Books).

O'Riordan, T (1976): *Environmentalisms* (London: Pion Ltd).

O'Riordan, T (1988): *Sustainable Environmental Management. Principles and Practice* (London: Belhaven Press).

Oduyoye, M (1986): *Hearing and Knowing: Theological Reflections on Christianity in Africa* (New York: Orbis Books), chapter 10.

Ostergaard, Lise (ed) (1992): *Gender and Development: A Practical Guide* (London: Routledge).

Pearse, J (1993): 'NGOs and Social Change' in *Development in Practice* (3)3.

Pepper, D (1984): *The Roots of Modern Environmentalism* (London: Croom Helm).

Pieris, A (1986): *An Asian Theology of Liberation* (Edinburgh: T & T Clark).

Platt, (1992): 'Poverty of Ideas', *New Statesman* (London: Statesman and Nation Publishing).

Pryer, J (1989): 'When Breadwinners Fall Ill: Preliminary Findings from a Case Study in Bangladesh', in *IDS Bulletin* 20(2).

Radford Ruether, R (1981): *To Change the World: Christology and Cultural Criticism* (London: SCM).

Ram, K (1991): *Gender, Hegemony and Capitalist Transformation in a South Indian Fishing Community* (London: Zed Books).

Rebera, R (ed) (1990): *We Cannot Dream Alone* (Geneva: WCC Publications).

Richards, H (1985): *The Evaluation of Cultural Action* (London: Macmillan).

Rogers, Barbara (1980): *The Domestication of Women: Discrimination in Developing Countries* (London: Kogan Page).

Rowlands, J (1995): 'Empowerment examined', in *Development in Practice* 5(2).

Sachs, W (1992): *The Development Dictionary* (London: Zed Books).

Sacred Congregation of the Doctrine of Faith, (1984): *Instruction on Certain Aspects of the Theology of Liberation* (Vatican City).

Said, E W (1978): *Orientalism* (London: Penguin).

Salgado, P (1991): 'Church and Violence: Philippine Experience', in *CTC Bulletin*, vol X, no 1 (Hongkong: Christian Conference of Asia).

Scheper-Hughes, N (1993): *Death Without Weeping: The Violence of Everyday Life in Brazil* (Berkeley and Los Angeles, California: University of California Press).

Scott, J (1985): *Weapons of the Weak: Everyday Forms of Peasant Resistance* (London and New Haven: Yale University Press).

Scott, J (1990): *Domination and the Arts of Resistance* (New Haven: Yale University Press).

Seabrook, J (1993): *Victims of Development: Resistance and Alternatives* (London: Verso).

Selznick, P (1966): *TVA and the Grass-Roots: a Study in the Sociology of Formal Organisation* (New York: Harper and Row).

Sen, G and Grown, C (1987): *Development, Crises and Alternative Visions: Third World Women's Perspectives* (London: Earthscan Publications).

Sharma, U (1980): *Women, Work and Property in North-West India* (London: Tavistock Publications).

Sharp, G (1973): *The Politics of Nonviolent Action: Power and Struggle* (Boston: Extending Horizons Books).

Solle, D (1990): *Thinking About God* (London: SCM Press), pp 1-6.

Sorrell, R (1988): *St Francis of Assisi and Nature: Tradition and Innovation in Western Christian Attitudes to the Environment* (Oxford: Oxford University Press).

Tamez, E (1982): *Bible of the Oppressed* (Maryknoll, New York: Orbis Books).

Tamez, E (1986): 'The Woman who complicated the History of Salvation', in *Cross Currents*, vol 36 (2).

Taylor, M (1990): *Good for the Poor* (London: Mowbray).

—— (1996): *Not Angels but Agencies. The Ecumenical Response to Poverty: A Primer* (London: WCC/SCM Press).

Thomas, K (1971): *Religion and the Decline of Magic* (London: Weidenfeld and Nicolson).

Thompson, E P (1980): *The Making of the English Working Class* (Harmondsworth: Penguin).

Teilhard de Chardin, P (1971): *Christianity and Evolution* (St James' Place, London: Collins).

Todaro, M (1982): *Economic Development in the Third World* (Harlow: Longman).

Torres, C (1971): 'Latin America: Lands of Violence', in Gerassi, J (ed): *Revolutionary Priest: Complete Writings of Camilo Torres* (London: Jonathan Cape).

Tugwell, S (1984): *Ways of Imperfection* (London: Darton, Longman and Todd).

Vallely, P (1992): *Promised Lands* (London: HarperCollins Religious).

Wallace, T and March, C (ed) (1991): *Changing Perceptions* (Oxford: Oxfam)

Wallis, J (1995): *The Soul Politics* (UK: Fount Paperback).

Warren, W (1980): *Imperialism: Pioneer of Capitalism* (London: New Left Books).

White, L (1967): 'Historical Roots of Our Ecologic Crisis', in *Science,* vol 155, no 3767.

White, S C (1991): *Evaluating the Effectiveness of NGOs in Poverty Alleviation: Bangladesh Case Study ODI Working Paper* 50 (London: Overseas Development Institute

—— (1992): *Arguing with the Crocodile: Gender and Class in Bangladesh* (London: Zed Books).

Willis, P (1977): *Learning to Labour* (Farnborough, Saxon House.

Whitehead, A (1984): 'I'm hungry Mum! The Politics of Domestic Budgeting' in K Young (et al) (eds): *Of Marriage and the Market: Women's subordination – internationally and its lessons* (Routledge, Kegan Paul).

Wink, W (1992): *Engaging the Powers: Discernment and Resistance in a Domination* (Philadephia: Fortress Press).

Wogaman, P (1988): *Christian Perspectives on Politics* (London: SCM Press).

Wood, G (1985): Labelling in Development Policy (London: Sage).

World Bank (1990-6): *World Development Report* (World Bank: Washington).

World Bank (1990-4): *World Development Report* (World Bank: Washington).

World Commission on Environment and Development (1989): *Our Common Future* (Oxford: Oxford University Press).

Worsley, P (1984): *The Three Worlds: Culture and Development* (London: Weidenfeld and Nicolson).

Wuyts, Mackintosh and Hewitt (eds) (1992): *Development Policy and Public Action* (Oxford: Oxford University Press).

Young, K (ed) (1988): *Women and Economic Development: Local, Regional and National Planning Strategies* (Oxford: Berg/UNESCO).

Young, K (1993): *Development Planning with Women: Making a World of Difference* (New York: St Martin's Press).

Young, K Wolkowitz and C McCullagh, R (1984): *Of Marriage and the Market. Women's Subordination Internationally and its Lessons* (London: Routledge & Kegan Paul).